THE
HOLOCAUST
CODES

THE HOLOCAUST CODES

CODES

The Untold Story of Decrypting the Final Solution

CHRISTIAN JENNINGS

First published by John Blake Publishing
an imprint of The Zaffre Publishing Group
A Bonnier Books UK company
4th Floor, Victoria House
Bloomsbury Square
London WC1B 4DA
England

Owned by Bonnier Books
Sveavägen 56, Stockholm, Sweden

www.facebook.com/johnblakebooks
twitter.com/jblakebooks

First published in hardback in 2024

Hardback ISBN: 978-1-78946-726-0
Trade paperback: 978-1-78946-728-4
Paperback ISBN: 978-1-78946-727-7
Ebook ISBN: 978-1-78946-725-3
Audiobook ISBN: 978-1-78946-724-6

British Library Cataloguing-in-Publication Data:

A CIP catalogue record for this book is available from the British Library.

Design by Envy Design Ltd

Printed and bound in Great Britain by Clays Ltd, Elcograf S.p.A

1 3 5 7 9 10 8 6 4 2

John Blake Publishing is an imprint of Bonnier Books UK
www.bonnierbooks.co.uk

CONTENTS

GLOSSARY OF NAZI AND SS MILITARY AND PARAMILITARY DEPARTMENTS AND RANKS

Allgemeine SS ('General SS') – main administrative branch of the SS

Einsatzgruppen ('Deployment,' or 'Action' Groups or Task Forces) – SS and German Police execution squads

Einsatzkommando – sub-group of the above

Gauleiter – a regional leader of the Nazi Party, and third-highest ranking of Nazi political officials

Gestapo (Geheime Staatspolizei, or 'Secret State Police'), a political and all-powerful Third Reich secret police agency

Judenrat – Jewish councils, especially in German-occupied territories

Kripo (Kriminalpolizei) – 'Criminal Police'

NSKK (Nationalsozialistisches Kraftfahrkorps) – the National Socialist Motor Corps or National Socialist Drivers Corps, a Nazi Party paramilitary organisation, which supplied the Nazi

Party with transport, highly skilled drivers and mechanics

OKW (Oberkommando der Wehrmacht) – Nazi Germany's supreme military command

OKW/Chi (Oberkommando der Wehrmacht Chiffrierabteilung) – the Cipher Department of the OKW

Ordnungsdienst ('Order Service') – the Jewish Ghetto Police

Orpo (Ordnungspolizei) – 'Order Police', the regular police force

Reichsmarschall – highest military office in the Wehrmacht, specially created for Hermann Göring, the head of the Luftwaffe

RSHA (Reichssicherheitshauptamt) – Reich Security Main Office. Most of the security and police agencies of Nazi Germany were consolidated into the RSHA

SD – Sicherheitsdienst (Sicherheitsdienst des Reichsführers-SS) – 'Security Service': the SS intelligence agency

SiPo – Sicherheitspolizei – 'Security Police', comprising Kripo and the Gestapo

SS – Schutzstaffel ('Protection Squadron') – Nazi Germany's most powerful and most feared military and paramilitary organisation; multiple police and military units came under its command

SS-Totenkopfverbände/SS-TV ('Death's Head Units') – the original name for the concentration camp guard units of the SS

Waffen-SS ('SS Weapons/Armed forces') – SS combat forces

Wehrmacht – Nazi Germany's unified armed forces comprising the Kriegsmarine (navy), Heer (army) and Luftwaffe (air force)

GLOSSARY

SS ranks and approximate British equivalents where they exist

(SS ranks also differed from regular German military ranks. Only the higher ranks are listed here as they are the ones encountered in this book)

Reichsführer-SS – title and rank created for the commander of the Schutzstaffel, the highest rank of the SS

SS-Oberst-Gruppenführer (und Generaloberst der Waffen-SS) – General

SS-Obergruppenführer (und General der Waffen-SS) – Lieutenant-General

SS-Gruppenführer (und Generalleutnant der Waffen-SS) – Major-General

SS-Brigadeführer (und Generalmajor der Waffen-SS) – Brigadier

SS-Oberführer – Colonel (senior)

SS-Standartenführer – Colonel

SS-Obersturmbannführer – Lieutenant- Colonel

SS-Sturmbannführer – Major

SS-Hauptsturmführer – Captain

SS-Obersturmführer – Lieutenant

SS-Untersturmführer – 2nd Lieutenant

SS-Sturmscharführer – Regimental Sergeant-Major

SS-Hauptscharführer – Sergeant-Major

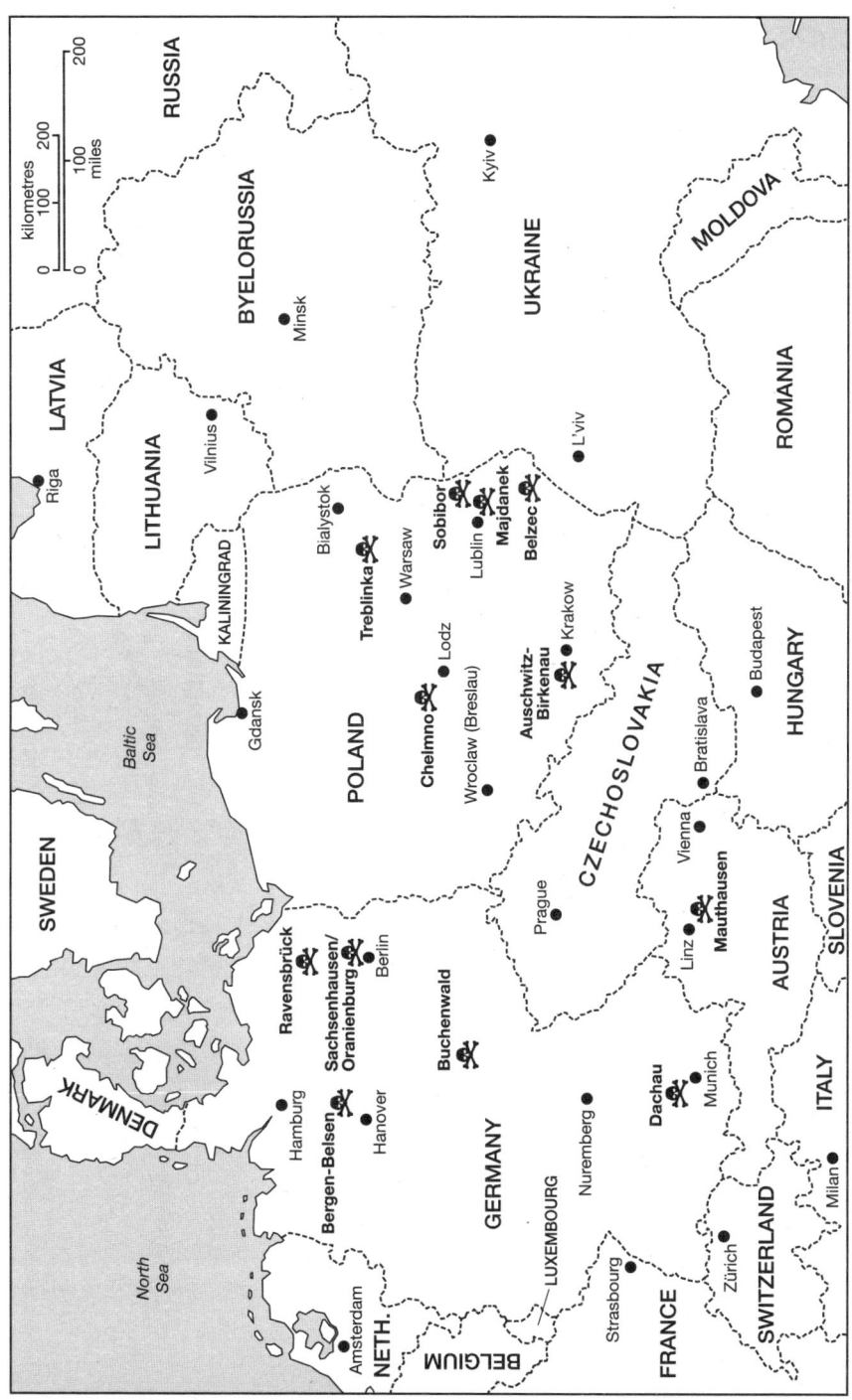

Europe in 1943, showing the main Nazi concentration and extermination camps

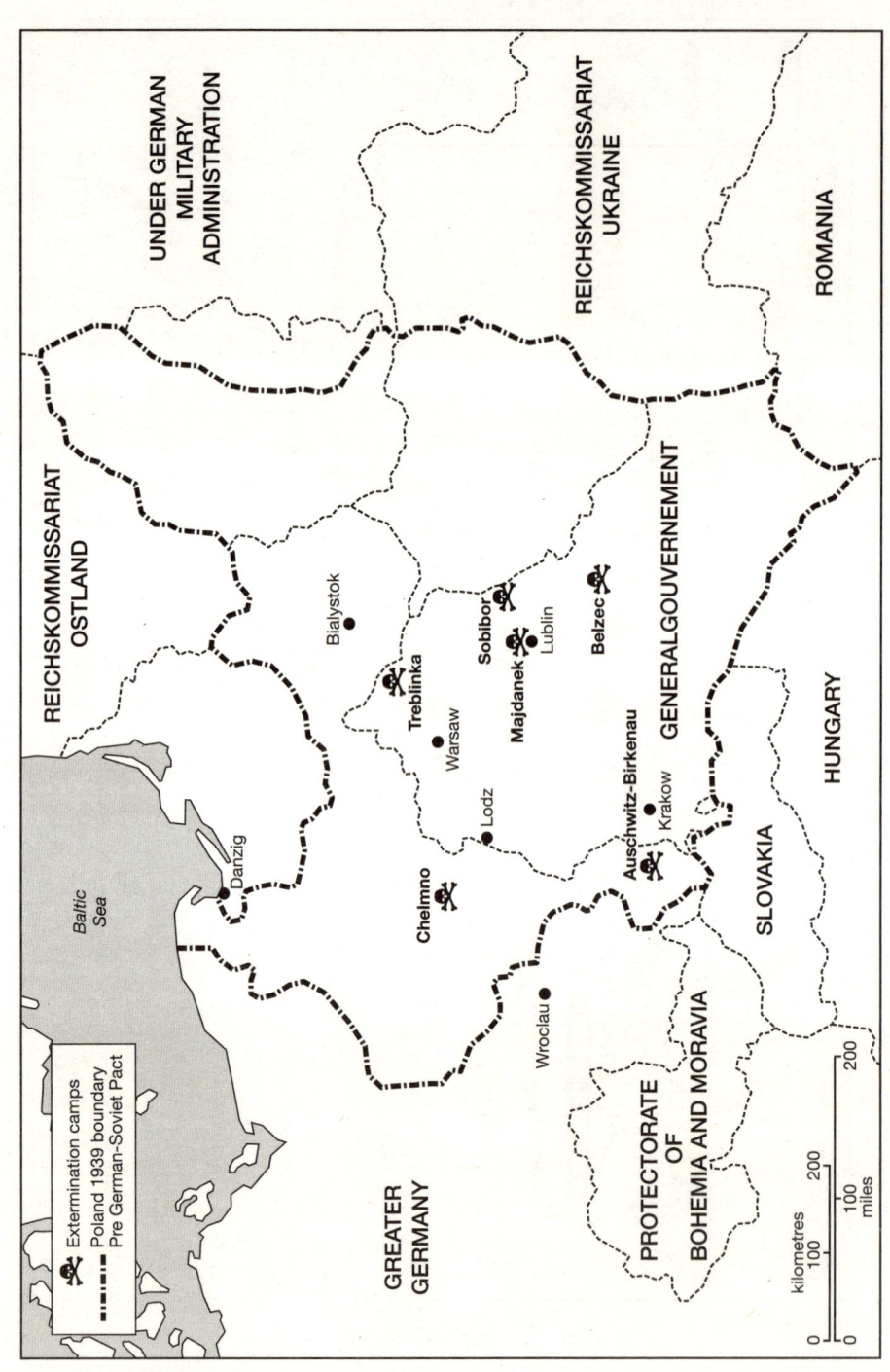

Nazi-occupied Poland

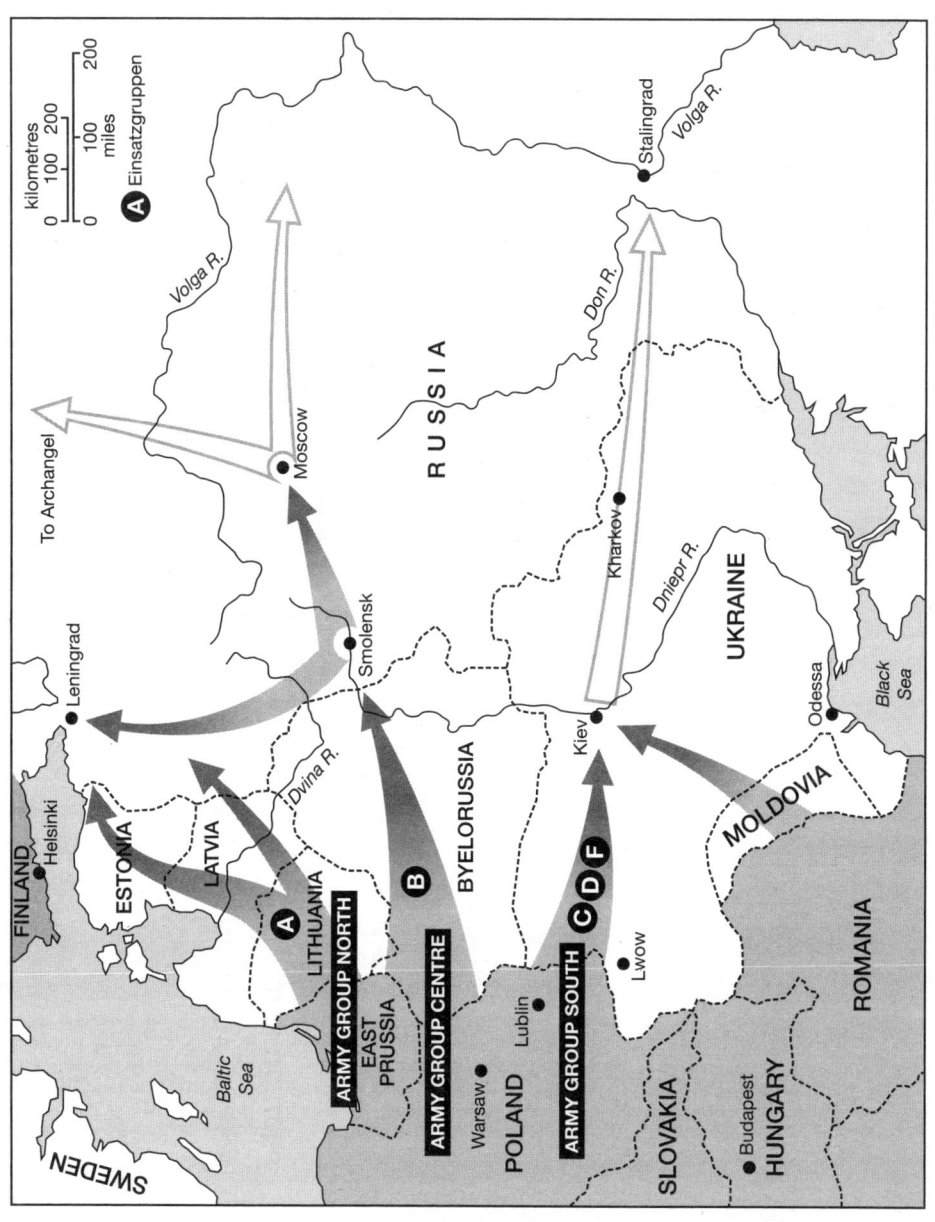

Operation Barbarossa: the German invasion of Russia, June 1941

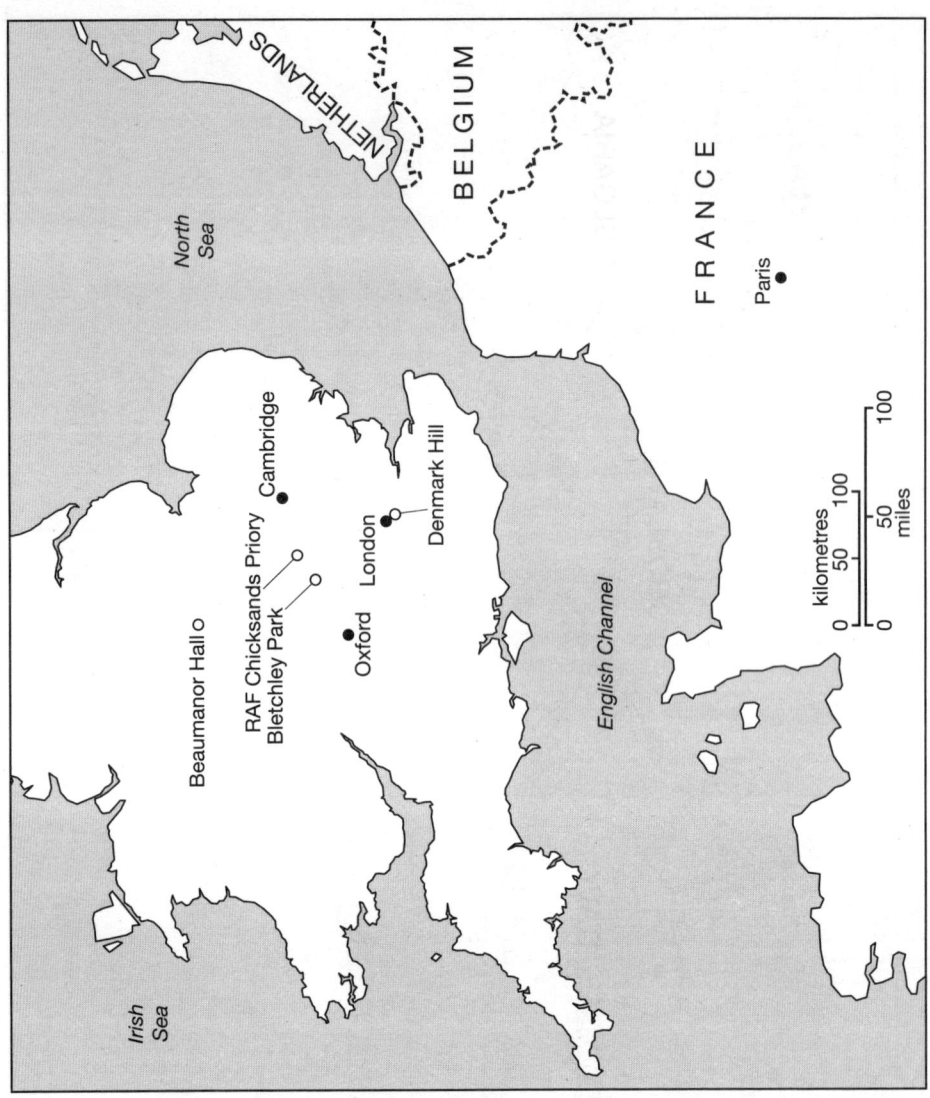

England in 1942 showing London, Oxford, Cambridge, Bletchley Park
and three of the main 'Y' or radio-intercept stations: Beaumanor Hall
(Leicestershire), RAF Chicksands Priory (Bedfordshire) and Denmark Hill
(Camberwell, London).

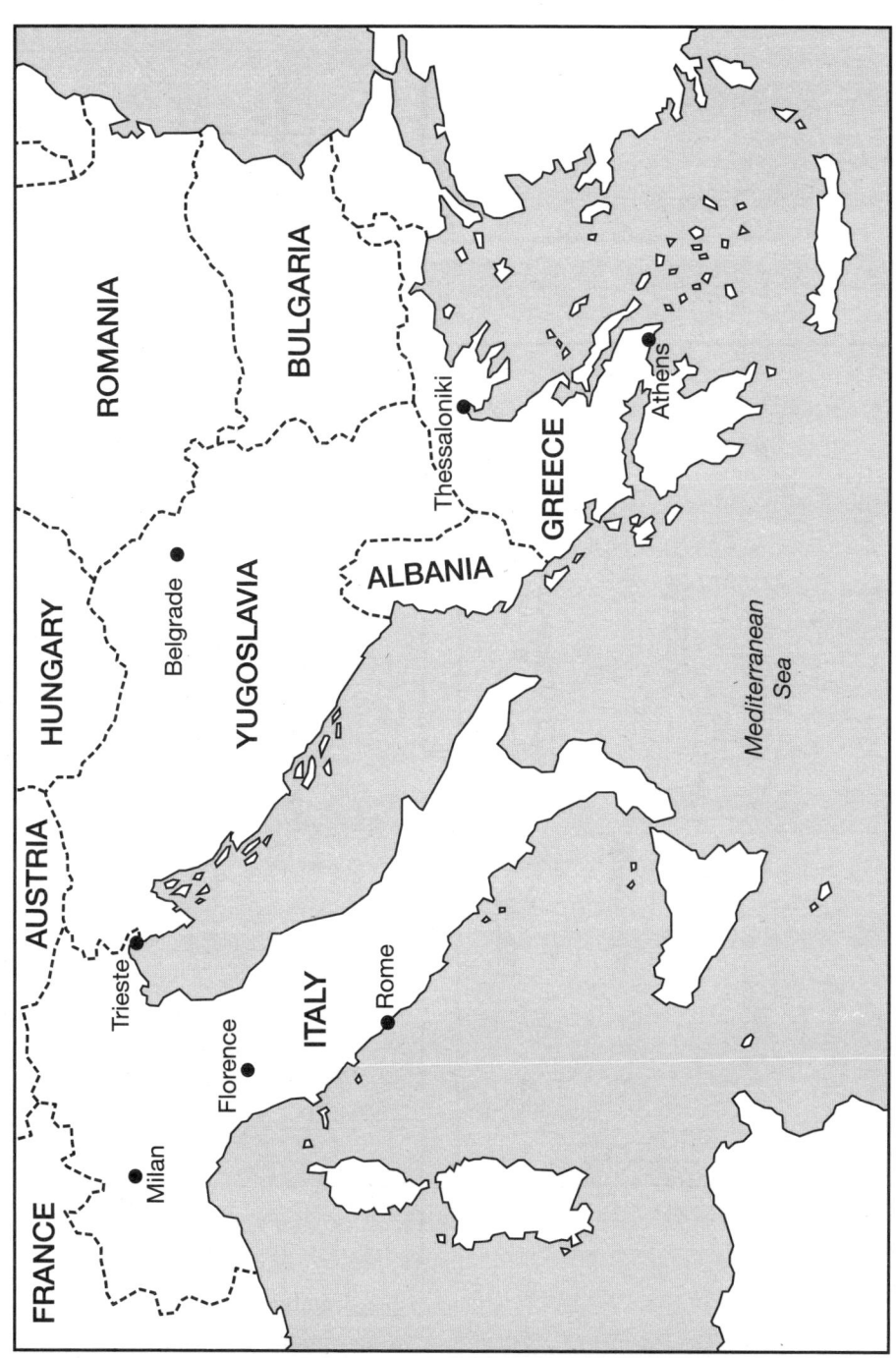

Central, South and South-Eastern Europe in 1944

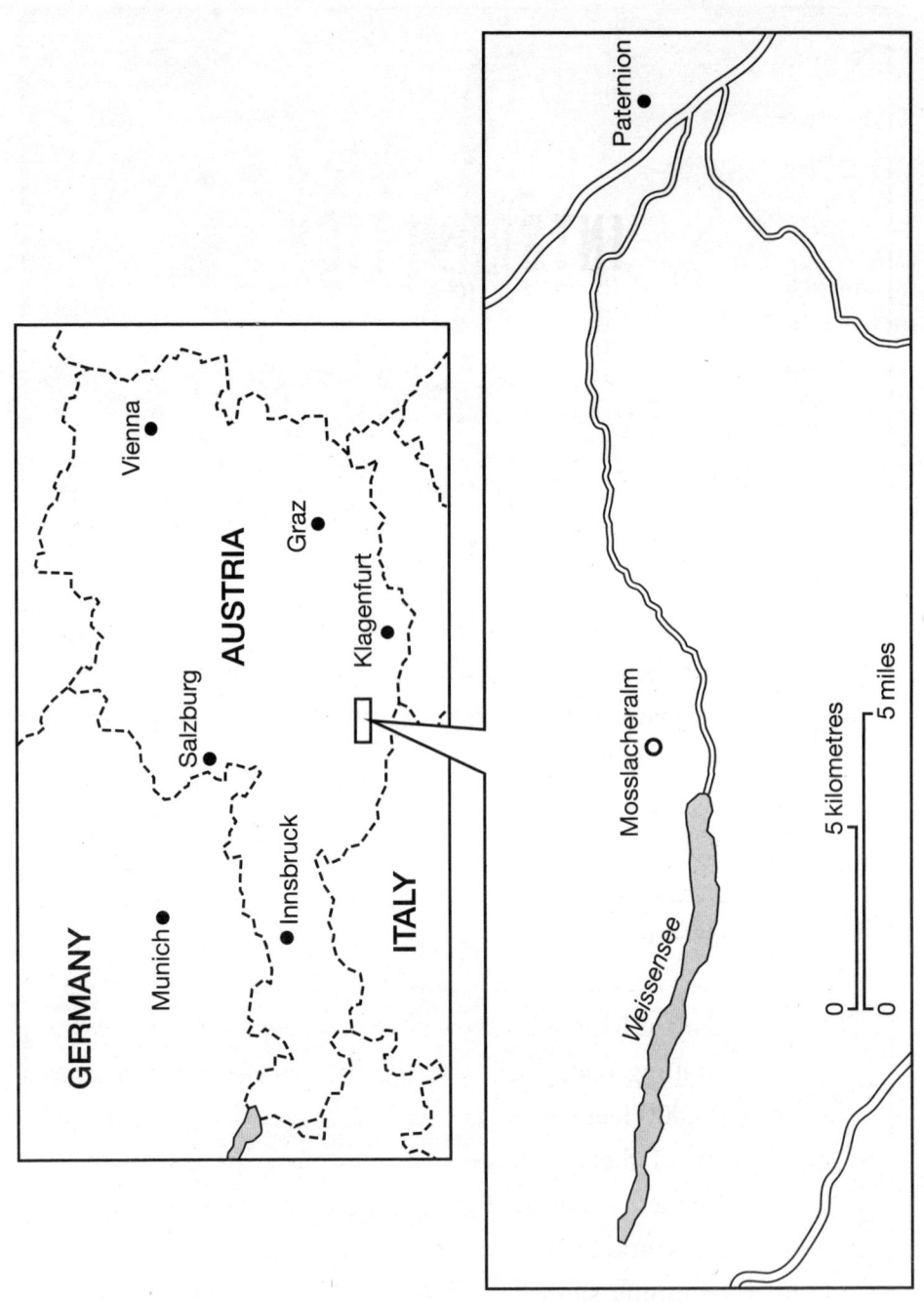

South-Western Austria, May 1945

INTRODUCTION

On the morning of 4 April 1944, a twin-engined De Havilland Mosquito from 60 Squadron, South African Air Force, took off on a reconnaissance mission from San Severo, near Foggia in south-eastern Italy. To save weight, the aircraft carried no machine-guns, cannon or bombs, but only two long-focal-length cameras, one mounted under each wing. The South African crew – pilot Lieutenant Charles Barry DFC and navigator Lieutenant Ian McIntyre – were tasked with photographing the huge I. G. Farbenindustrie AG (commonly known as IG Farben) synthetic oil and rubber plant at Monowitz in southern Poland in preparation for a possible bombing raid. The return flight took five hours, and at a height of 26,000 feet, they were over the target for four minutes. That day, one of the two cameras was malfunctioning, so, to be sure they obtained adequate images, the crew made two passes, from west to east and back again. On the second pass McIntyre left the cameras running slightly longer than usual to guarantee good coverage. Then the South Africans spotted enemy aircraft, and the unarmed Mosquito turned for home.

When the film of the second pass was developed back in Italy, the final frames were found to show a large site containing small buildings laid out in rows. Little attention was paid at the time to these: the target, after all, was the IG Farben plant five miles away. It was only in 1979, some thirty-five years later, that photo-analysts from America's Central Intelligence Agency recognised them for what they were: the first Allied aerial shots of Auschwitz.

Eighty years after the two South Africans flew that sortie in their unarmed Mosquito, it seems inconceivable that back then the world had not heard of Auschwitz, that the grisly images of rows of barrack blocks, the crematoria, the wire, the railway lines, now so imprinted on human consciousness, could then have been nothing but an anonymous image from the skies. One whose identity would only be recognised and admitted to in 1979. Yet that is how the Holocaust occurred, that is how its physical institutions were concealed, how its perpetrators murdered millions of people, precisely because it was anonymous, it was hidden and as much as possible of the documentation and evidence was covered up.

However, although the camp complex at Auschwitz-Birkenau may have been unrecognisable from a high-flying reconnaissance aircraft, by April 1944 its existence, and the existence of other extermination and concentration camps and programmes of mass execution, was the subject of a flood of reports and rumours from inside occupied Europe. Some of the precise details, however, had for some time been known to a select handful of Allied intelligence and government officials in London and Washington. One of the primary ways they had discovered what the Germans were doing was through cryptanalysis, the decryption of encoded SS and German Police and intelligence signals that gradually revealed how the Third Reich was murdering six million people. That cryptanalysis, that decryption, those signals and that discovery of a state-sponsored programme of mass murder is what this book is all about.

INTRODUCTION

I spent fifteen years as a foreign correspondent reporting on and investigating wars, genocides and ethnic conflicts across twenty-three countries, including Rwanda, Bosnia, Kosovo and Democratic Congo. Out on the red dirt tracks of central Africa's Great Lakes Region, in the sleety fog of frozen Balkans mornings, and across trails of mass graves and execution sites, I watched and learnt and reported on how genocide and mass atrocities happen. I wrote books on war crimes and international justice in these countries, as well as on the work of the International Commission on Missing Persons, which has revolutionised the science of DNA-assisted identification, helping to identify some of the thousands of people who go missing following conflicts in such areas as the western Balkans, Iraq, Syria and Ukraine.

Following on from this, I have also written four non-fiction books about the Second World War, focusing on both wartime Italy and the Holocaust, while in *The Third Reich is Listening*, I gave a detailed account of German codebreaking during that war, attempting to counteract the popular assumption of uncontested Allied superiority in this field. In many ways, it was as though all the different yet inter-connected topics of the past thirty years have led towards this current subject. The path has unwittingly progressed from the corpse-strewn interiors of Rwandan churches in 1994, to the machetes, burning villages and Kalashnikov tracer of civil war and ethnic cleansing in the eucalyptus forests and villages of Burundi – ironically, like Rwanda, one of the world's most beautiful countries. It has gone from the torched interior of a Kosovo coffee bar in 1999, the flame-blackened room strewn with the brass glimmer of cartridge cases, where Albanians were murdered by Serb paramilitaries, to the exhumed mass graves, the mortuaries and DNA laboratories of Bosnia, and to international courts in The Hague. At every step, the questions 'How?' and 'Why?' and 'What happened?' seemed to beg for answers.

Investigating genocide, knowing something of how wartime codebreaking had worked, and where the perpetrators had left their traces across twenty countries, has enabled me to look into the overarching drama behind one of the most extraordinary stories of all. How did the British and Americans use their stunning expertise in codebreaking to uncover parts of the Holocaust, almost as it was happening, and how did the SS use signals intelligence to try to hide what they were doing? And what then became of this information?

If the devil was in the technical detail, in the tangled mathematical forests of cryptanalysis where the war's secrets lay hidden, then the devil was also in human nature. The German signals clerks who inadvertently repeated key letters or words in messages, enabling codebreakers to gain a 'crib' into an otherwise unbreakable cipher. The SS general who changed a crucial code setting which the British had compromised, in order to conceal the electronic evidence of massacres committed by his men – and who then unwittingly chose as its replacement a code that was simpler to decipher, and then refused to change it for the remainder of the war. The inflexible mindset of key German officials who believed the Enigma system was unbreakable.

One of many systems Bletchley decoded was an arcane encipherment used by national Communist Party organisations around the world to send coded signals to and from the Communist International Committee in Moscow. On 25 June 1944 a signal was decrypted in this code from a Polish official telling a Hungarian colleague about the gassing of Hungarian Jews at Auschwitz. As the message was picked up from very long range, the British intercept teams were not able to make out all the incoming letters. But what was legible was clear enough.

INTRODUCTION

In the concentration camp at Oświęcim [the nearest town to Auschwitz] the Germans are gradually killing from five to ten thousand Hungarian Jews . . . approximately . . . thousand . . . have been gassed . . . month . . . Hungarian Jews about this. [word missing before 'Hungarian' estimated to be 'tell' or 'warn' or 'alert'].

Much has been written about Bletchley Park's extraordinary success in decrypting the coded wartime signals of Germany, Italy, Japan, and several other countries. The contribution of the codebreakers to the Battle of the Atlantic, the decryption of the German naval Enigma, their U-boat ciphers, the Luftwaffe's Vulture code, the Wehrmacht High Command's Tunny and Sturgeon keys on the Lorenz cipher machine, the Japanese Purple diplomatic cipher, and the naval JP25 – all these have been often and deservedly celebrated.

Much less well-known is the decryption of the Domino collection, and other ciphers used by German Police units, by the SS and Gestapo, by the Vatican and by the military and diplomats of a dozen countries around the world, which provided information not about military matters but on the genocidal policies of the Nazis as they played out behind the scenes. By breaking into these codes the Allies could see what was happening out in the remote villages and ghettos of Byelorussia, Poland and rural Ukraine, in the mud and blood and wire, and what diplomats and military officials around the world were reporting back to their own capitals about the ongoing persecution of the Jews. And all the while, thanks to their decryption of the Enigma coding system, the Allies were reading the Germans' own intelligence digests.

The Third Reich's ten different intelligence agencies had broken into some or all of the codes of forty-one different countries, and the Germans never knew that much of it was then decrypted by the Allies and used against them. This kaleidoscopic mix of coded sources can collectively be called the Holocaust Codes. The signals and their encipherments, their interception and decryption, the operations they described, and what became of the secret intelligence the Allies gained, all form the subject of this book.

Information about Allied codebreaking and the intelligence gained from it about the Final Solution has been emerging gradually since the first official histories were published in the 1980s, and the pace has quickened since the introduction of the Nazi War Crimes Disclosure Act in the United States in 1997 and 1998. As new documents are declassified in archives from London and Washington, more information becomes available. Nevertheless, it sometimes seems like the tip of an iceberg, and it is a crucial subject that merits ongoing investigation. The material is everywhere, in many languages, from Kew in London to Maryland in the United States, from Jerusalem, Berlin and Munich to Tokyo and Rome, from Helsinki and Berne to Ankara and Budapest, to name just a few of the main repositories. It is not hidden, but it is not obvious: it sometimes seems concealed in plain sight. Some of this information has been published by academics and by experts on cryptanalysis and the Holocaust. To find it you need to know where it is, to ask and to search. Some has not been printed before, and much of the detail of this book is derived from original archival research. This is an attempt to piece together as much as possible of what is known about the Holocaust Codes, and to give a picture of the way in which the Allies found out about Germany's genocidal policies.

CHAPTER I

THE POGROM PROCEEDS

London and Buckinghamshire, autumn 1939

At five minutes past two on the afternoon of 18 November 1939, a signals clerk from the General Post Office was on duty at a Foreign Office radio intercept station on Denmark Hill, in south London. He picked up one of a number of messages transmitted in Morse code. Focusing his receiving set on the high-frequency signal, he transcribed the incoming dits and dahs, or dots and dashes, into letter groups. The message was obviously encrypted, so he wrote down the groups of encoded letters in pencil on an intercept form, and handed the message to his supervisor. Although he had no idea as to the contents of the message, the clerk and his colleagues at the Denmark Hill listening station, with its high aerials standing tall over South London, were becoming increasingly familiar with the incoming signal's frequency. Since the beginning of September there had been dozens of such messages each day, coming in at all hours of day and night, sent by hundreds of different radio operators, all with very slight variations in their 'fist'. This was the way their individual fingers and palms moved on the Morse key as they tapped out messages, giving each operator their own electronic signature. From the way the clarity of the radio signal sometimes dipped in and out, faded and then reappeared, the clerks at Denmark Hill deduced that many of the messages were coming in from the extreme range of their receiving sets, in a semi-circle that stretched around the eastern fringes of the Atlantic, through central France, to eastern Germany and inside Poland. The latter seemed to the staff at Denmark Hill to be the most likely source of these signals, especially as the volume of messages had increased to over a hundred a day since 1 September. That was the day that Germany had invaded Poland.

That evening the intercepted message joined dozens of others in the sealed pouch of an army motorbike dispatch rider, who took them sixty miles up the A1 dual carriageway to the town of Bletchley in Buckinghamshire. The rider turned into the gates of a country house, past the army sentries and the sandbags, and handed his delivery over to a military policeman. He in turn took the messages down a series of gravelled paths to a single-storey Nissan hut, with the figure '5' painted on its wooden door. Inside was a small group of men, led by an army brigadier dressed in the tartan trews of a Scottish regiment.

The men in the hut laid out each message slip, and examined the way the different letter groups had been used to represent each encoded word. A lot of the signals that had arrived since the beginning of September had one unifying feature: they began with two lines of letter-group 'text', the first beginning with a two-letter group, the second with a three-letter group. These, the men knew by now, were the address lines, starting with 'to' and 'from'.

Next, they guessed, would follow the location, position and rank of the sender and recipient, followed by the text of the message itself. They were right. The messages were coming from inside Poland, as well as from Germany. The decryption of the first twelve letter groups of each message showed that it fell into a category that the men in the hut now called GP, or German Police, messages. These were the daily radio traffic, some routine and administrative, some urgent and operational, sent by the hundreds of different SS and German police units operating in Poland, Austria and Germany as the Third Reich stormed into war. The cryptanalysts had given the category of police messages a secret, one-word codename: DOMINO. The messages were all enciphered in a system known as a Double Transposition, and the first letter groups showed who had sent it, where, and to whom. On 18 November, the contents of one message in particular stood out:

From: Higher SS and Police Leader, Ostland
To: 11 Police Battalion, PULTUSK
This concerns 4 transports of 2,000 Jews each from Nasielsk to Nowydwor. To report there to commander on 14.11.39. Immediate radio reply. A) Who ordered them there? Is a Jew-Action ordered? B) Who carried out the transport? C). From which area did the Jews come? D). Who took the necessary measures regarding the remaining administration of the property left behind? If the Jews come from my area of command . . .[1]

Like everybody in Europe the women and men at Bletchley were all too aware of the events of the last three months. Germany had invaded Poland on 1 September, and Great Britain had declared war on the 3rd. The Polish capital, Warsaw, had capitulated on the 18th, as the Soviet Union and Nazi Germany occupied the country from east and west, partitioning the defeated country under the Brest-Litovsk Treaty. The persecution of Jews inside Germany and Austria had been continuing, and increasing, since Adolf Hitler had become Germany's chancellor in 1933. With war now under way, the decrypted SS and police messages showed that as the German forces moved into Poland, attacks on Poles and Jews had begun immediately, and German settlers were already moving into homes and land from which their Jewish and Polish owners had been forcibly evicted by the SS and German police. By late November 1939, the cryptanalysts in Hut 5 were decoding up to a hundred detailed messages a day, sent by the SS and police in the Domino encipherment.

By mid-November, Britain's army had mobilised in support of their allies across the Channel, and some 160,000 British troops had deployed to France and Belgium: meanwhile the SS had ordered all Jews to be removed from western Poland to make way for ethnic German settlers. The first Jewish ghetto had already been set up in the south-eastern city of Lublin. The message sent on 18 November showed that the Jewish inhabitants of the town of Nasielsk, north of Warsaw, had been forcibly moved to Nowydwor, a suburb of the capital: the senior SS commander in the region was asking the German Reserve Police Battalion 11 in the town of Pultusk what was happening. Had a 'Jew-action' already been ordered? The phrase, along with Sonderbehandlung ('special handling') and 'special duties' was, the cryptanalysts knew, used in SS messages to indicate a forcible evacuation of Jews from their property – or a mass execution.

Three days previously, on 14 and 15 November, a one-line message had been intercepted and decrypted: it originated from the same SS General, the 'Higher SS and Police Führer for the occupied territory of Ostland'. Bletchley's intelligence analysts estimated this meant parts of East Prussia and the Baltics, and northern parts of German-occupied Poland.

'By order of the Chief Police and Higher SS leader Ostland all executions which have just taken place are to be currently reported to me.'[2]

To decrypt the messages the analysts in Hut 5 had worked out each of several 'keys' – sets of different letters – required to read into the coded signals sent every day by the German police battalions operating with Wehrmacht and SS units in Poland. There were several keys in use, three of which Hut 5 were codenaming Reich, Ingot and Russian. The Germans were sending messages encrypted in a cipher known as a 'Double Transposition' system, based upon code words taken from codebooks. This involved taking a message and scrambling its component letters into another sequence. It was similar to moving around the pieces of a jigsaw puzzle. So the words UKRAINE PRISONERS could become NKRUIAE OSERRPNSI. The ciphered text could be broken into 5-letter groups, mixing the letters of the words with each other rather than keeping them separate. A message text might read:

UKRAINE PRISONERS ARRIVED THIS MORNING

Broken up into 5-letter groups it would become:

UIIAT ISIRE GOEDM RIKRH EORVN SNRRA SNPN

The 'Reich' and 'Russian' keys, for instance, were sets of words or phrases from the codebooks, instructions which enabled the encryption of the message. Under the word or phrase that made up that day's key, the plain text message would be transcribed in columns. So if the key is 'MUNICH' and the message is 'Ukraine prisoners arrived this morning' the encrypted square giving the encoded words would appear like this:

M U N I C H
U K R A I N
E P R I S O
N E R S A R
R I V E D T
H I S M O R
N I N G

The columns are then put in the alphabetical order of the letters of the key – Munich – so it gives:

```
C H I M N U
I N A U R K
S O I E R P
A R S N R E
D T E R V I
O R M H S I
G N N I
```

The message is, once in groups of five letters, encoded as INAUR KSOIE RPARS NREDT ERVIO RMHSI XGNNI, with 'X' being a dummy filler to ensure that each group contains five characters. This is a single transposition – a double transposition simply repeats the process on the already-enciphered text with a different key, to replace, in this example, 'Munich'; the codebook lists the keys and other instructions. These would include the page and line of the book on which to find the key for the given twelve-hour period of a given date. The keys also instructed the operator which additional letters to put as prefixes and suffixes, thus further complicating decryption. The key told the operator how to re-order each letter sequence, and security was further increased as the Germans changed the keys every twelve hours. The signallers would then send the encrypted message by radio in Morse code, or, if its contents were classified as highly secret, it could be in doubly-encrypted characters. The recipient of the message would have the same codebook and daily keys as the sender, thus enabling them to decrypt the message into 'plain text'. The British cryptanalysts at the Government Code and Cypher School (GC&CS), as the institution at Bletchley Park was formally known, had been able to break into the Domino code, enciphered in its Double Transposition system, from the first weeks of receiving messages encoded in it. The deputy director at the Code and Cypher School, a naval reserve officer and cryptanalyst called Nigel de Grey, had made notes about the encipherment system.

> The system, straightforward Double Transposition, was used too carelessly to stand up to a concerted effort. Depths were frequent . . . and standard beginnings the rule rather than the exception. The placing of the address at the beginning of the message and the signature at the end made the cryptographer's life a happy one . . . results therefore were quick in coming and results began to circulate.[3]

De Grey had been one of Britain's foremost codebreakers in the First World War, and like millions of other men between eighteen and sixty, had received call-up papers that year. Alongside his duties as deputy director, he now also worked as the Intelligence Coordinator at the Code and Cypher School, which, three months into the war, was expanding rapidly. It was calling in more specialised staff, spreading out over the grounds of the country house where it was based, and targeting as many as possible of the dozens of encryptions used by the Third Reich's different armed services. On 18 November, once the men in Hut 5 had decrypted the message referring to 'a Jew-Action', de Grey added the signal to a list of others, as part of a summary of intelligence to be sent to London. This summary would go first to 'C', as the Director-General of the Secret Intelligence Service was known, who would then pass it on to the Prime Minister and the members of the War Cabinet. At first the messages had been taken to London by courier, but then a plain-language teleprinter link was established between Hut 3 at Bletchley Park, and Sections III and IV of SIS at Broadway Buildings in St James's, which was then teleprinted on to various ministries.

The 'intelligence picture' from Poland was increasingly frightening. From the contents of the messages his colleagues had decrypted between September and 18 November, de Grey could work out parts of what was happening inside Germany and Poland. Putting the whole jigsaw puzzle together felt like catching hundreds of individual snowflakes and trying to build a complete snowman, but each successive signal added a little bit more to de Grey's understanding of the German's actions.

... 14–15 November, Police & SS HQ Warsaw ... A sector of Battalion 4 was fired on by persons trespassing beyond the barricades (of the ghetto). A Pole was sentenced to death by regimental court martial. A Jew was shot on the spot for sabotage and for assaulting members of the defence force, two other Jews were sentenced to death by court martial.[4]

... 7.11.39, From Brenner Warsaw to Police HQs Berlin, Krakow: 368 officers of all ranks of the former Polish army were arrested today on urgent suspicion of anti-German propaganda and taken to the Blonie prison camp, 15 m W Warsaw ...[5]

De Grey knew by now that the Germans were trying to resettle parts of the populations from their own country and from Austria inside Poland, forcibly evicting Poles and Jews from their homes and land, and confining them to ghettos. There were repeated mentions of gangs of ethnic German Volksdeutsche raised among the local German population to help control the Poles.

... 16.10.39, From SS Hauptsturmführer V Haller, to Adj Reichsminister Arthur Seyss-Inquart, Vienna: Re: promised land in Poland for South Tirolese / please call my flat urgently by 9 a.m. at the latest to tell me which areas are suitable for the settlement of the Sud-Tiroleans. Rf SS would like to have it immediately.[i] The Rf SS is apparently planning to visit these areas in a short time. If possible, instead of calling, radio. Heil Hitler.[6]

Every day, intercepted messages arrived at Bletchley Park from the 'Y' or intercept stations such as Denmark Hill, RAF Chicksands Priory in Bedfordshire, and Beaumanor Hall in Leicestershire. The German Police were meticulous in their documentation not just of their operations against Jews, Poles and Russians, but any perceived infractions by their own men who took matters into their own hands:

. . . 24.11.39: at about 10 o' clock a Jew named Ganz, Minka, born in Lithuania on 7.4.57 and domiciled here, was found on synagogue land in Memel[ii] severely injured with a dagger wound in his throat and his head battered in. He died about 15 o'clock. The perpetrator of this deed who is a member of the SA[iii] named Lunkeit Georg born on the 16.8.03 at Laugallen in the district of Tilsit gave himself up voluntarily. He maintains that he acted during a sudden brain storm; believes he was pursued by Jews and declares that he followed an inner compulsion. Has already been brought before the special court in Königsberg today . . . [7]

On 24 November, de Grey gathered the messages from the preceding seven days into a weekly summary: above the SS message

---

i 'RF SS' in German Police messages referred to the Reichsführer der SS, Heinrich Himmler

ii In October 1939, a strip of disputed land between Lithuania and East Prussia

iii The SA, or Sturmabteilung, were the original paramilitary organisation of the Nazi Party which helped Hitler come to power: they were purged by their rivals, the Schutzstaffel, or SS, on the 'Night of the Long Knives' in 1934

questioning the logistics of the evacuation from Nasielsk, he wrote the headline 'The Pogrom Proceeds'.

Nigel de Grey and the Zimmermann Telegram

On 12 January 1939, a letter had arrived for de Grey at the art publishers where he worked in London's Mayfair district. The Medici Galleries, with their distinctive company logo of Lorenzo de Medici, sold fine art reproductions, and the unassuming fifty-two-year-old de Grey had worked for them since leaving the Royal Navy at the end of the First World War. The letter that arrived that morning was from the Naval Intelligence Division at the Admiralty. Europe was sliding towards war, and like many of his friends and acquaintances, de Grey was on a list of reservist officers, and he knew that he could be called up. But when he opened the letter, he found its contents puzzling. It asked if he could give the Admiralty 'quite unofficially, information as to your naval training, and if you had any experience in intelligence work'.[8] It seemed to him a bizarre and rather ill-informed question to ask of a man who had been behind one of the greatest intelligence coups so far that century. So de Grey bided his time and waited. Two weeks later, another letter from the Admiralty arrived at the galleries in Grafton Street. It was apologetic.

'We are sorry that owing to some inexplicable omission on the part of our staff here, your previous record was not available when I wrote to you.'[9]

Along with the British Army and Royal Air Force, the Admiralty was looking for qualified staff who could join its newly formed cadre of cryptanalysts at the Government Code and Cypher School. This department of the War Office was responsible for Great Britain's decryption and analysis of the coded signals of foreign countries. Its headquarters was in a street in St James's, near Green Park.

De Grey wrote back and Admiralty Intelligence, who by now had realised exactly who he was and precisely what it was he had done in the previous war, asked him to attend an interview.

What had de Grey done in the First World War in the rarified world of cryptanalysis that had made the Admiralty write to him, and why were they so keen to recruit him? For the path that Nigel de Grey had wended to codebreaking was at once eccentric, and yet characteristic of the way the British upper classes functioned in the first half of the twentieth century.

His father, the Honourable Reverend Arnald de Grey, was a country parson in the village of Copdock in Norfolk, the youngest son of Thomas de Grey, the 5th Baron of Walsingham. Nigel de Grey grew up in the flat country of East Anglia, attuned to the rhythms of a rural parsonage set around services at the fifteenth-century church. Copdock had around two hundred inhabitants, and if de Grey or any of the other villagers had been asked to name one of note, they would probably have said William Henry Hewitt. Born in Copdock in 1884, the thirty-three-year-old lance-corporal won the Victoria Cross storming a German pillbox at the Battle of Ypres in 1917.

Arnald de Grey had married Margaret, the elder daughter of the Right Honourable Spenser Ponsonby-Fane, an aristocratic Somerset landowner who had been Private Secretary to three successive foreign secretaries, including Lord Palmerston. Ponsonby-Fane was a keen cricketer and was treasurer of the Marylebone Cricket Club, while as a diplomat in 1856 he had personally brought the Crimean War treaty from Paris to London for signature by the British government. The family's ancestral seat was at Brympton D'Evercy outside Yeovil in Somerset. Built in 1220, the handsome mansion was described in 1927 by the architectural writer Christopher Hussey as the house which best epitomised English country house qualities. Ponsonby-Fane was himself the nephew of Lady Georgiana Fane, a compulsive and highly eccentric socialite and gardener who spent half her life trying to pursue a relationship with Arthur Wellesley, the First Duke of Wellington. They met shortly after the Battle of Waterloo in 1815, when she was fourteen, he forty-seven, and she spent the rest of her life pursuing him. The situation was further complicated by the fact that Lord Palmerston, then Secretary of War, was having an affair with Georgiana's married half-sister, Sarah Villiers, but still proposed to Georgiana twice.

Nobody, therefore, could accuse Nigel de Grey of inferior pedigree. His father died in 1889 when he was three, and eight years later his elder brother Michael died tragically while getting off a train en route to school at Eton. De Grey himself left the college in 1904 and in 1907 sat the entrance exam for the Foreign and Commonwealth Office, which he failed. He joined the publishing company William Heinemann in the same year. The descendant of such aristocratic eccentricity grew up a shy, quiet boy, who seemed to quietly plod through his life. In 1910 he married his second cousin, Florence Gore, whose brother was the Post-Impressionist painter Spencer Gore. Her and de Grey's shared great-grandfather had been Home Secretary in 1834. Diplomacy, painting, the arts, public service and a certain maverick unruliness thus ran in the family blood, yet increasingly, de Grey seemed to become the opposite, almost as though he was tempering the flames of his forebears by becoming a man who said little. Rather, he was becoming a born organiser, a man who could administer. His unremarkability was remarkable.

When war was declared in 1914, he applied to be a special constable in London's Metropolitan Police: shortly after the outbreak of war, London's police force was issued with three very small anti-aircraft guns and told to deploy them to defend the whole of England's capital against German aerial attack. Almost immediately, feeling that anti-aircraft duties were not the expertise of policemen and detectives, the Met handed them over to the Royal Naval Volunteer Reserve, and so de Grey found himself drafted as a young sub-lieutenant into England's Senior Service. From December 1914, Germany used airships to stage wildly inaccurate bombing raids on London and southern England – so erratic was German aerial navigation that one raid on the City of London hit the port of Hull. Nonetheless, the raids killed some 550 civilians. Nigel de Grey spent night shifts as part of a searchlight crew, helping his colleagues rotate an enormous acetylene lamp very slowly as he and his crew scanned the skies over London for Zeppelins. When the British launched airships of their own, Chief Petty Officer de Grey crossed the Channel with them, and took up station at Dunkirk. At first he worked as a kite balloon observer, and twice a day his colleagues winched him up and down in a wicker basket to scan the skies over the Western Front for any German aircraft. After six months of ballooning, his commanding officer decided that the quiet, highly observant and very organised young man was wasted in the job.

Naval Intelligence was recruiting men to work in their signals intelligence department at the Admiralty in London, and de Grey fulfilled two of their principal criteria. They wanted men who were already naval officers, had been to Eton, and then preferably to Oxford or Cambridge too, and who spoke French and German. De Grey ticked three out of the four boxes. He returned to London, passed the selection interview, and from then on his headquarters was in the warren of rooms and offices in the Admiralty's main building in Whitehall. Collectively, these were called Room 40, and this became the unofficial name for the Signals and Defence Intelligence department of the Admiralty. De Grey was promoted to the rank of lieutenant-commander, and gradually introduced to the world of cryptanalysis, the making and breaking of secret codes.

British codebreaking and signals intercepts operations were in their infancy in 1914. This was to be expected, as the electronic medium they were trying to break into, wireless telegraphy, was also new. Guglielmo Marconi had perfected his invention only in 1907. In 1912, the high-power radiotelegraph transmitter installed on the Titanic for sending passenger 'Marconigrams' and for operational use was considered the height of technical innovation. At the Old Admiralty Building in London, in the rooms designated number 40, were the headquarters of the Royal Navy's nascent codebreaking unit. For the rest of the war it was simply called 'Room 40'. There was no shortage of wireless signals to work on. Three years earlier, in 1911, the British Imperial Defence Committee had made a far-sighted decision: German undersea wireless cables would be cut in the event of war breaking out. This, reckoned the committee, would force the Germans to send messages either by wireless networks owned by other countries, or in code on wireless networks not dependent on cables. In both cases, if the British could capture the codebooks, or crack the ciphers, the information would be accessible to them. They were proved right. Three days after war with Germany was declared on 4 August, the British cut five of Germany's transatlantic cables which ran down the English Channel. Coded German wireless traffic promptly increased.

By 1916, each German message was encoded using one of three codebooks, all of which the British had captured. The first, called the SKM book, came from a German cruiser captured by the Russians in 1914 in the Baltic, the SMS *Magdeburg*. The second and third, the VB and HVB codebooks, came from German ships boarded by the Royal Navy. This gave the British intelligence officers and civilian staff a huge amount of material to work on. Among those who arrived to lead and to staff Room 40 were the director of naval education, Alfred Ewing, who listed cryptology as a hobby. There was Nigel de Grey himself, and William Montgomery, a Presbyterian minister who had translated theological books from German. The eccentric classics scholar and papyrologist Dillwyn Knox came too: one of his more individual traits was to lie naked in a bath at the end of one of the corridors at Room 40, eyes closed, his mind working through cryptanalytical problems. He and de Grey had been at Eton together, from where Knox went on to Cambridge, after which Room 40 had recruited him immediately.

In no single incident in the First World War did the British signals intelligence operation achieve so much, or have its entire strategy so comprehensively vindicated, as in the Zimmermann telegram affair of early 1917. And in no single incident did every German failing in coding strategy since 1914 do that country so much damage. It was also to be the high point of Nigel de Grey's wartime service. On 11 January 1917, the German foreign secretary Arthur Zimmermann composed a telegram to send to his ambassador in Mexico City. It was then enciphered in the diplomatic code the Germans used. The Battle of Jutland had seen the British navies effectively deny the Germans definitive strategic control of the North Sea and the Atlantic. The Imperial German Navy had decided that submarine warfare against Britain and in particular the United States was their next strategic step. Knowing that this could lead to war with the United States, Zimmermann told the ambassador in Mexico that if and when the Americans entered the war on the British, French and Russian side, he was authorised to make a proposition to the Mexican government.

The famed 'Zimmermann telegram' laid out an extraordinary plan. The Germans would give the Mexicans funding and a military alliance designed to destabilise America's military capacity and undermine its desire to fight a war across the Atlantic. A successful outcome would see the Mexicans rewarded with parts of American territory. The Germans sent the telegram, but because its transmission required it to travel along radio telephone lines that passed through Land's End, the British intercepted it. De Grey and his colleagues deciphered much of it by the subsequent day. He used a German diplomatic codebook that had been captured in Mesopotamia in 1915, as well as the original German naval codebook, captured in 1914. Two days later the Admiralty, through three different and circuitous routes, made the contents of the telegram public. It coincided with the start of German submarine attacks on American merchant shipping, and saw the United States unsurprisingly join the First World War on the side of the Allies. Three days after the decryption was completed, de Grey stood up to address his colleagues:

'Ladies and gentlemen, we are going to win the war.'[10]

The subterfuge involved in the decrypting and publicising of the Zimmermann telegram was considerable: as he had been a central player in the affair, the Admiralty decided to give de Grey a break from London and sent him to work with Britain's Italian allies at Brindisi on the Adriatic seaboard. There, de Grey set up and ran interception stations monitoring Austrian and German radio traffic, passing the information gained to Sir Samuel Hoare, the Rome station chief of the newly formed MI6. Hoare had previously served in Petrograd in Russia as Britain's liaison officer with Russian intelligence: he had reported the death of Rasputin to London in 1916. In Rome, his chief priority was trying to persuade Italy not to drop out of the war, and he employed de Grey's cryptanalytical abilities for all his communications back to London. As a result of this work, based in both Bari and Rome, the quiet Old Etonian became familiar with many of the cipher codes then in existence, including German ones, and the Italians rewarded his work by making him a Knight Officer of the Order of Saint Michael and Lazarus. It was the second oldest Catholic order of chivalry, instituted by the House of Savoy in Turin.

The British, in turn, made him an officer of the Order of the British Empire in 1919, when Room 40 and the army's MI1 combined to form the Government Code and Cypher School. They asked de Grey to remain and work with them, but he declined. Some of his former colleagues, including Oliver Strachey and Dillwyn Knox did, however. Unemployed, de Grey tried to return to Heinemann, but there was no place available, so he accepted an offer of a position at the Medici Galleries. Twenty years later he was still there. The inter-war years saw him working quietly yet laboriously, raising three children, Roger, Barbara and Anthony, and painting. The first son studied art for three years at Chelsea Polytechnic, and was commissioned into the Royal Armoured Corps.

Over the inter-war years, de Grey remained in touch with his former colleagues from Room 40, and during the Spanish Civil War, he was aware that Dillwyn Knox was working on codes used by General Franco's forces. He also travelled to Poland to meet with cryptanalysts who were examining an encryption device the German armed forces were using. It was called Enigma. Oliver Strachey, another former colleague, also remained at the government's cipher school, working on Japanese codes. So a week after receiving the second letter from the Admiralty, de Grey reported for his interview. They told him they were sending him to the new headquarters of the Government Code and Cypher School, as it was now formally named (or, less formally, GC&CS), which had been moved from London to a requisitioned country house fifty miles north of London. As it had been twenty years since de Grey had done any codebreaking, said the senior naval officers who interviewed him, and things had come on somewhat, he would be put through a refresher course, and then would work alongside the director of the school. This was the Scottish naval officer and codebreaker Commander Andrew Alistair Denniston, who in 1914 had helped set up Room 40, and was now recruiting cryptanalysts to fill the ranks at the new codebreaking centre. There was no shortage of suitable candidates, and the established excellence of men like Knox and Strachey, combined with the shared knowledge of the Poles, meant that in technical terms, the British codebreakers were making advances. What they needed were people who could organise and supervise the technical brilliance of the often erratic and eccentric cryptanalysts, staff who could supervise the people, and build a functioning system that would administer them and the intelligence they produced. De Grey, although quiet, was extremely organised and an excellent logistical administrator with a love for detail. Both Alastair Denniston and Samuel Hoare from MI6 attested to this. He was unthreatening, too, so could handle the often volatile egos of highly intelligent scientists. His colleagues at Bletchley Park would nickname him 'the dormouse', but there was a core of steel to him, despite his unassuming and reticent exterior. Prone to whispering in meetings, writing in pencil and occasionally wearing a cloak, he was a codebreaker extraordinaire. The perfect cryptanalyst, said one historian, was 'Beethoven with the soul of an accountant'.[11] This described de Grey perfectly.

The new headquarters of the cipher school was called Bletchley Park, and the Secret Intelligence Service had chosen it for several reasons. It sat on the junction of two railway lines in Buckinghamshire, and was easily accessible.; there was a telegraph repeater station in a nearby village, making the high volume of electronic transmissions faster, and the final factor was the park's relative anonymity and seclusion. Hidden away in a grassy park, the Victorian country house, a hodgepodge of discordant architectural styles, inspired one codebreaker to describe its architecture as 'lavatory Gothic'.

In early August 1939, de Grey found himself standing on the lawn in front of the house at Bletchley, knowing, like everybody else in Europe, that war was only weeks away. 'There is no moment in time more beautiful than the first days of a fine autumn, such as were the last days of August, and the last days of peace . . . In such richly romantic atmospheric conditions, even the architectural vagaries of Bletchley Park were wrapped in a false mellowness and almost but never quite achieved the appearance of a stately home.'[12]

Britain's and Europe's Jews before the outbreak of war

In the months leading up to the outbreak of war the persecution of Germany's and Austria's Jews worsened dramatically: in one November night in 1938, Nazi Party paramilitaries ransacked and destroyed 267 synagogues and 9,000 Jewish businesses across Germany, Austria and the Sudetenland, the German-speaking region of Czechoslovakia. The Nazi party's paramilitary police, the Schutzstaffel, or SS, killed more than a hundred Jews that night, and over a period of subsequent weeks deported 30,000 Jewish men as political prisoners to concentration camps at Dachau and Sachsenhausen. Reporting filed by foreign journalists in Germany after Kristallnacht, or 'the night of broken glass', exceeded in volume any prior event in the Nazis' continuing persecution of Germany's and Austria's Jews.

'No foreign propagandist bent upon blackening Germany before the world could outdo the tale of burnings and beatings, of blackguardly assaults on defenceless and innocent people, which disgraced that country yesterday,' said *The Times* of London on the following day.[13]

Despite this violence, Nigel de Grey knew there had been very strong hostility in Britain towards welcoming unlimited numbers of Jewish refugees in the years prior to the war, a sentiment summed up in the country's newspapers. In the spring of 1938, Colonel Josiah Wedgwood, a Labour Member of Parliament, had tabled a motion before the house. Like Nigel de Grey, he was a former officer in the Royal Naval Volunteer Reserve who had served in the First World War. His gallantry commanding a unit of naval machine-gunners during the 1915 landing in the Dardanelles saw him awarded the Distinguished Service Order. It was at Gallipoli that he met Joseph Vulfovich Trumpeldor, a Russian Jewish dentist from the North Caucasus, whose left arm had been blown off by shrapnel while fighting in the Russo-Japanese War in 1904. By the time of the landings at Cape Helles, the former dentist was an officer in the Zion Mule Corps, and in his role as a Zionist activist was trying to help arrange Jewish immigration to Palestine.

As he and Wedgwood found themselves soldiering on the Turkish coast, a long way from their respective homes, the Russian Jew's views strongly influenced the naval reserve captain. Wedgwood ended the war a colonel, and twenty years later had become a vocal political critic of appeasement of Hitler, and of the strict quotas by the British government both on Jewish immigration to Palestine, and on German refugees trying to enter Great Britain. In March 1938 he tabled his motion in the House of Commons calling for a policy of wholesale admission and naturalisation of refugees fleeing mainland Europe. The vote went against him.

The editorial reaction by British newspapers to his proposal summarised the opinion of the country's media on the question of whether or not to admit into Britain unlimited numbers of the hundreds of thousands of German and Austrian Jews then trying to flee Europe.

'Shall all come in?' asked the *Daily Express* on 24 March 1938:

We need to ask, for there is a powerful agitation here to admit all Jewish refugees without question or discrimination. It would be unwise to overload the basket like that. It would stir up the elements here that fatten on anti-Semitic propaganda.

They would point to the fresh tide of foreigners, almost all belonging to the extreme left. They would ask: what if Poland, Hungary, Rumania all expel their Jewish citizens? Must we admit them too? Because we DON'T want anti-Jewish uproar; we DO need to show common sense in not admitting all applicants.

The *Daily Mail* of 23 March said that it would be disastrous to be ruled by the 'misguided sentimentalism of those who think with Colonel Wedgwood', and pontificated that 'once it was known that Britain offered sanctuary to all who cared to come, the floodgates would be opened, and we should be inundated by thousands seeking a home.'

On the same day, the *Daily Telegraph* tempered pragmatism with emotion, as did *The Scotsman*. 'The government is bound to qualify sympathy with practical and prudential considerations,' said the former, while the latter stressed that:

The policy of the fully open door is not practicable, and it is important that oppressed minorities should not assume that admission into this country is to be offered to all and sundry . . . the problem has an international character, and it is clearly impossible for this country alone to provide the necessary refuge.

The 1935 Nuremberg Laws had stripped German Jews of their citizenship, calling them 'subjects' instead, effectively making them stateless. By the time Wedgwood tabled his motion before the British parliament about half of Germany's and Austria's 900,000 Jews had fled or been expelled from their countries. Despite their widely publicised persecution, the United States had staunchly refused to increase their strict quota of immigration visas which they were prepared to give to the desperate Jews trying to flee the Third Reich. Britain had admitted some 50,000 of them, while around 450,000 had fled to France and 320,000 migrated to British Mandatory Palestine. This sudden influx on territory historically occupied by Arabs meant that tens of thousands of European Jews were also trying to occupy a finite amount of land, and the result was violent. Under the 1917 Balfour Declaration Great Britain promised to create a Jewish national homeland in Palestine. In turn, they also promised Hashemite Arab governors that, in return for supporting Britain against the Ottoman Turks during the First World War, they would create an Arab country in Syria. The arrival of the European Jews caused the Arab uprising of 1936-1939, and subsequently the British were overwhelmingly cautious about the number of Jewish refugees they admitted to Palestine, despite their ongoing knowledge of Hitler's increasing atrocities, and the determination of Winston Churchill – then out of government – and others to do something about it. The Conservative government led by Prime Minister Neville Chamberlain was the bedrock of this caution.

When United States President Franklin D. Roosevelt convened the Evian Conference in June 1938 at Evian-les-Bains, on Lake Geneva, it was a last-ditch attempt to help Germany and Austria's Jews. Hoping to persuade the governments of some of the thirty-one other nations invited to accept more Jewish refugees, the American premier also calculated he could deflect increasing criticism of the American State Department's immigration quota policy. The conference fell flat on its face. The Jewish representative from Mandatory Palestine, Golda Meir, was not allowed to speak or participate in any of the meetings except as an observer. Bar the Dominican Republic, none of the thirty-two participant nations managed to come to any agreement about accepting Jewish refugees. Roosevelt's failed grandstanding ultimately played directly into

Hitler's hands. Replying to the news of the conference's stalemate, the German Führer commented:

> I can only hope and expect that the other world, which has such deep sympathy for these criminals [Jews], will at least be generous enough to convert this sympathy into practical aid. We, on our part, are ready to put all these criminals at the disposal of these countries, for all I care, even on luxury ships.[14]

Jewish leaders themselves were unable to agree on a unified line of policy: Samuel Rosenman, the American Democrat lawyer and presidential speechwriter who had coined the term 'the New Deal', said increasing immigration quotas for Jews would backfire for the United States and other countries as it would simply create a Jewish problem in the country increasing its quotas. Zionist leaders Ezer Weizmann and David Ben-Gurion were firmly opposed to mass Jewish immigration into western Europe, hoping instead that the plight of hundreds of thousands of Jews trying to flee Germany and Austria would force Britain into allowing increased immigration to Palestine. The door was now almost closed for Europe's Jews. In July 1979, Vice-President Walter Mondale, addressing a UN conference on Indonesian refugees, alluded regretfully to the Evian Conference of forty years before:

> At stake at Evian were both human lives – and the decency and self-respect of the civilised world. If each nation at Evian had agreed on that day to take in 17,000 Jews at once, every Jew in the Reich could have been saved. As one American observer wrote, 'It is heartbreaking to think of the . . . desperate human beings . . . waiting in suspense for what happens at Evian. But the question they underline is not simply humanitarian . . . it is a test of civilisation.[15]

On 30 September 1938, Neville Chamberlain signed the Munich Agreement, which allowed Germany to annex the mainly German-speaking Sudetenland in Czechoslovakia. Churchill called this a 'total and unmitigated defeat'.[16] He was an ardent opponent of what he saw as the racist anti-Semitism of Nazi Germany, and any appeasement of Hitler. He had also foreseen the coming storm earlier than most. On 13 April 1933, two months after Hitler came to power, he had given a speech in the House of Commons in which he said: 'There is a danger of the odious conditions now ruling in Germany, being extended by conquest to Poland and another persecution and pogroms of Jews being begun in this new area.'[17]

By April 1937, he was stressing the importance of not limiting Jewish immigration to Mandated Palestine, of 'not closing the door against them'.[18] This was an unpopular political and social view in Britain at the time, and Churchill himself was seen as very pro-Jewish. One leading associate who had known him from the 1920s onwards said of him: 'Winston did have one serious fault – he was too fond of Jews.'[19] The same could not necessarily be said of Prime Minister Neville Chamberlain, who in a letter to his sister written after Kristallnacht, said, 'Jews aren't a lovable people – I don't care for them myself, but that is not sufficient to explain the pogrom.'[20]

The next nail in an almost-closed coffin came in May 1939, when Chamberlain's Conservative government issued the White Paper of 1939, which laid out Britain's policy towards Palestine from 1939 onwards. It was a response to the Arab revolt in Palestine, and the subsequent failure of the Arab-Zionist conference in London, which had aimed at finding a settlement between both parties. In the following year, an increasing influx of Jewish immigrants had worsened the situation. The House of Commons approved the paper in May 1939: it called for the establishment of a Jewish national home within ten years, to be set inside an independent Palestinian state. It rejected the idea of partitioning Palestine. The White Paper also contained a crucial clause – which became a matter of life or death for the Jews of Europe in 1939, fleeing the Third Reich's ever-increasing persecution. The paper ruled that for the successive five years, until March 1944, the maximum number of Jewish immigrants to Mandated Palestine would be 75,000. Further increases in this number would be decided by the Arab majority in the territory. From May 1939, this meant that of the hundreds of thousands of Jews trying to flee Europe, only a small number stood a chance of being admitted to safety in Palestine. Being trapped inside Europe, as a Jew, now meant a high chance of economic exploitation, extortion, arrest, deportation and quite possibly death. By November 1939, the messages which Nigel de Grey and his colleagues were decrypting were, day by day, showing how the Germans were putting their plan of persecution into action.

CHAPTER II

HERMANN HÖFLE AND THE AUSTRIAN SS

'Forget your Austrian softness'

On 16 October 1939, six weeks after Germany had invaded Poland, an SS officer called Ludolf von Alvensleben stood in front of some of the men he commanded. He was one of the Higher SS and Police Leaders in the newly occupied German territory, and the men were from local paramilitary groups, made up of ethnic Germans living in Poland with Polish citizenship, called Volksdeutscher Selbstschutz. These were the 'levies of ruffians raised among the local population to help hold down the Poles' as Bletchley Park described them.[21] Their title meant 'Volksdeutsche People's Self-Defence', and the men, trained and supervised by the SS (Schutzstaffel) and the Gestapo (Geheime Staatspolizei, the Secret State Police), had for two years been drawing up lists of Polish activists, intellectuals, politicians and trade union leaders targeted for elimination once Nazi Germany invaded. There were about 17,500 men in their ranks in West Prussia alone, and by the time Alvensleben gave his speech, they had killed around 4,250 Poles and Jews in six weeks.

You are now the master race here. Nothing was yet built up through softness and weakness... That's why I expect, just as our Führer Adolf Hitler expects from you, that you are disciplined, but stand together hard as Krupp steel. Don't be soft, be merciless, and clear out everything that is not German and could hinder us in the work of construction.[22]

The paramilitaries operated alongside German Police and SS units, and were already establishing concentration camps for Poles set near the main towns and cities where the SS and Wehrmacht were based. By mid-October, operations against these Poles and Jews were in full swing.

From Police Battalion 63, to the Commander of the Order Police, Krakow 19.10.39:

At the urgent request of the local field commander on Friday 20th October a platoon of the third comp[any] to be sent to Sandomierz to carry out a pacification operation: the deployment of the rest of the third comp in Nesto is probable by the 20th.[23]

The Germans had occupied Sandomierz on 9 September, and immediately started the segregation and rounding-up of the town's 3,000 Jews. The police units and the SS communicated with each other and with their command echelon using radio signals, encrypted on the handheld codebook system called Double Transposition, and then transmitted in Morse code. This was a different system from that of their colleagues in the Heer (army), the Luftwaffe and the Kriegsmarine, who used the newly issued encryption device called Enigma. Executions of Poles and Jews had begun the moment the SS, their colleagues from the 'action squads' (*Einsatzkommandos*) and the Wehrmacht had crossed the

German-Polish border. On 6 September the Germans burned down the synagogue in the town of Bedzin, and then shot 100 Jews and 60 Poles. In the town of Czestochowa, a unit from the Heer killed 200 Polish civilians after mistakenly thinking that Polish partisans had fired on them: 16,000 Polish civilians, including Jews, were killed in the first week following the invasion. On 14 September, as Jews were celebrating Yom Kippur, the Day of Atonement, the SS entered the town of Wloclawek in central Poland, burned both synagogues, and then arrested Catholic priests and politicians and deported them to Dachau. Families of murdered and deported Jews were immediately taken to ghettos in the General Government area. The SS started fires in Jewish houses and shops in Wloclawek, and watched as the occupants fled with their possessions into the city's streets, where many were promptly robbed by neighbouring Poles. Then the SS forced the Jews to sign confessions that they had actually set fire to their own houses, and had thus committed arson; 800 Jews were held ransom by the Germans, and only on payment of fines of 100, then 150, and then 250,000 zlotys could they avoid instant deportation. Following behind the SS and German police was Einsatzkommando III, who set up their local field headquarters in Wloclawek, and began 'evacuation operations' – as the SS designated deportations – of the town's Jews.

After the invasion of Poland, the Germans either incorporated their newly occupied territory into the existing German Reich, in the case of such areas as Danzig, Wartheland and West Prussia, or began to administer it under a newly formed area called the 'General Government'. Much of the land taken by German troops was quickly occupied by ethnic German settlers – the Volksdeutsche – arriving from eastern Europe. Five hundred thousand Jews now found themselves living on this new German territory, and their new occupiers aimed to deport as many of them as possible to the area in and around the city of Lublin, the designated capital of the General Government, a hundred miles south-east of Warsaw. There they would be concentrated in ghettos.

One of the SS officers who commanded a detachment of the Volksdeutscher Selbstchutz, or VDSS, was an Austrian officer called Hermann Julius Höfle.[iv] The VDSS were the Volksdeutsche 'Self-Protection' squads. That September the former taxi driver and mechanic from Salzburg was twenty-eight. He was now in charge of the ethnic German paramilitary unit based in Nowy Sacz, fifty miles south-east of Krakow, towards the Hungarian border. Like all other SS officers, he had read the Schnellbrief, or Orders Directive, which Reinhard Heydrich had sent out to all units of the SS on 21 September. In the message, the head of the Reich Security Main Office gave orders for how Jews in occupied Poland would be treated. Those in towns and villages would immediately be transferred to ghettos, administered by a small Judenrat, or Jewish Council, whose members would be selected by the SS. The Jews would provide a pool of labour for the Germans, until the SS had decided how 'the Jewish problem', as Heydrich called it, would be solved. Yet by the first weeks of September, the SS, Order Police battalions, the Einsatzkommandos and the VDSS were already beginning to tackle the problem, deploying extreme violence.

Hermann Höfle had worked as a mechanic and driver for his father's taxi company in Salzburg in Austria before joining the Schutzstaffel on 1 August 1933, driven by a desire for professional advancement, social status and a loathing of anything connected with Bolshevism. Born in June 1911, he was four when his father went off to fight for the Austro-Hungarian Empire against Italy. Life before the First World War for the family in Salzburg had been one of calm, ordered affluence: a lower middle-class stability where everybody in the town, socially and professionally, knew

---

iv   Not to be confused with Obergruppenführer Hermann Höfle (1898–1947).

their place and adhered to it. There was enough money, too. This changed by 1918 when the soldiers came home from fighting on the Isonzo river in north-eastern Italy, in sixteen increasingly bloody battles of mounting stalemate, against armies of Italian conscripts. The bottom fell out of the empire after Hungary terminated the union in October 1918. The 'turnip winter' of 1918 saw inflation, falling food supplies, the Spanish flu pandemic, all set against the backdrop of a collapsed political and national alliance. When the National Socialist German Worker's Party formed in 1920, it started to represent a light of aspirant, political hope for ex-solders like Hermann Höfle's father.

At the time Hermann Höfle left formal education and began to work for his father, the Nazi Party was still an illegal organisation in Austria, and the awkward, insecure cab driver, with his poor school record and terrible spelling, was arrested twice for belonging to a proscribed political party.[24] The second charge earned him a short spell in prison. When Adolf Hitler came to power in 1933, the Austrian SS received weapons, military training and political orientation from their colleagues in Germany, half a mile from Salzburg, to the west across the Saalach river. The boxy two-litre taxis, the Steyr-Daimler 45s from Höfle's company, became the unofficial transport for some local Austrian Nazis, taking them to political party meetings at cafés and restaurants owned by other SS members. One of the cafés they favoured for their meetings was called Café Lerch, in the eastern town of Klagenfurt, on the Hungarian border. Designed in the Art Nouveau style, it had arched ceilings, myriad glass and brass fittings, and a large billiard table: it was popular not just for its smart, modern style or its cakes made by a man who had worked in France's restaurants, but for its jazz and dancing, Ernst Lerch was the son of the owner, and was a professional waiter who had worked in Switzerland, Hungary and France, and brought back their recipes and influence with them.In Paris, he had met German Nazis in a café where he worked. He had also joined the SS in 1934. By early 1937, he and Höfle were both Untersturmführers, or 2nd lieutenants, in the paramilitary organisation.

Lerch then moved to Berlin to join the Reich Security Directorate, while Höfle, with his own platoon under his command, took place enthusiastically in the mass arson and vandalism of Kristallnacht in November 1938, which in turn brought him to the attention of another Austrian SS officer, called Adolf Eichmann. Further officer training at Dachau followed for Höfle, and then a posting to the 1st SS Totenkopfverbände, or Death's Head Guard Battalion, as one of the first units of concentration camp guards was named. He served with them in the occupation of the Sudetenland, before crossing the border into Poland on the night of 1 September 1939. After the 1938 Anschluss had seen the Nazis take power in Austria, SS men like Höfle were swiftly rewarded with administrative positions and fast promotion within SS military units. In September 1939, Höfle went over the Polish border as a subaltern, and by the time his platoon had advanced into the Polish drizzle at a rate of a hundred miles per week, taken two hundred prisoners and slept two hours in every twenty-four, Poland was on the verge of collapse, and Höfle close to promotion to captain. He was sent to Nowy Sacz in the south, an area of Poland that was earmarked for 'Germanisation', and took over the Volksdeutscher paramilitary unit. He and his men terrorised, tortured and killed local Poles and any Jews they could find – a role in which he succeeded. His insecurity, stemming from his partial dyslexia, made him feel constantly backfooted by other more confident and powerful people, so he strived to be more organised and to assert himself. Yet he looked confident, with a cheerful, round face and deep blue eyes above the SS uniform. As the summer of 1939 turned into a damp autumn, the wheat harvest rotted, sagging in the fields once the Polish farm labourers had fled or been shot, and the former taxi driver was promoted and sent to Lublin in Poland. His SS superiors earmarked him to run one of the first work camps, filled with Jewish slave-labourers. It was to be built outside a village called Bełżec.

Five men of the Austrian SS who changed Europe

Five Austrian men alone were to have more effect on the fate of Europe's Jews than almost anybody else from their country. On April Fool's Day 1932, in the city of Linz, one of them had made a decisive career choice. He was called Adolf Eichmann. A family friend had offered him some firm professional advice, and then afterwards had extended him an invitation. The advice was to become a Nazi. The invitation was to ask if he wanted to join a new organisation. It was called the Schutzstaffel, or SS. What did Eichmann think of this? asked the acquaintance, emphasising his recommendation to become a Nazi. The man who had made the suggestion was also an Austrian, called Ernst Kaltenbrunner; he and Eichmann, two and a half years his junior, knew each other because their fathers, respectively a lawyer and a mining official, were both based in Linz, sixty miles north-east of Salzburg.

The connection was more professional than personal, however, and the two men didn't know each other well, or mix in the same carefully delineated social circles. Kaltenbrunner was from a firmly established middle-class Austrian family, and already had his own law firm in Linz. He was twenty-eight in 1932, and at six-foot-four was physically imposing. He was well-connected, and the three deep scars on the left side of his face were, he claimed, from wounds sustained while duelling at Graz University. Others said they were injuries from a drunken car accident. He wasn't just an influential local lawyer, however: he was the speaker for the Nazi Party in

Upper Austria, and had also been a member of its paramilitary wing since 1931. This organisation was the SS, or Schutzstaffel – meaning 'protection squad' – and in the beer halls and cobbled streets of Austrian towns, its troopers guarded party meetings against violent political opponents. When things went wrong, and young SS troopers beat, stabbed or shot the supporters of conflicting factions, particularly communists, it was Kaltenbrunner and his legal team who came to their rescue.

Adolf Eichmann came from the same lower-middle professional classes as both Hermann Höfle, the son of a war veteran and mechanic, and Ernst Lerch, son of a restaurant owner. He was a bit older than the other two, and was twenty-five in 1932; for five years he had been working in a steady, plodding job as the regional salesman in Upper Austria for an American petroleum consortium, the Vacuum Oil Company. It was not interesting, but in the stringent times of a recession, people always needed oil, and Eichmann got paid. His family were originally German and his father, a bookkeeper, had moved to Linz twenty years before to work for the local tram company. In the tight-knit class system of Austria, the family was significantly below the affluent, middle-class Kaltenbrunners. With five children, money had always been tight in Adolf Eichmann's family. He went to the same secondary school in Linz that another Adolf, this one surnamed 'Hitler', had attended seventeen years before.

Like Höfle's, Eichmann's school performance was lacklustre, he didn't try, and so his ordered, worried and ambitious father removed him. He then enrolled his son in a local technical school, keen for him to learn about electronics. Again, Eichmann dropped out, this time without a trade qualification, so his despairing father gave him a job in his new mining venture that dug salt out of the surrounding Austrian mountains. For a third time, Adolf Eichmann couldn't make a success of it, so after two years as a salesman with a local electronics company, he applied to the Vacuum Oil Company. Could he try and sell their products for them?

For five years he moved repeatedly around a local sales circuit of small-town garages, factories and agricultural suppliers, across the valleys and Alpine passes of Upper Austria, selling motor oil. Yet he wanted something more. He most liked belonging to organisations, and being with like-minded people who shared his increasingly right-wing and nationalist views. What he was trying to escape and avoid was what he described as 'a leaderless and difficult individual life, where I would receive no directives from anybody, no orders or commands would any longer be issued to me, no pertinent ordinances would be there to consult'.[25]

In the evenings, after a day driving to sell oil to local garages, he attended meetings of the youth wing of the Front Freedom Fighters, a right-wing political party founded by an Austrian veteran of the First World War. It stood for the rights of former soldiers, was bitterly opposed to the terms of the Treaty of Versailles, which it saw pulling neighbouring Germany apart. It had no time for socialists or communists, who it saw, simplistically, as agents of what the 'fighters' termed international Bolshevism. And they promoted a right-wing brand of anti-Semitism as well, hating Jews, blaming them for both Austria's and Germany's political-economic failures. They also accused them in speeches of occupying land and houses and jobs and what they called *Lebensraum*, 'living space', that rightly belonged to nationalist people, pan-Germans who wanted to see Austria and Germany and its Germanic people united in one country.

For a man with little direction, an overbearing father, a repetitive but reliable job, and little in terms of self-definition, the youth wing of this party offered Eichmann what he seemed to want. So when the towering, confident Kaltenbrunner suggested he join the Nazi Party, and then by extension also become a member of the

Austrian SS, Eichmann jumped at the chance. Yes, was the answer. He officially joined the Nazi Party on 1 April 1932 and applied immediately to join the SS, a process which took some six months but he finally enrolled as member no. 45326. He stayed at work with Vacuum Oil, however, as the SS was, for now, an evening job. In Linz and Salzburg and Klagenfurt, Eichmann and his fellow Schutzstaffel troopers Hermann Höfle and Ernst Lerch were given a smart uniform and badge each, and as part of an SS-Standarte, or SS Guard Unit, they watched over their political colleagues at rallies, and stood outside the doors of meeting halls trying to prevent the frequent violence from opposing socialist or communist political supporters. The commanding officer of Eichmann's unit was the very man who had advised him to join up – Ernst Kaltenbrunner, who was by now legal adviser to all Austrian SS troopers and officials.

The Nazi Party seized power in neighbouring Germany in January 1933, and the Austrian SS was suddenly an illegal organisation in Kaltenbrunner's home country. He and other men from Standarte-7 would drive through the mountains, and across the border post in the town of Passau, which sits on the junction of the Danube, Inn and Ilz rivers. They would travel to Munich, and from German SS men pick up money, political pamphlets, handguns and explosives. Then they would cross back into Austria and return to Linz. Sometimes, if it was considered too risky to drive via Passau, the journey went through Salzburg, further south on the border, and there Höfle and his fellow members of Standarte-1 would help.

In 1934 the Austrian government briefly imprisoned Kaltenbrunner for being part of a plot to overthrow the then-ruling party of Chancellor Engelbert Dollfuss. By 1935 he had been inside prison twice, an experience he was determined not to repeat: Höfle's year in detention had the same effect on him. The Austrian SS, which Kaltenbrunner now effectively led, was under constant observation, and on one occasion when he went to meet SS officials Reinhard Heydrich and Heinrich Himmler in Passau, he hid first on a train, and then on a steamer going up the Danube. In 1937, he was again arrested for being the head of the Austrian Nazi Party. Yet he was biding his time and trying to avoid the limelight, until such time as Germany could take over Austria. He was developing a reputation for maintaining a low profile, being uncompromising with his enemies, and for getting results. One persistent characteristic that came across in Kaltenbrunner's character was his dislike of weakness, and one of his senior colleagues knew how to manipulate this:

> A tall, stoutish-looking man, with a singularly unpleasant face . . . he has never been very keen on publicity. A retiring individual, who does not really make friends . . . combined with ruthlessness . . . his parents were all supporters of pan-German nationalism. He was often criticised by [Heinrich] Himmler for being too easy-going, and that he should forget his 'Austrian softness'. [26]

Kaltenbrunner wanted to impose the political and ideological framework of National Socialism onto Austria, and the Vienna government saw this, and knew it. The SS leader's direct entourage was expanding, and he saw immediately that his old acquaintance, the oil salesman from Linz, had several qualities that would be very useful. He was obedient to those in higher authority, he was deeply resentful of the Austrian bourgeoisie, socialists, communists, and especially Jews; he was not particularly intelligent but was efficient and driven, and lastly, he didn't like people. Many SS men didn't. But, especially, they all hated Jews, not just the affluent, haute bourgeoisie of the Viennese Jewry, objects of their jealousy and resentment, with their furs, cream cakes, modern art, philosophical discussion and patronising levels of education; their business interests in Switzerland, and their endless, endless money. They also loathed the Jew of legend, Zygmunt the eastern European moneylender, in his muddy shtetl, with his communist, Bolshevik friends, his back-handing business dealings, his hand somehow in every despicable international pie.

Seeing that Eichmann shared with him both these perceptions of Jews commonly held by Nazis, Kaltenbrunner brought Adolf Eichmann very close into his personal staff. When the time came to empty Austria of its Jews, as the Nazis were already planning to do, Kaltenbrunner saw that Eichmann would be extremely efficient. The Jews would have their considerable financial assets seized for the benefit of the SS private economy, and tens of thousands of them, if not more, would be forced to emigrate, but not before the SS had effectively bankrupted each of them by extorting their funds before they were allowed to leave, and by making them pay to do so. The Jews would then become the responsibility of other countries – the SS were already imagining the United States, South American states, African countries such as Algeria and Madagascar – and the burgeoning Reich would have more space for Germans.

Eichmann had by now travelled north to Bavaria, across the border: when the National Socialist Party took power in 1933, Vacuum Oil had, on the instructions of its American owners, sacked any staff in Germany or Austria who were members of the Nazi Party. Eichmann underwent a short period of SS military training at Augsburg in Bavaria, which he hated, and then as a newly promoted SS corporal, was allowed to lead two reconnaissance teams that would regularly cross over the German and Austrian borders smuggling arms, propaganda and money into Linz and Vienna. It was a dangerous job Eichmann looked forward to – unlike soldiering: 'The humdrum of military service, that was something I couldn't stand, day after day always the same, over and over again the same.'[27]

Inside Germany, Eichmann and his colleagues were posted to a headquarters in a suburb of Munich, where they stayed in, and operated out of barracks next to a camp and detention centre for political prisoners and criminals. The suburban town was called Dachau. When he was not crossing over the Danube into northern Austria, Eichmann had determined to do anything he could to avoid the military 'humdrum' he so hated. So he decided to join the SS fledgling intelligence service, which was called the Sicherheitsdienst, SD for short. Expecting to be given a position where he could begin to make plans for the Germanisation of Austria, centred around the removal of Jews, the former oil salesman was surprised to be told to sit in an office next to Dachau camp, and there to compile lists of all Freemasons in Germany and Austria. But this he dutifully did. His superiors told him that Freemasons were to be considered in the same category as Jews and communists, so Eichmann got down to work: he even dreamed up a travelling museum exhibition which aimed to describe the dangers of Freemasonry. To his surprise his commanding officer approved the plan, and so Eichmann left the barracks at Dachau, and moved around Germany. When Kaltenbrunner, Himmler and the head of the SD, Leopold von Mildenstein, saw the exhibition, they were impressed. Kaltenbrunner made the introductions: Eichmann was invited to join the SD in Berlin and was assigned to the Jewish Affairs Office.

Further to the east of Salzburg, Linz and Klagenfurt was the Adriatic port city of Trieste, formerly part of the Austro-Hungarian Empire, and by 1936 the easternmost city in Italy. It was the birthplace and home town of Odilo Globočnik, another of the quintet of Austrian SS men who were to have such profound effects on Europe's Jewry. Born in 1904, his father had been a lieutenant in a Slovene cavalry unit, and his mother was half-Serb and half-Croatian. Globočnik's surname was categorically Slav – and thus despised by the National Socialists as being *untermensch* or 'subhuman' – although Globočnik argued his father was Aryan and had been forcibly Slavicised. Regardless, the large, lumbering Slovene was picked on and bullied at school by wealthier Austrian and Italian Catholics. His father had been too poor to summon up the requisite money needed for an army officer's marriage licence in the Austro-Hungarian army, so had been obliged to resign and join the empire's Royal Post and Mail. His son grew up with a deep loathing and resentment of Catholics, and a hatred of poverty. The family moved to Klagenfurt in the eastern Austrian province of Carinthia, and the young Odilo worked as a railway porter to help support his parents.

In the early twenties, he was one of the first in pre-Nazi Carinthian paramilitary organisations to sport a swastika emblem. In 1933 he joined the Austrian SS, and like the other men, was arrested and spent a year in prison. Himmler intervened on his behalf, and he was freed. Within the Austrian Nazi party his star rose: he became a deputy regional political leader in Vienna, and then from 1936 chief of staff of the Austrian Nazi Party. Dishonest to the core, resentful, and sadistic, Globočnik had his eyes fixed on power. Following the Anschluss, Ernst Kaltenbrunner recommended him to Hitler, who made him Gauleiter, or party chief, in Vienna. At the same time, Adolf Eichmann recommended another Austrian SS man to the now-powerful Globočnik. Reliable, dedicated, and one who had done prison time for the SS cause, said Eichmann – he was called Hermann Höfle. He met Globočnik around the time of the first anti-Semitic political exhibition held in Vienna, one of whose centre pieces was a propaganda film called *Der Ewige Jude*, or *The Eternal Jew*. Globočnik's SS career seemed to be in its ascendancy, until Himmler discovered he had been dealing fraudulently in foreign currency speculation, so demoted him, removed him from his position, and made him a junior sergeant in the 'Germania' infantry unit in the Waffen-SS. With them he took part in the invasion of Poland.

Meanwhile, the head of the SD, von Mildenstein, knew that Adolf Hitler, Heinrich Himmler and Hermann Göring were determined to deport, arrest, or forcibly emigrate the Jewish population of Germany, and that of Austria as well, now that it had come under Nazi rule. He needed Jewish experts, he needed to know about Zionism, and he needed to know what motivated Jews, how they ran their personal and business economies, what were their weak points, and what, in due course, would make them move, fast, en masse, under orders. In Section B4 of Department IV of the SD, he and Eichmann considered the problem. By 1936 the latter had been a sergeant, by 1937 a second lieutenant. His fellow SS man from Linz, Kaltenbrunner, was rather higher in the ranks: a full colonel by this point, awaiting promotion to SS-Brigadeführer. He had been, Eichmann knew, focally involved in the planning for the takeover of the two men's home country, and so in his SD office in Berlin, he watched and waited and tried to learn more about Jews, how they lived, worked and how their society functioned.

Back in September 1935, the anti-Semitic and racially orientated Nuremberg Laws had essentially stripped German Jews of their citizenship. The Reich Citizenship Law decreed that only Germans or those of German-related blood were eligible to be citizens – Jews became stateless people. Barred from all forms of government employment and the civil service, which included medicine and the economy, and subjected to increasing violence and intimidation, many decided to emigrate. Despite the fact that the Reich forced them to pay a tax of 90 per cent of their assets before leaving, half of the country's Jews fled, to thirty different countries, regions and territories, including South America, Shanghai, other western European states, South Africa, Poland, Sweden, and a limited number to the United States and Britain. In 1937, Hitler, Himmler and Goring then decided to empty Germany and Austria of their remaining Jewish populations of 650,000 people. Violence, intimidation, theft and bankrupting them were deemed to be the four most effective ways. An obedient, asocial and manipulative man, Eichmann saw how Jews who refused to emigrate, give up their assets, or who broke one of the myriad clauses of racial regulation that governed their every movement, were arrested and sent to Dachau or Sachsenhausen prison and concentration camps. Run by one of the new SS Totenkopfverbände or Death's Head regiments, the regime in the prison centres, for Jews especially, was of violence, poor diet, and frequently death. What seemed effective for Germany's Jews, he thought, could be equally effective for those of Austria.

Eichmann suggested to Kaltenbrunner and von Mildenstein that if they could possibly persuade Jewish nationalist organisations inside Palestine to guarantee immigration and living space for Germany's Jews, the entire population could simply be deported to what was, after all, their Promised Land. The main obstacle to this was that Palestine was now British Mandated, and Westminster knew that if a large influx of hundreds of thousands of extra Jews arrived, then the resultant demonstrations by Palestinian Arabs would turn violent, and British soldiers would be killed and injured. Germany, too, wanted to avoid mass deportation to Palestine: Hitler believed that an independent Israeli state would mean a permanent, vengeful enemy for the Thousand Year Reich, sitting in a geo-strategically vital part of the Mediterranean.

Eichmann and one of his fellow SD officers sailed to Palestine and Egypt in 1937, posing as journalists: they met with Jewish officials from the nationalist Haganah organisation. No, the German intelligence officers were told. We cannot guarantee the safety of half-a-million German and Austrian Jews, but we would like it to happen. But, the two SS men were also told, the British will decide, and they will cap their immigration quotas again, soon. So with Israel and the Palestine option looking increasingly unworkable, Eichmann returned to Berlin. Then Germany marched into Austria, and the Anschluss was under way.

The word can be translated as 'joining' and this is precisely what happened. At dawn on 12 March, a Wehrmacht reconnaissance unit on motorbikes and half-tracks crossed the border into Austria. Their first sight was lines of cheering, flag-waving, flower-throwing families lining the road, and thankfully for them, not units of the Austrian army. Hitler himself crossed the border south of Munich, driving over a bridge on the River Inn into his home town of Braunau. Another Austrian had come home: by nightfall he was in Linz, and by midnight he and Kaltenbrunner were in contact, arranging for the entire Austrian SS to be instantly deployed in each town, city and village, and at key road junctions. Kaltenbrunner had foreseen this: his men were already out in force. In a day, Austria's Nazi Party had gone from being an illegal terrorist organisation to the country's ruling party. Its leader, Arthur Seyss-Inquart, was made head of state. Kaltenbrunner was made the Secretary of Public Security, and was given control of one of the two areas into which Austria was now divided. They were called Alpenland and Donau – Alps and Danube.

The latter was Kaltenbrunner's fiefdom, and Himmler also made him the Senior SS and Police leader. His remit included transforming the administration and bureaucracy of his half of Austria into an exact replica of Nazi Germany's. This included the adoption of precisely the same criminal and racial regulations as existed, and which would be mirrored across the Third Reich as it expanded. Kaltenbrunner's next priority was the establishment, in

Vienna, of the Central Agency for Jewish Emigration. To reward him for his ultra-loyal service since the early 1930s, Hitler made Kaltenbrunner a brigadier-general in March.

Now the senior SS officer in the country, the former lawyer from Linz knew he needed determination, knowledge, ruthlessness and efficiency from the SS officer who was going to be appointed to run the Central Office for Jewish Emigration in the capital. There were officially 192,000 Jews in Austria, as well as an undocumented number of up to 28,000 German Jews who had taken refuge there as well. This composite of around 220,000 contained some of the most affluent and economically well-established families in Europe's Jewish communities, and the SS wanted their money. Before extermination was to be the order of the day with Europe's Jews, extortion, emigration and economic violence were the watchwords. The SS was expanding, it needed money for its own economic affairs department; Himmler didn't trust the three component parts of the Wehrmacht – the Heer, the Kriegsmarine and Luftwaffe – and extorting the Jews of their money and terrorising them into leaving Reich territory seemed an effective, profitable and viable solution.

Kaltenbrunner contacted the SD in Berlin: SS-Lieutenant Adolf Eichmann drove to Vienna, and on arrival was promoted to Hauptsturmführer, or captain. His plan was to make Jews emigrate, but only on receipt of an exit visa, to obtain which they had to pay a series of costly taxes and permissions. Wealthy Jewish families would pay for the poorer ones. Eichmann saw that in this way the country's entire Jewish capital would be internally self-distributed, and then simply appropriated by the SS. The Jews, as refugees, would then become the problem of the outside world, who would either be forced to harbour them as penniless immigrants, or provide sponsors and funding for them. Either way, they would be gone, and as a result of this financial extortion their money would belong to the SS.

I immediately said: this is like an automatic factory, let us say a flour mill connected to some bakery. You put in at the one end a Jew who still has capital and has, let us say, a factory or a shop or an account in a bank, and he passes through the entire building, from counter to counter, from office to office – he comes out at the other end, he has no money, he has no rights, only a passport in which is written: You must leave this country within two weeks; if you fail to do so, you will go to a concentration camp.[28]

The senior SS generals and the invasion of Poland

By autumn 1939, Germany had invaded Poland, and Hermann Höfle was in Nowy Sacz. Himmler pardoned Globočnik, whom he liked and approved of, and in a characteristic whimsical sleight-of-hand, promoted him to the rank of brigadier, and made him Higher SS and Police Leader in Lublin. Ernst Kaltenbrunner was now the senior SS leader in Austria, and Ernst Lerch an SS-Hauptsturmführer, with the Reich Security Directorate in Berlin. The latter had married a female Gestapo officer, a fellow Austrian from Klagenfurt, and Odilo Globočnik had been his best man. He worked in the same building in the German capital now as Eichmann, who now ran the RSHA Department IV B4, the Jewish Affairs Office. By September 1939, overseeing the fates of the five men, their operational and personal futures, were a triumvirate of senior SS officers.

SS-Obergruppenführer Kurt Daluege was one of them. Höfle knew the rumours about the head of the Ordnungspolizei, the Order Police, of how in the First World War he had been hit in the head and upper back by shrapnel on the Western Front. He survived, declared a quarter disabled due to lasting neurological damage. He had been in at the start, joining the Nazi Party in

1923, and then its paramilitary wing, the Sturmabteiling, or SA. These were the party's uniformed detachments; its stormtroopers, the men who provided security at party meetings, and went head-to-head and fist-to-fist in street brawls with the trade unions and opposing political parties. In 1930, Hitler had ordered Daluege to join the SS, a personal bodyguard detachment formed in 1925, which by summer 1931 had expanded to over 10,000 members. Increasingly, Hitler distrusted the SA, and the fledgling SS was a devoted inner-circle of followers loyal only to him. Kurt Daluege was among the first group of twelve hundred recruits, and his membership of and commitment to the SS put him in direct confrontation with his former colleagues in the SA. When the latter attacked the Nazi Party headquarters in Berlin in 1930, it was Daluege who went out on the streets and led the resistance, and Hitler wrote to him afterwards. This devotion to the Nazi cause, said the Nazi leader, showed that Daluege's 'honour was loyalty', or *'Ehre heisst Treue'*, a phrase which, as *Meine Ehre heisst Treue*, became the motto of the SS. Hermann Höfle, like every SS man, now had it emblazoned on his belt-buckle.

At the same time this deeply scarred veteran of the trenches, the angry, unpredictable man from provincial Silesia, was given command of the SS in the whole of northern Germany. The head of the SS, Heinrich Himmler, controlled the south. The third member of the SS triumvirate who oversaw the world of Hermann Höfle was the sadistic Reinhard Tristan Heydrich, the Catholic altar-boy from Saxony whose father had given him the Christian names of two opera characters. The first came from one of his father's own operas, the second was from Wagner. Even the Führer called Heydrich 'the man with the iron heart'.[29]

The three ran the different centres of power of the SS: the office of the Reichsführer, Heinrich Himmler, the second the SS Main Economic and Administrative Office, and the third the different officials in charge of each department at the Reich Security Main Office, or RSHA. In August 1941 the ruthless and deeply anti-Semitic SS-Gruppenführer Heydrich was in charge of the RSHA, overseeing a variety of departments. These included the Gestapo, the Criminal Police, or Kripo, the Jewish Affairs Office, and the Sicherheitsdienst or SD, which was the SS Intelligence and Police Service. Heydrich himself had formed the Einsatzgruppen in 1939, and given them orders to round up Jews as the SS and Wehrmacht units advanced into each different country. The 'action' or 'command' squads were paramilitary groups normally made up of a combination of policemen, SS men, local national auxiliaries, and sometimes German army soldiers.

Everybody knew there was friction among the powerful trio of SS leaders: Heydrich despised Daluege as a former political rival who could usurp his position at the head of the RSHA. He thought he was incompetent too, and nicknamed him '*Dummi-Dummi*', the Idiot. There was suspicion as well. The head of the RSHA reportedly believed that the police commander was among those responsible for spreading repeated rumours that Heydrich was partly Jewish. His parents were Catholic and Protestant, his social and professional background impeccably upper middle-class German, but since 1932 his opponents had been alleging that he had Jewish ancestors.[30] If proved true, this would have been ample reason for Himmler to remove the then SS-Sturmbannführer Heydrich from the organisation. Wilhelm Canaris, who in the mid-1930s was still a serving naval officer and yet to take over the Abwehr, Germany's military intelligence service, allegedly made the initial claims about Heydrich in 1932. He claimed he had papers that showed Heydrich's Jewish genealogy. The Nazi Party's race and ancestry expert was a politician called Achim Gerke, and he carried out an investigation,[31] concluding Heydrich to be German, without any evidence of Jewish ancestry.

Himmler, reassured, then appointed Heydrich to be head of the Sicherheitsdienst, or SD, the SS intelligence police.

In 1934, Hermann Göring put Daluege in charge of the German uniformed police, and when all of these civilian police officers from every branch of law enforcement in the Third Reich were subsumed under SS command in 1936, Daluege took control of them. He now commanded more than 120,000 uniformed policemen who made up the Ordnungspolizei, or 'Order Police'. By 1941, these included the 12–15,000 men from the different police battalions working on the Eastern Front, in Poland, and in such territories as the Protectorate of Bohemia and Moravia. The Order Police were the foot soldiers of law and order in the Reich. They were the police from the railway service, or *Reichsbahn*, the coastguard, fire brigades, customs and traffic officers, and security guards from government buildings – every police official in the new Germany who wore a uniform. In 1938 and 1939 Daluege enforced the forced emigration policies for German, Austrian and Czech Jews when he signed the deportation orders that authorised the SS and the Gestapo to take them to camps in Byelorussia and Latvia. Höfle understood the force of Daluege's commitment to a solution to the Jewish problem from a comment of his, that 'the consciously asocial enemies of the people must be eliminated by state intervention, if it hopes to prevent the outbreak of complete moral degeneration.'[32] It was in Poland, too, that most of these asocial enemies of the people could be found. As a result of their hard work, their connections to Odilo Globočnik and Eichmann and Kaltenbrunner, Höfle and Ernst Lerch were now in a position where they would be called on to do something about the elimination of their enemies. As Christopher Browning wrote in his book, *The Path to Genocide*:

> The Warsaw ghetto contained more Jews than all of France;
> the Łodz ghetto more Jews than all of the Netherlands.

More Jews lived in the city of Krakow than in all of Italy, and virtually any medium-sized town in Poland had a larger Jewish population than all of Scandinavia. All of southeast Europe – Hungary, Romania, Bulgaria, Yugoslavia, and Greece – had fewer Jews than the original four districts of the General Government.[33]

The German operations to deport Jews to the General Government, and many Poles to ghettos, continued in the bitterly cold winter of 1939 to 1940. On 17 December, SS-Brigadeführer Odilo Globočnik, now the Higher SS and Police Leader in Lublin, sent a baffled message about the confusion on the country's railway lines as wagonloads of Jews and Poles, forced out of their homes and 'evacuated', criss-crossed the country. Cattle cars were used for the deportation operations where necessary, or third-class compartments in public train transport. The former were unheated, and in the logistical chaos, often found themselves stranded in sidings overnight. Globočnik had heard reports about the transports arriving at the wrong stations, children and old people frozen to death, their bodies glued solid to the wooden sides of the cattle cars by ice and frost. A train of 720 Jews and Poles forced and burned out of their homes in Włocławek, and heading for a new ghetto in Tarnow, in south-western Poland, turned up by mistake in Lublin, leading Globočnik to send an exasperated message of complaint.[34] New Year's Eve 1940, meanwhile, was as joyless as the Germans could make it: a circular radio message went out to all duty stations:

From: Higher SS & Police Führer, General Government
I forbid anybody in the General Government to sell any alcohol to Jews and Poles from 20.00 hrs.[35]

Odilo Globočnik in Lublin said on 10 January to Heinrich Himmler that by the end of January or the end of the first week of February 1940, the 'whole resettlement should be finished'.[36] Meanwhile, Globočnik's attitude towards what he called 'the Jewish question' was simple: he said he would not recoil from radical solutions required to resolve it.

CHAPTER III

UKRAINE AND ULTRA

France and Buckinghamshire, 1940

On 5 December, a cold clear day with snow on the ground, two British officers and three non-commissioned men arrived at a French chateau near the River Marne, north-east of Paris. The castle in the small town of La Ferté-sous-Jouarre had become the headquarters of a new joint British and French cryptanalytical operation, codenamed Mission Richard. Its aim was simple: to try to intercept and decrypt more Domino traffic. This was the codeword used by Bletchley Park to describe the German police and SS messages sent between themselves and their headquarters in Germany. The British intercept stations at Denmark Hill and elsewhere could not pick up much of the low-frequency police radio traffic from inside and around the big cities in the industrial heartland of Germany, whereas the French, being geographically closer, were intercepting dozens of messages per day.

By the beginning of December 1939, Great Britain and Nazi Germany had been at war for just over three months, but physical confrontation between both sides was still mainly limited to short, sharp naval actions. Magnetic mines laid by U-boats sank and damaged Royal Navy ships, including the battleship HMS *Nelson*, and the brand-new light cruiser HMS *Belfast*, to be put out of action for over two years by one mine laid in the Firth of Forth. In October submarine captain Gunther Prien had taken U-47 into the anchorage at Scapa Flow and sunk the battleship HMS *Royal Oak*. The Kriegsmarine's commander-in-chief, Admiral Erich Raeder, ordered in November that all Allied merchant ships should be sunk without warning. Shortly after the cryptanalytical team from Bletchley Park arrived on the River Marne, the Royal Navy then balanced the account in a spectacular piece of combat seamanship in the South Atlantic. Three British cruisers fatally crippled the German heavy cruiser *Graf Spee* in the Battle of the River Plate. In London, a magnetic mine dropped by the Luftwaffe into the Thames estuary in November had failed to explode, allowing British scientists to use it for research as they invented the process of degaussing, reducing a mine's magnetic signature; this crucial development was to make Germany more dependent on the use of torpedoes to attack British ships.

The news from Poland was of a country in a tortuous freefall of atrocity and occupation. The Polish government-in-exile had fled their home country and made a temporary headquarters in France, at Angers in the Loire valley. Thousands of Polish soldiers had fled the country to Romania and Hungary, while other senior officers and officials had made their way to London. In Poland, they said, Germans had forced Jews to wear yellow Star of David armbands, and deported Polish university professors to concentration camps. The Germans and local militias were arresting, deporting and often executing Poles and Jews. The East was edging towards total war. On 30 November Russia attacked Finland and bombed Helsinki, beginning the Winter War. Focusing their operational attention on the north, Russia had divided all of Polish territory with the Germans, as tens of thousands of Polish refugees fled the SS and took a false refuge in Soviet territory, only to be deported even further eastwards by the NKVD, the Russian interior ministry police.

The deployment with the French doubled the British intercept capability, and Hut 5 at Bletchley reaped the benefits, both in terms of signals decrypted and intelligence gained, of the joint work breaking into signals transmitted in the German Police Code. By January, Nigel de Grey and his colleagues had written a summary of the hundreds of messages they were intercepting and decrypting about Poland, and noted that 'the migration of the nations continues, Polish refugees being handed over to the Soviets, Poles being hunted out of the district marked down for Germanisation, Germans being repatriated from Russia.'[37]

As Nigel de Grey and his colleagues had by now deduced, the German Police organisation was so widespread and the networks it used so various that satisfactory interception could only be achieved by having a number of different stations at widely distributed points in the British Isles, and the mission to France, sent with the cooperation of the Deuxième Bureau of French military intelligence, greatly increased successful interceptions. It meant the flood of information coming in from occupied Poland gave both British and French a picture, clearer by the day, of what the Germans were doing to the Jews and Poles.

At the chateau on the River Marne, the two sides had different ways of operating, as the French only allowed officers to work on the mission, even for duties such as typing. British records noted:

The mission had an uphill task, for the French, with individual exceptions, regarded the mission with the eye of rivalry, rather than of friendly cooperation, however the work went on successfully enough to warrant the enlargement of the mission.[38]

An extra thirteen men arrived from Bletchley in February, and the two sides split their duties: the French decrypted on even days, the British on odd, and both sides succeeded in maximising the decrypts and the information they could gain from them. The decrypts detailed movements of German Police battalions, deportations of Poles and Jews, coal allocations in the frozen Polish winter, and endless movements of transport trains across the railway network of German-occupied Poland. The British and French continued to break into the different encrypted daily settings of the Domino system, and the prickly atmosphere between the two nationalities softened.

> The entente grew continually more cordial . . . the French showed a prodigality in their expense of manpower, with their twenty-two officers to our three officers, and fourteen other ranks, and in their time. Lunch at their mess was a matter of three hours, with little likelihood of much exacting intellectual work being possible thereafter.[39]

The team in France continued operating until 9 May 1940, when they and their French colleagues were taken by surprise. The Wehrmacht invaded France. Decryption slowed, and then halted, as the British officers and NCOs moved out of the castle as quickly as they could. With their French colleagues, they travelled south to the town of Ussel in central France, south-east of Limoges. They said a sad farewell to their new French counterparts, travelled west to Bordeaux, and were taken off by the Royal Navy. With their departure, the interception and decrypts of the German Police codes came to a temporary stop, almost for three months, until new intercept stations in Great Britain were allocated. Known as 'Y' stations, from the phonetic equivalent of 'WI', for Wireless Intercept, these became the home of 'the Listeners'. These were

Army, Air Force and Navy staff, normally women, who twenty-four hours a day scanned the radio frequencies the Germans used. A country house at Beaumanor in Leicestershire became the lead Y station for the German Police traffic.

> Traffic had [by September] meanwhile increased, the German police having spread its net over western Europe. This was met by an allocation of 12–16 [interception] sets at Beaumanor which quickly became the leading 'Domino' [German Police] Interception station . . . It was during this period that the first signs of anxiety on the part of the Germans about the security of their cypher was shown. The German monitoring station in Berlin, always efficient in jumping on minor breaches of discipline, called for a wider variety in lengths of messages, and as an added security measure addresses and signatures were placed in the body of the text. Continuity breaking had made available a wider knowledge of the habits of each individual station, as well as the kind of content and jargon to be expected from given texts.

With the extension of police activities in Russia the quantity of traffic steadily increased, but here again security measures followed quickly. A separate key and new frequencies were instituted for the traffic of messages encoded in the 'Russian' key. In quantity this was too small to allow more than 50 per cent success.[40]

Back at Bletchley Park, Nigel de Grey's colleagues had made huge advances. The burgeoning cryptanalytical and intelligence operation was physically spreading from the manor house and outbuildings where it had initially started. Further buildings, known as 'huts', were built on the grounds. The codebreakers in Hut 6, led by a mathematics fellow from Cambridge, Gordon Welchman, broke into one of the keys of the Luftwaffe's Enigma system on

22 May. Polish cryptanalysts had worked on finding a way into the Enigma system before the outbreak of war, and had shared their knowledge with the British. A team led by Dillwyn 'Dilly' Knox, had met with the Poles, and combined their knowledge with their own. Along with the Cambridge mathematician Alan Turing, and the two chess champions Hugh Alexander and Stuart Milner-Barry, Welchman was one of the four original recruits to Bletchley Park whom de Grey had nicknamed 'the Wicked Uncles'.

As the volume of intercepted signals increased with the first decryption of an Enigma cipher, de Grey looked back a few months to how things had been in January 1940, the calm before a phenomenal storm. 'The German Army & Airforce Enigma Reporting Section' – its formal title from January 1940 – was soon just called Hut 3, the Intelligence Centre of GC&CS.

> In a small bleak room with nothing but a table and chairs . . .
> the first bundle of Enigma decodes appeared. Here lay a pile
> of dull, disjointed enigmatic scraps all about the weather,
> or the petty affairs of a Luftgau no-one had ever heard of, or
> trifles of Wehrkreis business; the whole sprinkled with terms
> no dictionary knew, and abbreviations of which our only
> guide, a small War Office list, proved completely innocent.
> Very small beer, in fact, and full of foreign bodies . . . The
> original idea in London had been that GCCS had no business
> to do with intelligence. We were merely to break, decode
> and translate . . . [41]

Not for long.

The Luftwaffe key which Welchman had broken into was used to communicate between the Wehrmacht headquarters at Zossen, south of Berlin, and commanders in France and Scandinavia, including those around Dunkirk, where a desperate rescue operation was under way to evacuate the remains of the British Expeditionary Force. With the Battle of Britain at its height in August and September 1940, breaking into the Luftwaffe Enigma meant that the Royal Air Force had another electronic weapon in their armoury, to add to the Chain Home network of radar stations. The Luftwaffe painstakingly transmitted encrypted messages about every supply of fuel, pilots, ground crew and aeroplanes to France and the Low Countries. Hut 6 followed them.

On 24 September, they decrypted a message from the Luftwaffe containing details of air-sea rescue vessels the Germans had deployed to the Scandinavian, North Sea and Channel coasts to support an operation codenamed 'Seelowe', or Sealion. On 9 October the Luftwaffe requested half a million gallons of aviation fuel to be held in readiness at Rotterdam and Antwerp.[42]

Winston Churchill had become Prime Minister on 12 May 1940, and recognised the extraordinary intelligence breakthroughs that Bletchley Park had made. On no account whatsoever, he knew, could the secret be compromised. On 16 October, he wrote urgently to his chief staff officer, Major-General Hastings Ismay, protesting at the number of senior officers and government officials who were being given security clearance to receive and see the information. At first, the intelligence was circulated in summaries codenamed 'Boniface', suggesting it came from a specific human intelligence agent, and then 'Ultra', from the words stamped at the top of each message decrypt, 'Top Secret Ultra'.

> I am astounded at the vast congregation who are invited to study these matters [Churchill wrote]. The Air Ministry is the worst offender and I have marked a number who should be struck off at once, unless after careful consideration in each individual case it is found to be indispensable that they should

be informed. I have added the First Lord, who of course must know everything known to his subordinates, and also the Secretary of State for War.

A machinery should be constructed which makes other parties acquainted with such information as is necessary to them for the discharge of their particular duties. I await your proposals. I should also add Commander-in-Chief Fighter and Commander-in-Chief Bomber Command, it being clearly understood that they shall not impart them to any person working under them or allow the boxes to be opened by anyone save themselves.[43]

By 7 November, the number of Ultra-cleared officials was set at thirty-one. The selection of these individuals was extremely strict. One man who was on the list was Lieutenant-Commander Ian Fleming from the Naval Intelligence Division. According to his biographer Nicholas Shakespeare:

Not even Churchill's confidential adviser on Intelligence, Desmond Morton, was in the 'charmed circle' that had ULTRA clearance. Ian [Fleming] was initiated from the beginning. His name features as one of only twenty-four on a 'Most Secret' list dated 8 April 1940 of those 'having access to Huts 1 and 6 GCCS [Government Code and Cypher School] or to whom the source of the reports is known.[44]

Each day Nigel de Grey, as Bletchley's Intelligence Coordinator, sent summaries, selected decrypts and passages of intelligence analysis to the office of MI8, the Directorate of Military Intelligence responsible for Signals, who passed them to Stewart Menzies, known as 'C', the Director-General of the Secret Intelligence Service, or MI6. He in turn passed them on to Churchill and thence the other twenty-nine officials who by November were Ultra-cleared. The signals were sent on a teleprinter link to Sections III and IV of SIS at Broadway Buildings in London, for onward transmission to ministers; then shortly afterwards, as the volume of traffic increased, a direct teleprinter link to the Admiralty was added to the communications chain.

Menzies was, like de Grey, a veteran of the First World War and an Old Etonian. He had served with the Household Cavalry, and then as an intelligence officer on Field-Marshal Haig's staff. He showed aptitude in combat and King George V personally decorated Captain Menzies with the Distinguished Service Order for resourcefulness, coolness and gallantry in December 1914, for bravery during the Battle of Ypres. The Military Cross followed in 1915, when Menzies was gassed in a German operation and taken off active service. On Haig's staff as a counter-intelligence officer, he was instrumental in removing Brigadier John Charteris, the Field-Marshal's intelligence chief, for his lacklustre and amateurish performance. Charteris had claimed to be behind one of the most notorious of Britain's propaganda stories of the war – that the Germans rendered down the corpses of their own soldiers to be turned into soap. His involvement was not just subsequently to be dis-proved, but the circulation in newspapers of the story itself gave ammunition for the Germans to accuse the British of being liars.

After the war Menzies became a staff officer, then deputy Director General of SIS. In 1939, on the death of the incumbent, Admiral Sir Hugh Sinclair, he became Director General. As MI6 grew fast, and broadly, Menzies took charge of the operations of the GC&CS, and by extension the intelligence generated by Ultra. Not an academic, not a scientist, Menzies was a traditional upper-class soldier, brave and loyal, determined that Bletchley Park and its endeavours and successes should help win the war. He could be impatient and brusque with people who were not from his own strata in the rigid social and professional rank structure that then so defined much of Britain; he was accused of being intellectually inflexible and unimaginative, but he knew about conflict and he knew about fighting, and under his directorship MI6 expanded, and became a part of the war machine. Bletchley Park was one of its most effective weapons, and Menzies was fiercely protective of it.

The Ultra information, once decrypted, was sent, either physically by courier or by encrypted radio signal, to the Prime Minister, and when he was in Britain, the papers were given to Churchill in locked buff-coloured boxes. Only the Prime Minister had the key, and could read them. His Assistant Private Secretary, John Colville, went with Churchill to the Prime Minister's country residence at Chequers in Buckinghamshire:

> The PM, tempted by the warmth, sat in the garden working and glancing at me with suspicion from time to time in the (unwarranted) belief that I was trying to read the contents of his special buff boxes.[45]

In February 1941, an American military mission visited Bletchley Park, after Churchill agreed with President Roosevelt that Great Britain and the United States could, and would, share information with each other. The Americans brought details of their vital decryption of the Japanese Foreign Office cipher device called 'Purple', which had enabled the United States to break into Japanese diplomatic codes. The Purple cipher was the Japanese foreign office's supposedly unbreakable diplomatic code, and the Americans had brought the secrets of it to Bletchley Park when their first mission visited the Government Code and Cypher School. They had constructed their own copy of a 'Purple' machine, which had enabled them to piece together messages sent on it by the Japanese. The code was first broken in September 1940 by a former mathematician and railway annuity statistician called Genevieve Grotjan, one of the American women recruited into cryptanalysis from universities, public utilities and scientific backgrounds. She had noticed the way in which the different patterns and repetitions of Japanese syllabaries were used in circular and cyclical ways in intercepted messages. Purple was employed by Japanese ambassadors and consuls worldwide, who reported on everything from German military developments, their relations with other countries outside the Third Reich, and such matters as Jewish refugees.

In return for sharing their information about Purple with the British, the Americans received a limited amount of technical data about the decryption of Enigma, although Nigel de Grey's colleagues who were decrypting the German Naval Enigma were extremely wary of telling the Americans about their successes.

While Beaumanor and other intercept stations were picking up SS and German police signals sent from Germany, Austria and eastern Europe, Bletchley Park's cryptanalysts were simultaneously decrypting the encoding settings used on the German Enigma machine, and on other of their encipherment systems. Out in the Battle of the Atlantic, the cracking of the Kriegsmarine's Enigma setting, codenamed Hydra, then Shark, meant that the Royal Navy could sometimes have advance warning of where U-boats might be lying in wait for Allied convoys. Great Britain needed a million tons of supplies per week to survive, and by October convoys were being attacked and merchantmen sunk at an alarming rate by U-boats using 'wolfpack' tactics. On 21 September, four U-boats attached Convoy HX-72, and sank eleven ships out of forty-two. The protection of the Atlantic convoys was a priority for national survival: if the decryption of Enigma could help prevent

Britain losing the Battle of the Atlantic – and thus the war – then everything had to be done to protect the secret of Ultra. Subsidiary intelligence discoveries based upon signals decrypts, such as the persecution of Europe's Jews, could not be allowed to endanger or compromise Ultra.

'The only thing that really frightened me during the war was the U-boat peril. I was even more anxious about this battle than I had been about the glorious air fight called the Battle of Britain,' Churchill was to write in *The Second World War: Their Finest Hour*.

The Royal Navy had first captured parts of the German Naval Enigma wiring system in February 1940, when the minesweeper HMS *Gleaner* depth-charged U-33 in the Firth of Clyde. Crew members of the submarine were given parts of the U-boat's Enigma machine, including its rotors, to put in their pockets as they jumped overboard, and then drop into the sea. Several of them failed to do this. The resulting technical leap made by Frank Birch and Alan Turing in Hut 6 at Bletchley, on receipt of the captured rotors, began the lead-up to breaking into Hydra. By August 1940, the first 'bombe' computer prototype arrived at Bletchley Park, partly designed by Alan Turing. The system was fed the enciphered text of a German Enigma message, and it then threw up suggestions of what rotor and wiring settings the sender's machine might have been set to. These were then entered back into the bombe, with an example of plain text, resulting in an encryption that 'reverse-decoded' the original received message, and suggested options of what the original German encipherment settings had been.

The run of success continued. When the Royal Navy captured codebooks and parts of an Enigma machine from the German trawler Krebs, off the Lofoten Islands in March 1941, Turing and Birch's team's work advanced. The *coup de grâce* came when, on 9 May, a Royal Navy ship depth-charged U-110 off Iceland, and a boarding party from HMS *Bulldog* captured an Enigma machine, and its codebooks. By July that year the German Naval Enigma was being read with a maximum delay of seventy-two hours, and often with a delay of only a few hours. Yet U-boat sinkings of merchantmen continued: the British were only just holding their own. If the Kriegsmarine, or the SS and German Police, or the Luftwaffe, were to suspect their encryption devices were in any way compromised, and they changed them or switched covert signalling techniques altogether, then each one of the Third Reich's signals intelligence services would alert the other and Ultra would be dead in the water within twenty-four hours. Domino could not be allowed to threaten Hydra. Britain's survival in the Battle of the Atlantic depended on it.

Protecting the Ultra secret had other operational and strategic costs, some of them seemingly excessive, even when operationally crucial to the desired aim of protecting the Holy Grail of Britain's signals decryption. German, Hungarian and Italian troops had attacked Yugoslavia and Greece on 6 April 1941. By 30 April both countries had been occupied by the Wehrmacht and the SS. The British, Australians and New Zealanders fought a fierce and dogged rearguard action between 24 and 30 April, after which more than 30,000 British, Australian and New Zealand troops were evacuated from Greece to Crete.

When Luftwaffe Enigma decrypts revealed that the Germans were planning an air assault on the island, Churchill informed General Wavell, the Commander-in-Chief in the Middle East, in Cairo. But because the New Zealand General Bernard Freyberg, who had just days before been appointed commander of the Allied forces on Crete, was not Ultra-cleared, Wavell could not tell him about the impending assault and thus let him into the secret of Bletchley Park's operations.

The codebreakers in Hut 6 knew that the Germans were planning to parachute onto the strategically important Maleme airfield:

Freyberg had to concentrate his defences there. Yet the British Secret Intelligence Service insisted that, unless the New Zealander could be seen to have some non-Enigma related reason for any tactical deployment he carried out, he should not be allowed to see Ultra decrypts showing what the Luftwaffe intended – any sign that he had knowledge of the Germans' operational intentions would reveal that the British had decrypted the Luftwaffe's encipherment systems, which would lose the British a priceless weapon.

Churchill, however, was very anxious for Freyberg to see the actual texts of the decrypts regarding German plans for glider and parachute attacks, and wrote to the three Chiefs of Staff on 10 May:

> So important do I consider all this aspect that it would be well to send a special officer by air to see General Freyberg and show him personally the actual texts of all the messages bearing upon this subject. The officer would be answerable for their destruction in the event of engine failure en route. No one should be informed but the General, who would give his orders to his subordinates without explaining his full reasons.

At Churchill's insistence, Stewart Menzies decided that Freyberg should be allowed to see Ultra decrypts but that he must not act on them operationally unless he could demonstrate that he had at least one non-Enigma source for his intelligence. He could not.

The Allies did not deploy sufficient forces to Maleme airfield in time to successfully counter the Luftwaffe's assault on this most important area and most strategically vital element. No officer was sent to Crete. No defensive preparations were made that took account of the Enigma-generated intelligence advantage. The island fell. The goose of Ultra had laid a golden egg, but in the interests of protecting the goose, the egg had proved worthless. Ultra was indeed not compromised, but at the cost of eight Royal Navy warships, 5,300 Allied casualties, 12,000 prisoners, and the loss of Crete, a strategic outpost in the eastern Mediterranean arguably as important as Malta. The Allied intelligence services would, it seemed, go to the wall to protect Ultra: once again, maximising the intelligence gained from Domino, and alerting the world to the persecution of Europe's Jews and Poles, seemed out of the question if it threatened Bletchley's secrets. So how could the British and the Americans use the increasing amount of information that Nigel de Grey and his colleagues were generating about this persecution, without losing one of Britain's only strategic advantages, that might just prevent it from losing the war? The answer became even more complicated, even more vital, even more operationally pertinent, when on 22 June 1941, Nazi Germany invaded the Soviet Union.

The secret messages of Domino

On 21 August 1941, an intelligence analyst at the GC&CS at Bletchley Park began to type out a succinct summary. It was headed MSGP 27, or Message Group 27, entitled G.P. Ds 237–323. With a few exceptions, for the period 3 July to 14 August 1941, these were summaries of decrypts of Domino, the German Police signals. The summaries themselves were on beige paper, typed in black, with red headlines.

> MOST SECRET – TO BE KEPT UNDER LOCK AND KEY. NEVER TO BE REMOVED FROM THIS OFFICE.

> This is very secret. If future circulation is necessary it must be paraphrased, so that neither the source of the information nor the means by which it has been obtained is apparent.[46]
> [To be noted: * Letter R next to message indicates msg sent in new 'Russian' key]

The first section of the summary was called 'Police Activities in Russia'.

The most [important] development since the last summary is the extension of GP activities in Russia. This has been on a very large scale and the importance attached by the Germans to the operations is indicated in the fact that a separate key and a new frequency (6900) is used for messages on this front. There are thus two keys to break each day. Fortunately in the continuity of the breaking of the previous police messages [it] made it possible to break into the new ones. At the same time lack of material has made breaking impossible on more than half the days of each month, and for this reason the gaps in the following summary are considerable.

The distribution list included seven people, and a file. One copy was to Section 8 of Military Intelligence, or MI8, which handled signals intelligence and ran the British network of Y stations. A second copy went to the Director of the Code and Cypher School, another to Frank Birch in the Naval Section, a third to Joshua 'Josh' Cooper, a Russian linguist who headed the Air Section, and then three other recipients noted only by initials.

The German Police Forces, says the summary, are divided into three groups, North, Middle, and South, each one corresponding to the Army Group behind which it follows. In charge of each group is a Gruppenführer, or SS general, with Gruppenführer Prutzmann at Riga, in the middle von dem Bach, with his headquarters at Baranowicze, in western Byelorussia, while the general in the south is not yet identified. These three are responsible to Himmler, who is taking a very active part in the campaign, to SS-Obergruppenführer Daluege, the chief of the Ordnungspolizei, and SS-Gruppenführer Heydrich, head of the SD.

In the section called 'Personalities involved' the intelligence analysts began to compile a list of those officers and civilian officials whose names appeared in the decrypts. First among these in the messages from July and August was the Reichsführer-SS, Heinrich Himmler, who is constantly travelling between the different operational areas, sometimes by road in a convoy, sometimes by rail, on his Sonderzug, or personal train. He has a signals staff with a permanent transmitting station, whose callsign is DSO, which keeps him in touch as he is on the road.

'By the nature of our decodes,' noted the summary, 'we have not been able to discover the Reichsführer doing much else but travelling . . . for instance on the "sonderzug" [special train] to Minsk.' Daluege has been confined to the northern sector, first at Rastenburg, although the summary (and presumably the decrypts) do not mention any meeting with Hitler at his Wolf's Lair headquarters, three miles from the town, in the middle of a pine forest. On 24 July he sends a telegram to Heydrich, saying after consultations with Prutzmann, that:

> I request that Brigade-Leader Dr Stahlecker[v] be kept at it, weiterbelasten, at any rate until Petersburg is occupied and cleaned up. Dr S' relations with the army are so good that his relief will certainly be disadvantageous.

It is clear that the 'cleaning up' that Stahlecker is undertaking is something the SS want to continue. It is in the Central Sector, behind Army Group Centre, that most of the recent fighting involving the police has taken place: fifteen police battalions, as well as part of the whole of the SS Cavalry Brigade, are involved.

---

v This refers to SS-Brigadeführer Franz Walter Stahlecker, formerly Adolf Eichmann's senior officer at the Central Agency for Jewish Emigration in Vienna. By summer 1941 he was commanding Einsatzgruppe A, which followed behind Army Group North.

With their HQ at Baranowicze and bases at Bialystok and Minsk, these forces have been given the task of 'cleaning up' the whole of the area swept across by the task forces of the centre.

'The campaign starts,' says Bletchley Park's signals summary, 'as far as our decodes are contained, with the move of the leader of the police forces of this area, SS-Gruppenführer von dem Bach,[vi] into his HQ at Baranowicze on 14.7.'

An 'R' following the date on the page of the summary indicates that the original message was encrypted using the key that Hut 5 have codenamed 'Russian'. Along with 'Reich' and others soon to follow, these formed part of the group of sub-codenames for the entire German Police traffic, which, as previously explained, was codenamed Domino. Then at the urgent request of the commander of the Army Rear Areas, Police Regiment Mitte (Middle) follows, with battalions 316, 322 and 307.

> They have 'special duties' (*besondere Aufgaben*) ahead of them. This phrase last appeared in our decodes after the cleaning-up in Poland, when participants were told they were to strictly hold their tongues as to what their '*besondere Aufgaben*' had been. This time the phrase appears in a message asking the authorities in Bialystok, Baranowicze and Minsk if they can lay their hands on any 'sound-film' apparatus since these are needed to help the troops in face of their special duties. The troops had to do without their atrocity films as a later message (no.13) shows.[47]

---

vi   SS-Brigadeführer Erich von dem Bach, the Higher SS and Police Leader in Byelorussia in July and August 1941. He was born with the surname Zelewski, but changed it for expediency's sake, sometimes alternating between the two names if politic. He was promoted Obergruppenführer in November 1941

The first report of these duties comes on 18 July, when Police Battalion 307 has taken part in 'pacification' in the woods south-east of Baranowicze. Police Battalion 316 undertakes similar operations in Ulsnin near Baranowicze. And also in the area covered by Police Battalion 307, Police Battalion 322, based at Bereza Kartuska, whose job is to guard the railway, has also participated in these operations. Police Battalion 309 based at Stozek near Bialowieza has had similar work in the woods around the latter. Then comes the decrypt of the first signal describing the numbers of victims of the 'special duties':

On the 18.7. a more laconic message of the same day informs Himmler that 'in the cleaning-up operations in SLONIM by Pol Regt Mitte of 17.7.41 1,153 Jewish plunderers were shot.'

The summary continues. Von dem Bach sends a document about the proportions of the population of Baranowicze, which, with 35,000 people, is made up of 17,000 Jews, 9,000 Russians and 9,000 Poles. The next situation report is on the 27th, announcing that Police Battalions 307 and 316 are to start on the following day with 'cleaning-up operations 25km north of Minsk'.

On 12 September another summary followed: 'Police Activities in Russia: August 15th–31st.' The first paragraph explained two things: the comparative successes the British were enjoying in cracking German police signals sent from the Eastern Front in the last two weeks of August, and the large numbers of Jews executed there. British cryptanalysts at the codebreaking centre in Buckinghamshire were breaking into a cipher they had named German Police Code Number 2, a sub-division of Domino. To decrypt it they had worked out each of two 'keys' – in reality different words – required to read into the coded signals sent every day by the German police battalions operating with Wehrmacht and SS units in Ukraine and Byelorussia. There were two keys in use each day, which Bletchley now codenamed 'Reich' and 'Russian'. The Germans were sending messages encrypted in the same Double Transposition system, which, as explained earlier, was based upon words taken from codebooks, then enciphered. The 'Reich' and 'Russia' keys, as they were known, were specific words from the codebooks that served as de facto instructions which enabled the senders to encrypt their message, and the recipients to decrypt it. These 'keys' changed every twelve hours. As described earlier, the German signallers would send the encrypted message by radio in Morse code, or, if its contents were classified as highly secret, the already-encrypted characters could be further encoded with a second encipherment. An Enigma machine could be used as an alternative. The recipient of any message, of course, would have the same codebook and daily keys as the sender. In the seventeen days of August 1941 covered by the summary described above, the analyst at Bletchley Park typing the report estimated that on eight days his colleagues had broken the Russian key, and the Reich on twelve days. The signals encrypted in these two keys represented approximately half of the messages sent by the German police units during the period in question.

> This fact should be borne in mind when assessing certain items of information: the number of executions is probably double that recorded . . . the execution of Jews is so recurrent a feature of these reports that the figures . . . have been brought under one heading. Whether all those executed as 'Jews' are indeed such is of course doubtful, but the figures are no less conclusive as evidence of a policy of savage intimidation if not of ultimate extermination.[48]

The report then summarised the tactical and administrative details of the operations the German police units were carrying out in the area of southern Byelorussia and northern Ukraine that they had occupied in the second half of August, and the executions of Jews they had carried out across this territory. Police Battalion 323 had arrived at Bialowicze on 18 August, followed closely by *Einsatzkommando Kompanie Gotenhafen*, part of Einsatzkommando B, one of the SS-run 'action squads' tasked with the rounding up and executions of Jews, Communist commissars and partisans behind the whole German front-line. The units had attacked the Russian-held town of Turov, in southern Byelorussia, on the 21st, meeting fierce resistance. The summary quoted a German Police message:

SS Cavalry Regiment 2, reinforced by a battalion of Cavalry Regiment 1, this day took TUROW, 50 kms east of DAVIDGRODEK [David-Gorodok]. There was con-siderable opposition. Prisoners reported the Russian strength as one battalion acting as advance detachment to stronger forces. The battalion was destroyed by artillery fire and hand-to-hand fighting. Only a few of the enemy got away to the southeast over the STWIGA, a tributary of the PRIPJET. As a corrective measure TUROW and nine other places were razed to ground. Only a few Russians escaped.[49]

By the 25th, Regional HQ is established in Mogilev, a town on the Dnieper River sixty miles east of Minsk. Then in an encounter thirty kilometres south of Mogilev between Police Battalion 307 and 'Russian hordes', the SS Cavalry unit moves forward. During this period up to 27 August, 16 guerrilla fighters, 25 partisans, 174 'plunderers', and 21 Red Army soldiers are shot. More operational detail follows. The SS Cavalry moves against partisans, some of whom are wearing German uniforms and carrying German rifles. Twelve more plunderers are shot. On the 26th Russians in retreat burn villages as they go. Kaunas in Latvia, meanwhile, is becoming an important police centre in the north. Order Police (Ordnungspolizei) Command for the East is installed there with the telephone number 29775 Kauen, operating via the army system, and they also have access to the army teleprinter. Their own will be ready in fourteen days. (This is reported on 18 August, and for the codebreakers in England the information about the German technical communications logistics was vital, enabling them to know how information was being transmitted.)

On 21 August, as the SS Cavalry units take Turov, and burn it to the ground, the Higher SS and Police Leader in Byelorussia, SS-Gruppenführer Erich von dem Bach uses the police encrypted network to send happy birthday wishes to his wife. The message summary also reports on the movements across the northern and central sector of the front of SS-Obergruppenführer Kurt Daluege, the commanding officer of Germany's Ordnungs polizei, or Order Police. This huge grouping includes every single police and customs officer, border guard, coastguard and railway police officer across the whole of Germany and its occupied territories. Its ranks included the different police battalions operating across Ukraine and Byelorussia. From decrypted messages the analysts at Bletchley deduce that the two generals loathe each other. Von dem Bach is a self-centred aristocrat, a martyr to his health, in particular his kidneys, whose condition he worsens through use of opium. Daluege is a policeman's policeman, down to earth, badly wounded in the First World War, left with neurological damage. Both hate Jews. Zelewski (von dem Bach) is not above using his personal Fiesler Storch reconnaissance aircraft to fly him bottles of spa water for his renal problem. Both complain about each other behind the other's back to Himmler, who is forced to remind them that he has other more urgent matters to attend to.

Prior to the August bi-monthly summary, Bletchley Park had reported each execution individually, but from 12 September, as noted, these are included in one complete section.[50]

'These are those referring specifically to Jews,' says the GC&CS report, ' . . . many, no doubt, were not Jews, but the fact that this heading invariably produces the biggest figures shows that this is the ground for killing most acceptable to the Higher authorities.'

- On 25 and 30 August, in the Central Sector, Regt Mitte & SS Cavalry Regt, execute 150 and 84 people respectively.
- In the Southern Sector, Police Battalion 314 and 1st SS Cavalry Brigade execute groups of 367, 294, and 65 people, all on the 23rd.
- On the 24th, a Police Regiment, Police Battalion 45 and a Police Squadron kill 70, 113 and 61 people.
- On the 25th, the 1st SS Brigade kill 283 in a mass execution, the Police Regiment South 1,342
- On the 26th the 1st SS Brigade execute 82 and the Police Regiment South another 549. Staff Headquarters SS and Police Forces kill 546, and Police Battalion 314 then put 69 people into a ditch and execute them.
- On the 27th the 1st SS Brigade shoot 16 people, Police Regiment South 914, and Police Battalion 320 another 42.
- On 30 August Police Regiment South kill 45, the 31st Police Regiment South 911, and Police Battalion 320 2,200 more prisoners.

The total of killings for the second half of August 1941 was 12,361, just in the sectors run by von dem Bach.

The report continues: as Bletchley Park writes 'administrative details defy classification.'[51] Items of interest that are logged include: a trip to Minsk by SS-Oberführer Professor von Arendt to 'secure' the picture gallery; sixty pigs are taken by an abattoir unit to Warsaw, and fifty typewriters are ready for delivery to police units in Minsk. A corporal in Königsberg sends a case home to Cologne, labelled 'Books'. It contains 55kg of butter and 55kg of oil, sugar, fish paste, flour, cheese. This has given the police 'food for thought', says a message. Meanwhile, from another operational area, a German communist arrested in Yugoslavia is believed to be plotting to assassinate Hitler. On 21 August Police Battalion 56, in between rounds of mass executions, sends a radio request to Berlin for 396 steel helmets, 376 pairs of handcuffs and 415 bathing costumes.[52]

Nigel de Grey and his teams of codebreakers and intelligence analysts had been decrypting dozens of similar German police messages since late June 1941, when the Germans invaded the Soviet Union. From the signals the British intercepted and decoded it was clear that as the Wehrmacht and SS units fought their way forward, behind the front lines execution squads were engaged in organised mass killings of captured Jews. On 18 July, an army intercept station at RAF Chicksands Priory in Bedfordshire picked up the first such signal from the town of Slonim in Byelorussia. This was the message that said that an Einsatzkommando, 'action squad', had shot 1,153 Jews. On 7 August, one of the SS cavalry units operating in Ukraine reported back to the headquarters of the Gestapo that it had carried out 7,819 executions since Operation Barbarossa began. The police commander of Army Group Centre said that since his units arrived in Russia in the last week of July, they had collectively carried out approximately 30,000 executions. The messages were all going to the same destination – SS and Gestapo headquarters in Berlin. Himmler and Heinrich Müller, the head of the Gestapo, were keeping close track of the killings. In the week between 23 and 31 August, covered by the two-weekly summary of German Police messages, different Einsatzkommando leaders also sent seventeen separate radio messages detailing executions of individual groups of prisoners numbering between 61 and 4,200.

What de Grey's cryptanalysts deduced was that out on the scorching midsummer steppes of Ukraine and Byelorussia, platoon and company leaders in each SS and police unit were compiling their after-action reports and sending them to their group headquarters, located in each large town strung behind the 1,000-mile-long front line. By late summer this stretched from near Leningrad in the north, to southern Ukraine. The signals staff of each Einsatzkommando encrypted the plain text of the messages in German Police Code No.2, with the coded key setting that changed twice a day, and then transmitted the reports to Berlin in Morse code. Gestapo cryptanalysts working in their headquarters would have decrypted them immediately. What they did not know was that Allied intercept stations were picking up their signals, while Bletchley Park had also broken into the settings of their army, navy and air force colleagues' Enigma enciphering machines.

On 2 September 1941, one of his cryptanalysts showed Nigel de Grey a signal that had just been decoded: instantly de Grey knew this was something for the Prime Minister, who was due to visit the codebreaking centre in Buckinghamshire in four days' time. This was Churchill's first visit to Bletchley Park. When he arrived his Principal Private Secretary, John Martin, who was travelling with him, did not come into the headquarters in the manor house, but stayed outside.

De Grey and his staff showed the Prime Minister the decrypt of the specific decoded signal. A German police officer on the Eastern Front had transmitted it a week previously. From the terse details contained in it, he was almost certainly operating with an SS and police killing squad in northern Ukraine, and had sent the message to the office of Heinrich Himmler. A radio intercept station in eastern England had picked up the signal as it was sent, and Bletchley Park's analysts decrypted it within hours.

> A report from the Berditschew Korosten area mentions that Russians are still retiring and burning the villages. Prisoners taken number 47, Jews shot 1,246, losses nil.[53]

The message in question had already been sent to London by de Grey, and on receipt of it Churchill had circled with a red pen the figure 1,246. By the time he was visiting Bletchley Park, more than 1,500 miles distance from the summer plains and forests of the Eastern Front, three radio intercept stations in Britain were picking up the coded German signals. One was at Beaumanor in Leicestershire, one at RAF Chicksands Priory in Bedfordshire and another, the one run by the General Post Office and the Metropolitan Police, at Denmark Hill in south London. By July and August 1941, as the German killing squads were sending their messages in, there were already forty women and men working in shifts at Bletchley Park, decoding the Domino messages that Beaumanor, Chicksands and Denmark Hill were intercepting from the Eastern Front. The Bletchley signals analysts decrypted between thirty and a hundred messages per day. The Double Transposition system was hard to break, but as was so often the case with codebreaking, human error on the part of the Germans gave the British an unexpected break. The German police were disciplined with language, and would frequently open a radio message with the same phrase: *An den Befehlshaber der Ordnungspolizei in Frankfurt am Main / Berlin / München* [for the commander of the Order Police in Frankfurt am Main / Berlin / Munich].

Nigel de Grey saw that these opening encoded words would often be subsequently repeated in each message, in each of the two daily encipherments, which gave the British a series of coded versions of the same words which they could then compare with each other. When differently enciphered versions of the same plaintext words appeared like this, it was known as a 'crib'. The messages which the SS and German police units sent back in July and the first half of August, and which Bletchley Park decrypted, provided the British with some of the first information on the mass executions being carried out on the Eastern Front.

Regardless of which hut it originated from, the relevant contents of each signal then went into a daily and weekly summary of intelligence. At first Bletchley had called this by the codename of 'Boniface', to make it appear as though it came from a human agent, then changed it to 'Ultra'. This referred to the single governmental security classification that was even higher than 'Most Secret' – 'Ultra Secret.' The intelligence summaries were distributed to a small list of government and defence officials. These included the Prime Minister, the senior ministers at the War Office, the respective Chiefs of the Imperial General Staff from the Army, Navy and the Royal Air Force, and the heads of the Joint Intelligence Committee, as well as MI6 and MI5.

Stewart Menzies, the Director-General of the Secret Intelligence Service, did his utmost to bring the Ultra intelligence, and its distribution, under the control of his agency. The Prime Minister himself received weekly summaries of the intercepts, although as the summer and autumn of 1941 progressed, and reports of mass executions continued to be decoded, he asked for intelligence updates to be given to him every day. He was adamant, determined to make the German atrocities public, while simultaneously being urgently aware of the vital need to keep Ultra secret. The two imperatives were often to prove mutually incompatible, and the handling of the information about mass executions on the Eastern Front was the first example of this. On 24 August 1941, Churchill had returned from meeting President Franklin Roosevelt, aboard the battleship HMS *Prince of Wales*, which had transported him across the Atlantic to Placentia Bay in Newfoundland. The Atlantic Conference, at which the two leaders discussed their goals for a post-war world, took place on 14 August. The speech on the 24th formed the basis of a radio broadcast by the British Prime Minister, called 'Broadcast to the World', and at 3,500 words long, the equivalent of ten pages of a book, it provided a huge amount of material for the Germans to listen to.

> The aggressor . . . retaliates by the most frightful cruelties. As his Armies advance, whole districts are being exterminated. Scores of thousands – literally scores of thousands – of executions in cold blood are being perpetrated by the German Police-troops upon the Russian patriots who defend their native soil. Since the Mongol invasions of Europe in the Sixteenth Century, there has never been methodical, merciless butchery on such a scale, or approaching such a scale. And this is but the beginning. Famine and pestilence have yet to follow in the bloody ruts of Hitler's tanks. We are in the presence of a crime without a name.

To protect the sources of the information, he did not refer to Jews directly in this message, simply to 'Russian patriots'. Yet the key words of 'German Police troops' and 'executions' were almost certainly enough. The British knew enough by now about the administration of the SS and the Third Reich to know that when German police and SS units on the Eastern Front sent the encrypted radio reports of their mass executions back to Berlin, the principal recipients of the messages would be three different SS departments. The first was the office of the Reichsführer of the SS, Heinrich Himmler; the second the SS Main Economic and Administrative Office, and the third the different officials in charge of each department at the Reich Security Main Office, or RSHA. De Grey knew that in the middle of the SS vicious intrigues, the Germans' suspicious nature and operational astuteness foresaw personal and organisational risk and threat everywhere. They would be very concerned that the British, the Soviet Union and possibly the Poles could be intercepting and reading their men's encrypted communications. For de Grey this was like a deadly form of electronic chess – the Third Reich's leaders would be convinced that the Allies could be deciphering signals whose encryption many other senior officers in the SS, and the Wehrmacht, assumed to be secure. So the mentions of 'German Police troops' and 'executions' in the Prime Minister's speech would have been enough to alert them.

A signal that Bletchley Park decoded on 13 September confirmed this. SS-Obergruppenführer Kurt Daluege, the SS officer in charge of the Ordnungspolizei (Orpo), sent a priority message to his senior SS and Order Police officers who commanded the Einsatzkommandos and the police battalions on the ground in Ukraine, Byelorussia and the Baltics.

The danger of decipherment by the enemy of wireless messages is great. For this reason, only such matters are to be transmitted by wireless as can be considered open . . . (decoding groups missed . . .) . . . Confidential or Secret, but not information which is containing State Secrets, calls for especially secret treatment. Into this category fall exact figures of executions (these are to be sent by courier).

Once his colleagues had intercepted and decrypted this particular message, de Grey added a sidenote on the piece of paper on which the transcript was typed. This happened some time later, before the translated signal was added to the weekly intelligence update which the Government Code and Cypher School sent to London. The German signal showed that Churchill's desire to publicise and condemn German atrocities was actively and immediately endangering the very intelligence sources on which his information was based.

> The scale of these executions [read de Grey's sidenote] was a clear indication of the utter ruthlessness of the Germans in Russia. The anxiety (of SS Police chief Daluege) may have been increased by a speech by the Prime Minister drawing the attention of the world to this carnage. In any case the German authorities evidently demanded more drastic steps still, and these culminated in a complete change of cypher in mid-September. Double Transposition (a straightforward system, and relatively simple to break) was dropped (never to appear again) and Double Playfair took its place.[54]

The German Police had changed their codes. Not only was Bletchley Park's ability to break into Domino now in question. Hydra, the German army and Luftwaffe Enigma codes were also, by extension, at stake.

CHAPTER IV
'SPECIAL DUTIES' IN THE EAST

Lublin and Mogilev, autumn 1941

In an average week at the SS headquarters in Lublin, Odilo Globočnik, his clique of Austrian SS officers, his civilian staff and their wives and girlfriends drank some three hundred bottles of champagne. They consumed about forty on a normal night, but when a larger celebration was planned, the total could go up to fifty or sixty. The large house on Wienawska Street where the SS General had his headquarters was filled with thousands of bottles of champagne, wine and spirits, and the men ate prodigious amounts of ham, pork, bacon and eggs too. SS-Corporal Willy Natke, Globočnik's batman, said the headquarters ate and drank twenty-five pounds of butter, thirty pounds of coffee, a hundred and seventy eggs each week, all food given to the SS by local Polish businessmen and officials, men desperate to curry favour, obtain dispensations, and, often, avoid death. It was no wonder that Globočnik was getting fat, said his girlfriend, Irmgard Rickheim. Before moving to Lublin to work as a secretary she had been stationed in the Berlin headquarters of the Hitler Youth. The SS officers in the capital of the General Government, like Hermann Höfle and Ernst Lerch, were literally living high on the hog. Outside much of Poland was near starvation, living in ghettos or under the close supervision of the SS or German police, but every morning Globočnik and his team would plough through their work, stomachs full, stoked with coffee, some of the men shuddering with hangovers.[55]

After the Volksdeutscher Selbstschutze were disbanded in mid-1940, Himmler and Globočnik posted Höfle to run a small labour camp of Jewish slave workers building anti-tank ditches along the river Bug, near the village of Bełżec. This lay near the Ukrainian border, some fifty miles south-east of Lublin. After this, he transferred to Globočnik's headquarters. Höfle was by now an SS Hauptsturmführer, or captain, as was his compatriot Ernst Lerch, his Austrian SS colleague from the pre-war meetings at the café in Klagenfurt. Many of the SS men around them in Lublin seemed to come from Klagenfurt or Linz or Salzburg or Vienna: as Higher SS and Police Leader in the city, Globočnik had surrounded himself with his cronies. Ernst Lerch was particularly close to the mean-tempered officer from Trieste, who was described by his batman as a brute, who would not hesitate to kill his own subordinates. Ernst Lerch had access to Globočnik's personal radio communications too, so it came as no surprise when he told Höfle in the first week of September that a priority message had arrived from SS Police headquarters in Berlin. The recipients were all the generals serving as Higher SS and Police Leaders inside Germany, in Poland and out in Ukraine, the Baltic states and Byelorussia where the SS and Wehrmacht were now operating.

As seen earlier, the message warned that the 'danger of decipherment by the enemy of wireless messages is great,' and stipulated that no messages containing state secrets, including those with 'figures of executions' should be transmitted over the radio.

Senior commanders had either intercepted or heard a radio

broadcast made on the BBC by British Prime Minister Winston Churchill at the end of August, in which he had made reference to 'executions' and 'German police troops'. The message about radio security came from the head of the German Order Police himself, the testy, unpredictable SS-Obergruppenführer from East Prussia, Kurt Daluege. Adding on to his warning that the enemy could easily be deciphering German coded messages, he was determined to improve radio security, and so as an extra precaution he ordered that all units were to change their encryption codes immediately.

Another message followed shortly afterwards: the Reichsführer der SS, Himmler himself, would be paying a three-day visit that month to the three main German headquarters operating inside the Soviet Union. Following the German invasion, which had begun ten weeks before, the front line in the east now stretched more than a thousand miles from Leningrad in the north to the Crimea in the south, split between Army Groups North, Centre and South. Höfle knew, as well, the secret news that in mid-October Himmler would either be coming to Lublin too, or 'Globus', as Globočnik was nicknamed, would be going to see him in Berlin. Either way, all of his SS subordinates knew what would be on the agenda: not just the SS plans for building ghettos, labour camps and fortifications out here in the east, but what to do about 'the Jewish problem', as Heydrich and Göring preferred to call it.

Overseeing the Reich Security Main Office, Heydrich was simultaneously a guiding light for Höfle and the bane of his existence. With their orders, draconian edicts, quotas, deadlines, and ceaseless demands for updates and information, the vast Berlin office ran the Reich's security, and it saw everything. There were spies and informers everywhere, even among the loyal ranks of Himmler's SS, even this far away in southern Poland. The city of Lublin felt a thousand miles from civilisation to Höfle and his colleagues. They were men and women from Salzburg, Innsbruck, Graz –

and now they found themselves a thousand miles from flowering linden trees, boating on the Saalach river, and the Alps adorning the skyline.

To be fair, Lublin was sizeable, and had an urban centre of faded, turn-of-the-century Austro-Hungarian affluence that reminded Höfle of parts of his home country. At the outbreak of the war, when Hermann Höfle had crossed the Polish border, there had been some 120,000 people living in Lublin, of whom about a third were Jewish. There were three synagogues, a Jewish hospital, and two newspapers published in Yiddish. Jews owned a third of the manufacturing, the small shops and factories too. The Germans had entered the city on 18 September, and immediately the Jewish community was ordered to pay money to the Wehrmacht, and clean up the bomb damage, while their shops and businesses were robbed without delay. The German soldiers beat some of them, and threw the books from the large Talmudic library out of the windows, before collecting them in a pyre in the main square and setting them alight. As some of the town's Jews crowded round the fire, a German military band played to try to drown out their protests. The Germans lost no time creating a new administration, and renamed a city park after Adolf Hitler, while a thoroughfare was renamed after Reinhard Heydrich and another became 'Ostlandstrasse'. From late November, Jews over the age of ten then had to wear the yellow Star of David armband. The Lublin Town Council, or 'Judenrat', had been established at the end of 1939, with twenty-four members, all elected by the Jewish community.

Tens of thousands of other Jews from all over Poland were shipped to Lublin in late 1939, and the first months of 1940. The SS and German police rounded up thousands of them and sent them to work in hastily built labour camps around the village of Bełżec, some fifty miles south-east of Lublin. In a frozen winter, with meagre diets, constant illness and barely heated huts to live in, they slaved to build the so-called Eastern Wall, between the General Government and Soviet territory. Along with the Germanisation of Lublin and other areas, this was one of Odilo Globočnik's engineering priorities. In the city itself the Germans established a ghetto for the Jews; others settled outside the town in poor, rural settlements, and waited for the Germans to decide their fate. There was enough to eat, just. Black marketeering was rampant. Following the occupation, the town seemed to be a tawdry cluster of Austro-Hungarian buildings, destroyed and looted cafés, half-torched municipal offices, smashed windows. As for the outskirts, the alleyways were of wooden-walled buildings, dusty earthen streets and runner beans sprawling in the gardens, panic-eyed cats scuttering like fleeing wraiths. And Jews. For Jews were Höfle's business, here in Poland, and the tempo of business was increasing.

Yet it was not half as busy as it was across the border: from the signals Globočnik's officers saw, it appeared the number of executions on the Eastern Front was increasing. In Vilnius in Lithuania, the Germans imprisoned 40,000 Jews in a ghetto, and from July onwards, had begun executing another 30,000 in the nearby Ponary Woods. Two days after the incoming message about radio security came news that on 15 and 16 September the Einsatzkommandos had carried out mass executions of 42,000 Jews in two separate incidents in the towns of Berdichev-Kostichen and Uman in Ukraine. Then came yet another message about communications:

On 13/9 the three officers commanding the North, Centre and Southern Russian Front are reminded that the danger of their messages being decoded was great. Among other secret matters that should not be sent by wireless was the number of executions carried out.

Meanwhile, the SS, the Wehrmacht and the Order Police were meanwhile planning a further meeting in October, where they would discuss the situation behind the lines on the Eastern Front. The Wehrmacht's commander of the Army Group Centre Rear Area, Max von Schenkendorff, gave the meeting the formal title of The Mogilev Security Conference, and Colonel Max Montua from Police Regiment Centre had arranged that it would be held in the eastern Byelorussian city in mid-October. Under the auspices of an anti-partisan training conference, the officers involved, from the Wehrmacht, the SS and the Order Police, would be meeting to work out how to expand their operations against partisans, fighters behind the lines, how to control rear-area security, and to increase the pace and scope of the killings of Jews. Arthur Nebe was going to be one of the conference attendees. A former Berlin police officer who had joined the SS, he had risen through the ranks by 1936 to command the Kriminalpolizei, the Kripo, Nazi Germany's criminal police. He had then volunteered to command Einsatzgruppe B, now operating behind Army Group Centre. His men had been killing since the unit crossed the Soviet border in July, and Nebe now reported that there were, simply put, more Jews to kill than the men under his command could handle. Einsatzgruppe B just did not have the resources to deal with all the Jews they found, and as far as he was concerned in Army Group Centre, the solution to the Jewish problem so far was proving impractical. The number of people to be executed had also increased since the SS had added Jewish women and children to their killing-lists in August.[56]

One SS officer who was not invited to the conference was one of the squadron commanders from the 2nd SS Cavalry Regiment, called SS-Hauptsturmführer Franz Magill. The regiment had had units based in Poland, including Lublin, since December 1939. Along with the 1st SS Cavalry, they were now operating in the rear areas of Army Group Centre, and by late August had killed over 10,000 Jews. Himmler had addressed the cavalrymen personally on 5 July, shortly after the launch of Operation Barbarossa. Any man who did not want to take part in forthcoming operations, which would include special duties, could transfer to another unit.[57] Himmler reportedly did not describe that these duties included participating in mass executions. Magill was an SS riding instructor, and one of the 2nd Regiment's squadron commanders. On 1 August 1941 the commander of the 1st SS Cavalry Regiment, Hermann Fegelein, gave orders to his men who were operating in the rear areas of Army Group Centre in Byelorussia and northern Ukraine. They were carrying out an operation to find and kill Jews in and around the huge, black muddy expanse of the Pripyat marshes. Magill's men were now put under his command. Himmler had criticised Fegelein's performance in July, saying that the numbers of Jews killed to date by his men were too low: so his latest Regimental Order no.42 specified that all male Jews over the age of fourteen were to be shot, the women and children driven into the swamps and drowned. Magill, however, interpreted his orders literally, and said afterwards that it had not been possible to drown the women and children since the waters in the marshes in question were not deep enough. So they were shot. The final number of Jews killed in the lengthy operation, in Fegelein's report of 17 September, was 14,178.[58]

Fegelein had influence: he was a favourite of Himmler's, and would become the brother-in-law of Eva Braun, when he married Gretl, one of her two sisters. Magill's operational performance, despite his unit having accounted for over 6,000 Jews, was deemed lacklustre and weak, as he was seen to have only wanted to kill Jewish men, and not the women and children. This showed clearly how the wind of mass death was blowing, and so for Magill a seat at the Mogilev conference table was not forthcoming.

By the time the preparations for the meeting were under way, one SS officer employed another piece of euphemism to join the expanding vocabulary of phrases being used to describe atrocities, while simultaneously being used to try to camouflage their meaning in subsequent radio signals. The men in Mogilev would 'exchange experiences', as the SS officer put it, of what the different units had learnt so far about rounding up, arresting and executing Jews, partisans, and residual Russian communist personnel living, operating and trapped behind the ever-moving front line.[59] The meeting would include a training exercise for SS troops and the German Police on how best to surround Soviet villages, and 'screen' their Jewish inhabitants.

Heydrich, Himmler, the RSHA, the SS and German Police were increasingly making ample use of words like 'exchange of experiences' and 'screening'. Others phrases being used included 'special handling', 'special duties', 'activities according to the usages of war', 'anti-social elements', 'intervention', 'purification' and 'evacuation'. Hermann Höfle knew that out on the midsummer steppes, in the trampled, sprawling fields of unharvested Ukrainian wheat, the waters of the Pripyat marshes, and through the stands of pine forests of Byelorussia, in reality these phrases meant one thing: bullets and bodies. German bullets, Jewish bodies. By late summer 1941, as he stood in his office in Lublin hundreds of miles away from Salzburg, his star was in the ascendant, and the collar tabs on his uniform bore the twin lightning flashes on one side, on the other the three diamonds and two bars of a captain in the SS.

Höfle had heard about what had happened in Mogilev, too, like in so many other towns and cities the Germans had occupied. He was due to visit the town in coming weeks, to coordinate with other officers over SS-Brigadeführer Globočnik's forthcoming operations. What the SS and Einsatzkommandos had done in Mogilev was similar to what he and his Volksdeutsche unit had done in Poland, but on a far larger and more decisive scale. The Wehrmacht had pounded the Byelorussian city for two weeks before the Red Army fled at the end of July, leaving ruined buildings, shell holes, corpses putrefying in the ninety-degree summer heat. The Germans counted nearly 6,500 Jews who were still alive in the city, of whom a third were children. While the Wehrmacht and the SS waited for the arrival of an Einsatzkommando, the Jews were confined to a muddy ghetto on the edge of the city, their clothes emblazoned with yellow cloth stars.

On 17 July Hitler had ordered Himmler that the SS were to be responsible for all behind-the-lines security in occupied Soviet territory. He in turn had appointed three new Higher SS and Police Leaders for each Army Group, responsible among other duties for what was termed, again euphemistically, as 'rear-areas security'. This involved the increased arrests, confinement and execution of Jews in the North, Centre and South operational areas. The job was entrusted to the Einsatzkommandos, or 'action squads', made up of SS units, local auxiliaries and battalions of officers from the Ordnungspolizei. By mid-July, the German advance on Operation Barbarossa had pushed 200 miles east in a month, leaving behind it hundreds of thousands of Red Army prisoners, captured Communist Party officials, partisans and Jews to fall into German hands. The SS task was to imprison the first, capture and interrogate the second, and execute as many of the third and fourth as they possibly could.

On 31 July Reichsmarschall Hermann Göring had instructed Heydrich to take measures to implement what he called 'a Final Solution to the Jewish question'. By August and September, the SS and Police were already establishing large ghettos in towns and cities such as Minsk, Riga, Mogilev, Lublin, Vilnius, Kaunas and Bialystok, which they were filling with large groups of Jews rounded up in Poland, Ukraine, Latvia, Estonia, Lithuania and

Byelorussia. Jews from Germany and Austria were soon to follow. At the Auschwitz concentration camp at Oswiecim in the southern part of the General Government, the SS were about to trial the use of an odourless pesticide called Zyklon B as a means of executing human beings. The first inmates in line to be killed were Soviet prisoners of war.

Operation Barbarossa had only been under way for five weeks when on 1 August Heinrich Müller, the SS general commanding the Gestapo in Berlin, added yet another task for each one of the SS and police units. Each action squad and SS detachment operating behind the advancing German front line, from Leningrad in the North to the Black Sea in the south, were to send a regular radio update detailing the number of executions they had carried out, and the numbers of Jews moved to ghettos, and those awaiting deportation to them. This meant fresh work and complication for every unit's commanding officers and their signals NCOs. In Höfle's case, these new duties included more tasks for his secretary Berta Gottschall, who was also a Salzburger.

Berta had been the Leader of the *Salzburg Bund Deutscher Madel* (BDM), or League of German Girls, which was the female arm of the Hitler Youth. Membership of this organisation was compulsory in Nazi Germany – which included Austria – from the ages of ten to eighteen, and girls were only excluded if they had hereditary diseases or were considered racially impure, which could mean having one grandparent who was part-Jewish. Their role was simple – to prepare for a life as a mother, home-maker and wife in the Third Reich, and to take Germany forward into the next generation. She also served in the older girls' section, called 'The Faith and Beauty Society', which in turn instructed the younger girls. During the invasion of Poland, the BDM taught its members that Poles were truly subhuman, worthy of disgust, suited to be ruled by a master race. While the younger girls stayed behind on the home front, growing vegetables, helping in hospitals, the older ones like Berta Gottschall had served in Poland, alongside the teenage boys of the Hitler Youth, helping to evict Poles from their homes to make way for German settlers. Much to the fury of Himmler and Hitler, Germans liked poking fun at the BDM. During the summer months, the girls would go on large camping trips in the Alps or the Black Forest, living outside under canvas alongside detachments of their teenage male counterparts from the Hitler Youth. In 1936 large contingents of teenagers of both groups travelled to Bavaria, to participate in the annual Nazi Party rally at Nuremberg. Nine hundred of the BDM girls returned home pregnant, leading a group of anti-Hitler cynics in Berlin to dub them 'The League of German Mattresses'.

Meanwhile Höfle was also waiting for his deputy and friend to arrive. Helmut Ortwin Pohl was a fellow Austrian, an accountant, with a matchless head for figures, which was exactly what Höfle needed right now. Another friend was his driver, Lieutenant Max Meirhofer, also a dependable Salzburger. Max was a keen amateur photographer, an enthusiast for duplicate pictures, which he sent back to Austria as souvenirs. In one instance, he was to take two photographs of an old Jewish woman in Poland: in the first, she was sitting in a wheelchair. In the second, she was lying sprawled on the cobbles after Meirhofer had pushed her out of the chair. Then he shot her, and posted the photographs home. The number of enemies Hermann Höfle had seemed to increase the further he went from his headquarters. The SS was full of factions, favourites, officers preening for advancement and patronage, Germans versus Austrians, the clique of Himmler, the clique of Heydrich, who liked whom, who distrusted whom, who would or would not promote who to this post or that. Sycophantic senior officers displaying their loyalty, sending birthday wishes to Hitler and Himmler over a radio net that half the units on the Eastern Front used; while SS-Gruppenführer von dem Bach was having bottles of curative pure mineral water flown to his headquarters in the Fiesler Storch aircraft meant for urgent transport, and reconnaissance. In his office in Lublin, Globočnik, and by extension Höfle, surrounded themselves with close, proven allies, men and women who were not just part of the SS hierarchy, but who were mostly Austrians too. They understood each other: they all came from the same regional, historical and cultural background, and nothing needed to be explained. They had been illegal, loyal SS men before the Anschluss: now their time in the sun had come. Höfle and his fellow SS officers knew they were out on the front lines not just of a global war, but of a new world. Poland, Ukraine, the Baltics – the whole east – had to be emptied of Slavs and Jews to make way for the wave of German settlers who were going to arrive, as the Aryan population of the Third Reich expanded. What was it that the fellow Austrian SS man, Franz Stangl, called these Jews? Cargo.

Höfle and the two generations of Germans and Austrians who had grown up in the preceding forty years had long recognised the necessity of confronting, and eradicating Bolshevism. To be doing that, and simultaneously creating Lebensraum, 'living space', in the east for German settlers was Höfle's principal mission, and he was devoting himself to it. He was convinced of the rectitude of what he was doing. Around him were those who weren't: the Russians and Ukrainians would be defeated, killed or imprisoned. The British, French and Americans? Well, thought Höfle, they should be on our side, but they were not, so we will have to defeat them, or make peace. The Jews? That was simple. Special duties.

Hermann Höfle's enemies were people who were not himself or of himself, who were obstructing his mission, and they had to be defeated, destroyed or diverted. Any of the British or their allies who were trying to listen in to his secure communications –

and Höfle, like many of his fellow commanders, was convinced they were – had to be defeated and obstructed. He was a former taxi driver, he had run a transport firm, he knew the nuts and bolts of mechanics, but he was no mathematician, and as for electronics . . . ? His chronically bad spelling and awkwardness had always hindered him at school, making him angry and frustrated, but as he worked in Lublin, life seemed to have fallen into place. For a man who was possibly borderline dyslexic, the complexities of Double Transposition, of Enigma encipherments, of one-time code pads were sometimes beyond him, but he had very capable signals staff. As always, the SS provided, as they had since the moment Höfle enlisted.

Höfle's SS superiors were impressed by his energy and determination in executing the mission to rid the newly conquered territories of what the SS dubbed 'undesirables': the captain from Salzburg brought a ruthless and mechanical approach to the task. By September 1941, at the headquarters of the Higher SS and Police Leader in Lublin, Höfle and Lerch also oversaw budgets, administration and signals security, making sure that the daily and weekly signals sent back to Berlin were properly encrypted in the prescribed cipher. Each sub-unit of the German army and the SS had its own Enigma encoding machine, and signals operators were trained to use it. Höfle, like many of his colleagues, was extremely wary about radio discipline, partly because other SS officers had told him how easy it had been to break into and read the Soviet codes used by the Red Army and NKVD interior ministry troops. The Enigma, though, was a different beast to the simple, outdated codebooks the Russians used.

When one of Höfle's operators sent a message, he took the plain text, written on a signal transmission form in pencil, and encoded it on the Enigma. The typewriter-sized machine had a keyboard with a 26-letter Roman alphabet, and above it a panel with

26 lights, each representing a letter. Each time the signals clerk pressed a letter on the keyboard another one would flash up as the encoded version. There were three or four rotors inside the Enigma machine, each bearing the 26 letters of the alphabet, and each of these rotors rotated one click, or one letter, each time the keyboard was pressed. There was a plugboard inside, too, with ten pairs of letters connected. In this way the combination of the alphabetical letters on the keyboard, and even just three different rotors, gave hundreds of billions of potential letter options. The device could not be broken, the signals generals said, and so Hermann Höfle believed. However, were there ever a chance that it was, he had two separate codebooks to encrypt a message, both based upon the system known as a Double Transposition. He felt confident that his signals were secure.

The German police and SS signallers on the Eastern Front were using two encryption devices. They enciphered some of the plain texts of their messages on Enigma machines. With other messages they employed codewords taken from codebooks, enciphered with the use of word keys. This was based on the Double Transposition encoding system. Each day the German signallers had a choice of two 'keys'. These were words from the codebooks that enabled them to encrypt their message. Each key was made up of a word or sometimes a group of words which told the radio operators how to lay out the patterns of words prior to encrypting them by using the codebook. These keys changed every twelve hours. The signallers would then send the encrypted message by radio in Morse code, or, if its contents were classified as highly secret, the already-encrypted characters could be further encoded by using another key on the same message. The recipient of the message at, say, Gestapo headquarters in Berlin would have the same codebook and the daily keys as the sender, and would be using the same Enigma setting, so would be able to decrypt the signals.

The cleansing of Mogilev

In September 1941, the commander of the 322 Order Police Battalion had signalled the SS officers in Mogilev to tell them that he and his men from Einsatzkommando 8, operating in northern Ukraine, would be arriving in Mogilev shortly to assist with 'the Jewish situation'. In preparation for this, the SS gave orders that the 6,500 Jews in the temporary ghetto should be moved by force to the other side of the Dnipro river, which flowed through the city. At dawn the following day, SS troopers, German police officers and Ukrainian auxiliary policemen surrounded the streets where the Jews now lived. They kicked in the front doors, unleashed Alsatian guard-dogs, and shot those too old, slow or argumentative to move. In the end, the SS and German policemen had killed 113 of the Jews before the operation was completed, but by nightfall they shoved some 6,400 of them, with boots, rifle-butts and whips, into a forest on the other side of the river. They surrounded the makeshift encampment with barbed wire and armed guards, and gave the captives no food or water, and left them to await the arrival of the men from Einsatzkommando 8. These arrived by 2 October. The unit commander kept a record of events, but following SS-Obergruppenführer Daluege's warning about radio security, no mention was to be made of it on the signals net.

On October 2nd [. . .] at 15:30, the 9th company . . . together with HQ staff of the Higher SS and Police Leader 'Center' and the Ukrainian auxiliary police, carried out an action in the ghetto in Mogilev [. . .] 65 were shot trying to escape [. . .] October 3 [. . .] Companies 7 and 9 [. . .] executed 2,208 male and female Jews in a forest outside of Mogilev.

A second action took place two weeks later, on 19 October, as described in the report of the Einsatzgruppen written on the day following the murder:

> On October 19, 1941, a large-scale operation against the Jews was carried out in Mogilev with the aid of the Police Regiment 'Center'. 3,726 Jews of both sexes and all ages were liquidated by this action [. . .] On October 23, 1941, to prevent further acts of sabotage and to combat the partisans, a further number of Jews from Mogilev and surrounding area, 239 of both sexes, were liquidated.[60]

Following these actions, Heinrich Himmler spent the last week of October on inspection visits to different units, before which he met with Odilo Globočnik for two hours in Lublin, and gave him approval to begin building an extermination camp for Jews at Belzec. The following day Himmler travelled back to Munich and met for five hours with Reinhard Heydrich. The main subject on the agenda was 'executions'.

CHAPTER V

CODE ORANGE

Bletchley Park, November 1941

The decision by the Germans to change their encryption system for the Domino signals was a blessing in disguise for de Grey and his colleagues:

The gradual tightening up of cypher security measures came to a head on September 12th when an entirely new form of cypher was inaugurated for the 'Russian' messages. Continuity in the breaking of the previous keys made it possible however to break into the new one too, and the net result of the change is whereas up to the 12th only 3 of the 'Russian' keys were broken, since the 12th only one Russian key has not been broken. Against this must be set the fact that the new form of cypher makes for more corruption in the text, so that names – particularly Russian place names – are often hard to decipher.

. . . General Daluege alarmed perhaps by our apparent awareness of the unspeakable activities of his police in

Russia, sent the following signal [about radio security and the use of the word 'executions'] on the 13th to the HSSPFs (Higher SS and Police Leaders) in North, Middle, South. The effect of this was that situation reports from the 14th onwards contained the enigmatic phrase 'action according to the activity of war' under the heading which had formerly contained the figures of executions. If there were any doubt as to the meaning of the phrase it is dispelled by a slip on the part of the HSSPF South, who in his situation report on the day before the General's order reports:

'Police Regiment South . . . Action according to the usage of war (3): Successes – Police Regiment South liquidates 1,548 Jews. (11.9.41). The only other figures recorded are Sept 2, 45, Sept 6, 494.' [61]

In the section of the regular summary titled 'Personalities involved', there was mention of Himmler travelling a lot, to all his commands, to Smolensk. Then came a name which had not appeared before in the signals updates. 'NSKK Obergruppenführer Höfle' [with the umlauts added on the page in fountain pen] visits units of his command with the Police Forces of the Centre.'

Who was this new SS general on the Eastern Front, visiting units who were carrying out mass killings? This Hermann Höfle was the leader of a brigade attached to the Nazi Socialist Motor Corps, a Bavarian general rather than an Austrian captain (see p. 279).

'Police Activities in Russia. General,' then began the signals decrypt summary of Domino for October and the first half of November. De Grey and his colleagues were astounded that the Germans had tried to improve their radio security by relinquishing one encipherment and replacing it with another that was much simpler to decrypt – despite the appalling contents of the SS and

Police messages from the Eastern Front, the way into Domino was still open, still secret, and now made simpler.

> The change from 'transposition' to 'Playfair' noted in the previous summary was completed on 1 November, when the latter was adopted also for messages inside Germany. This has made it possible to break all but four of the Reich keys, and all but two of the Russian keys (in all cases Sundays when traffic is at its lowest). Had they kept to 'transposition' it is likely these figures would have been doubled. A message from HQ in Berlin (4.11.41) sent out soon after the final change to 'playfair' was made is illuminating in that it shows complete ignorance of the weak points of both types of cypher, and the possible methods of breaking.[62]

One unit, however, appeared to have made a switch away from one-time pads to a mechanical device, and were now possibly using an Enigma encryption system: 'the use of machine-cyphers by the SS Cavalry Brigade at Police Eastern HQ at Arys is indicated in a message of the same date. (4.11.41.)'.[63]

The Germans were now convinced they had improved their signals security: Hut 5 at Bletchley Park knew that, at a stroke, they had made the work of the British cryptanalysts easier. The signals summary quoted above then details the movements of Himmler in the last week of October 1941, criss-crossing parts of the Baltic States, Byelorussia and Ukraine, including Mogilev. There is a changeover of command between the Higher SS and Police leaders operating behind the different Army Groups: SS-Obergruppenführer Jeckeln leaves the post of HSSPF South and moves to take over 'North' in Riga; his opposite number Prutzmann on promotion takes over 'South'. No mention is made in the signals summary as to why this might have happened. Was Jeckeln more capable at dealing with the logistics of mass executions than Prutzmann? Von dem Bach, leader at 'Centre', is promoted.

Of him, the summary observes:

He is a sick man and over the radio net makes a special appeal to General Daluege to allow a certain medicinal water to be flown to him by courier plane. Since in the meantime he was forced to relieve his pain by opium injections.[64]

The summary continued. Six different police battalions arrive for extensive 'cleaning-up' in the area around Mogilev, while a new enemy has arrived. The weather. Mud and rain and extraordinarily bad roads are the order of the day as SS men and Police carry out a forced march to Konotop, north-east of Kiev. The cleaning-up operations which follow then move in a north-easterly direction from Konotop, and the only 'successes' mentioned are nine partisans and twenty 'functionaries condemned' on 30 November.[65] Reading between the encoded lines, the message was clear: the German army was advancing east, running headlong into the mud and rain that preceded winter. Executions continued, but the numbers and locations were deliberately obscured. Fighting became harder.

A Double Playfair, meanwhile, was a German adaptation of a British encipherment system which Nigel de Grey and Room 40 had used in the First World War. It was more complicated, and allowed a greater number of permutations than the Double Transposition system. It involved two squares of letters from the alphabet, five written vertically, five horizontally, with the words that needed to be encrypted written into the top of each square, after which the blank spaces were filled with the remaining letters of the alphabet not already used. If the words POLICE and PATROL are to be encrypted, the squares would appear like this:

P O L I C P A T R O
E A B D F L B C D E
G H J K M F G H I J
N Q R S T K M N Q R
U V W X S T U V W

Using a codebook and a predetermined daily key, the sender then chose random pairs of horizontally or vertically linked letters from the alphabetical remainder in each square – not including the original message words – and enciphered these. So POLICE could become QV or DK, for instance.

On 11 September de Grey had annotated some of the German Police decrypts which were being sent to Stewart Menzies at SIS. His teams were, he said, decrypting so many signals from the Eastern Front describing mass executions that 'the fact the police were killing all Jews who fall into their hands should now be sufficiently well appreciated. It is not therefore proposed to continue reporting these butcheries (in a special summary).'[66]

Grey was at that point sending a 'special' summary to Menzies and Churchill each week summarising the intelligence about mass executions from the latest signals he and his staff had decrypted. Should he and his staff continue sending these messages on to London in this 'special' update, or simply include them in the regular, weekly intelligence brief that Bletchley sent to London, which contained information from other cryptanalytical sources, such as the Luftwaffe and Kriegsmarine Enigma?

How was the vital intelligence generated by Bletchley Park being acted upon by the Cabinet Office, MI6, MI5 and the Joint Intelligence Committee in London? thought de Grey. He needed to know how to proceed. Churchill wanted to do anything possible to impede or halt the mass killings, but could not use the information in further public broadcasts without risking betraying the Enigma secret. British military and intelligence chiefs were desperate to protect the Ultra intelligence, and publicising the ongoing killings was not a vital priority of national survival. The Battle of the Atlantic and the fighting in North Africa were, and both the Foreign Office and the Joint Intelligence Committee were determined not to let the Prime Minister distract any vital resources from these critical areas of operations.

By October and November 1941, Bletchley Park had formed an intricate, thorough and secret cryptanalytical operation, which was expanding every day. Some six hundred analysts and technicians, three-quarters of them women, worked in a series of drab wooden and brick huts on the country estate in Buckinghamshire, handling and decrypting intercepted messages. This was the second year of the war, and Britain was the only country in Europe that was still fighting, undefeated, unoccupied. There were urgent priorities for the Bletchley staff and their time: by this point Hut 6 was trying to decrypt as many signals as possible from the German Army, the *Heer*, after it launched Operation Typhoon, an all-out attack on Moscow. In North Africa Rommel was pushing towards Cairo, but then retreated unexpectedly, allowing British and Australian troops to liberate Tobruk. The Atlantic had become a vast maritime battleground, a definitive contest of national survival. Huts 4 and 8 were the centre of the constant daily struggle to keep decrypting radio messages sent and received by German U-boats, enciphered in the German naval Enigma setting that they called Triton, and which Bletchley had dubbed 'Shark'. With the Japanese army and navy thundering across Asia, Hut 7 was decrypting Japanese naval codes.

Churchill, meanwhile, had said he wanted as many decryptions as possible of German Police and SS messages, so there was no shortage of resources in Hut 5, where Domino, the German Police, Einsatzkommando and some Gestapo signals were read.

Yet compared with such priorities as the German naval Enigma, these often took second place. The British had already begun breaking into Enigma-encrypted signals sent by the German Army and the Luftwaffe. The entire operation, from intercept to decryption, was kept secret.

The Y station – as signals intercept stations were called – that handled the most Domino intercepts was located in a large Victorian country house at Beaumanor, in Leicestershire, and was considered to be a potential target of considerable value to the Germans, were they to discover what work was being done there. So the British had made extensive efforts to disguise and camouflage the huts in the grounds to resemble the normal, outlying buildings found on a large country estate. The sides and roofs of one of the large Nissen huts, where the intercept work was done, were even painted in a colour scheme that looked like glass. The aim was to disguise the building as a greenhouse, to deceive any German aircraft who tried to bomb it, or any of the other huts around it. The ATS operators sitting in the Nissen huts under the lime trees had one job: to intercept and transcribe coded German messages.

Twenty-four hours a day, teams of women from the British Army's Auxiliary Territorial Service scanned dozens of radio frequencies which they knew or suspected the Germans were using; they then transcribed the Morse-coded letters they heard, sometimes taking down as many as 125 characters per minute. The women entered these onto Wireless Telegraph transcription forms, and at the end of each of their eight-hour shifts, dispatch riders on their BSA motorcycles took the forms full of rows of letters sixty miles down the dual-carriageway to Bletchley Park.

From the German signals de Grey's analysts were reading, it appeared the number of executions on the Eastern Front were on the increase. In Vilnius in Lithuania, the Germans imprisoned 40,000 Jews in a ghetto, and between the months of July to October, executed another 30,000 in the nearby Ponary Woods. On 15 and 16 September the Germans carried out mass executions of 42,000 Jews in two separate incidents in the towns of Berdichev and Uman in Ukraine. The Germans reported each of these incidents in precise detail, either in a radio signal encrypted in a Double Playfair cipher, or in an Enigma encipherment, or alternately in a message carried by a personal police or SS courier. Then, on 13 October, Churchill read the translated and decrypted summary of a series of German police messages that Nigel de Grey's team had deciphered two days earlier, on the 11th.

> On 26/9 arrangements were being made for a 3 or 4 day visit by Himmler to the Southern area of the Russian front . . . on 13/9 the three officers commanding the North, Centre and Southern Russian Front were reminded that the danger of their messages being decoded was great. Among other secret matters that should not be sent by wireless was the number of executions carried out.

Nigel de Grey had signed this decrypt 'de G' on 11 October, and Churchill had again underlined the last two sentences in red ink. [67] An electronic war and a battle of wits between the British and the Germans was under way, between two opposing groups of men and women who had never met, who did not know each other, who recognised the other by small slips of information, a name in a decrypt, the electronic signature of a Morse operator's hand. By November, despite German fears about their signals security, they had changed their codes only once since mass executions on the Eastern Front had begun. If Winston Churchill or any allied or neutral leader gave another revealing speech, or made a declaration based upon intelligence about German mass killings which had been obtained through cryptanalysis, then Great Britain could very easily lose the vital advantage of Ultra intelligence. Priorities of national survival were at stake, and winning, or keeping an even hand in the Battle of the Atlantic was just one of them. The Enigma secret could not be compromised. Ultra intelligence often helped to give the Allies a crucial edge, and was a vital advantage which could not, under any circumstances, be lost.

Following his visit to Bletchley Park, Churchill received a letter, dated 21 October 1941. It came from the four 'Wicked Uncles' – Gordon Welchman, Stuart Milner-Barry, Alan Turing, and Hugh Alexander. In their letter, they made an urgent request to the Prime Minister to give them more funding and resources. Turing explained that decoding manually was extremely time-consuming. He thought that a machine he had devised, called a 'bombe', could make the process faster, but to build it he and his colleagues needed more money and more staff.

As Milner-Barry was to say later:

The cryptographers were hanging on to a number of 'keys' by their coattails and if we had lost any or all of them there was no guarantee (given the importance of continuity in breaking) that we should ever have found ourselves in business again.[68]

Given that the secrets of Ultra and the work being done at Bletchley were so secret, he took the letter by train to 10 Downing Street. He later reflected: 'The thought of going straight from the bottom to the top would have filled my later self with horror and incredulity.'

On receipt of the letter, Churchill wrote to his senior chief of staff, General Ismay, known as 'Pug' for his jovial, canine resemblance. The Prime Minister marked the letter 'Action This Day' and wrote 'Make sure they [the GC&CS] have all they want on extreme priority and report to me that this has been done.'[69]

'Almost from that day,' Milner-Barry recalled, 'the rough ways began to be made smooth. The flow of bombes was speeded up, the staff bottlenecks relieved, and we were able to devote ourselves uninterruptedly to the business in hand.'

The analysts in Hut 5 at Bletchley Park had also begun to decrypt some German SS and Police messages originating away from the Eastern Front. They showed that the German plan to deport, imprison or execute Jews was not confined to the mass executions being carried out by the Einsatzgruppen. The SS had begun to deport German, Austrian and Czech Jews to camps and ghettos in Poland, Ukraine and the three Baltic republics. The Russians had occupied Latvia, Lithuania and Estonia in 1940 under the provisions of the Molotov-Ribbentrop pact with Nazi Germany. As Operation Barbarossa began, the Germans had then occupied all these three territories. British analysts had now begun to decrypt some messages sent by the SS and the Gestapo. The latter came under the administrative authority of Heydrich's Reich Security Main Office, and operated as a sister organisation to the SS intelligence police, the SD. The messages Bletchley Park had begun to read into contained details of the rail transport and logistics of deportation of convoys of Jews.

> On November 17 1941 at 18.25 hrs transport train No.DO26 has left Berlin for Kovno [Kaunas, Lithuania] with 944 Jews. Transport escorted by two Gestapo and fifteen police officers. Transport commander is Kriminal Oberassessor Exner, who has the transport list with him . . .[70]

This was the text of a German police message sent on 20 November to the Commander of the Security Police in Riga, SS-Sturmbannführer Rudolf Lange. On 18 November, Lange received another message about an incoming transport that had

Top left: Flight Sub-Lieutenant Nigel de Grey, RNVR, during the First World War. In 1917, he was one of the team that decoded the Zimmermann Telegram, thereby helping to ensure the USA's decision to enter the war on the Allied side in April that year.
(courtesy of and © the de Grey family)

Top right: A formal portrait of de Grey taken in the 1930s, when he would have been in his forties. *(courtesy of and © the de Grey family)*

Below: A more relaxed photograph of de Grey (right), taken not long before the Second World War. A brilliant cryptographer, he was nicknamed 'the dormouse' by colleagues at Bletchley Park, but his modest and unassuming nature belied a core of steel.
(courtesy of and © the de Grey family)

Left: Sir Stewart Menzies, photographed with his second wife in the 1930s. As Director-General of the Secret Intelligence Service (MI6) – or 'C' – from 1939 to 1952, he received de Grey's intelligence summaries and analysis and passed them on to Churchill. *(© Evening Standard/Getty Images)*

Right: A three-rotor Enigma encryption machine of the type widely used by the German armed forces. On 1 February 1942 the Kriegsmarine added a fourth rotor, leaving Bletchley 'blind' to the U-boats' signals.

(© Bletchley Park Trust/SSPL/Getty Images)

Below: Interior of the machine room in Hut 6 at Bletchley Park, where the codebreakers worked on decrypting German Army and Luftwaffe signals. *(© Bletchley Park Trust/SSPL/Getty Images)*

Top left: The Austrian-born Hermann Höfle, a former taxi driver and mechanic from Salzburg who became a Hauptsturmführer in the SS, and was later in charge of five of the concentration camps in German-occupied Poland. In decrypting Höfle's signals, de Grey and colleagues provided proof of the mass killings of Jews in Ukraine, Russia and Poland. *(© Yad Vashem)*

Top right: SS-Hauptsturmführer Ernst Lerch, Höfle's fellow Austrian and partner in Operation Reinhard. *(© Yad Vashem)*

Below: Heinrich Himmler, head of the SS (left), with Reinhard Heydrich (centre), head of the organisation's intelligence division, the SD, in Paris, c. 1940–2. The two men were the principal architects of the Final Solution. *(© Everett Collection Historical/Alamy)*

Operation Barbarossa: on 29 and 30 September 1941, following the German invasion of Russia in June, 33,771 Ukrainian Jews were massacred by units of Einsatzgruppe C at Babi Yar, a ravine outside Kiev. The image shows a woman trying to shield her child as a German soldier takes aim at them.

(© CPA Media Pte Ltd/Alamy)

Jews rounded up in Mogilev in Byelorussia, July 1941. The SS and the Ordnungspolizei ghettoised and systematically murdered them. The Higher SS and Police Leader in Byelorussia, SS-Gruppenführer Erich von dem Bach, established his HQ in the town.

(© Deutsches Bundesarchiv/ Wikimedia Commons)

Von dem Bach (left) in Russia. His signals – which included a birthday message to his wife – were decrypted at Bletchley Park.

(© Deutsches Bundesarchiv/ Wikimedia Commons)

Above: Himmler (left) with SS-Obergruppenführer Kurt Daluege, who commanded the Ordnungspolizei (Order Police or Orpo). These police battalions carried out untold numbers of killings of Jews and others in Byelorussia, Ukraine and Russia. Daluege, like Höfle but unlike many of his fellow SS, was alert to the need for signals security, as de Grey noted from his decrypts.

(© Deutsches Bundesarchiv/Wikimedia Commons)

Left: Odilo Globočnik in 1938, when he was Gauleiter of Vienna; he is in the uniform of an SS-Standartenführer. Yet another Austrian SS officer, he was to play a leading role in Operation Reinhard, the systematic murder of some 1.5 million Jews, mostly Polish, in the camps at Majdanek, Treblinka, Sobibor and Belzec.

(© Sueddeutsche Zeitung/Alamy)

Above: Heydrich's car after the attack in Prague on 27 May 1942 by two Czech agents parachuted in from Britain – he died from his injuries on 4 June.

(© Deutsches Bundesarchiv/CBW/Alamy)

Right: Himmler speaks at Heydrich's state funeral in Berlin, 9 June 1942.

(© Scherl/Suddeutsche Zeitung/Alamy)

Above: The bodies of villagers massacred at Lidice, in Bohemia and Moravia, in reprisal for Heydrich's assassination, 10 June 1942.

(© Everett Collection/Shutterstock)

Left: German troops in Lidice during its complete destruction. Almost all the surviving villagers were transported to concentration camps.

(© Hulton Deutsch/Getty Images)

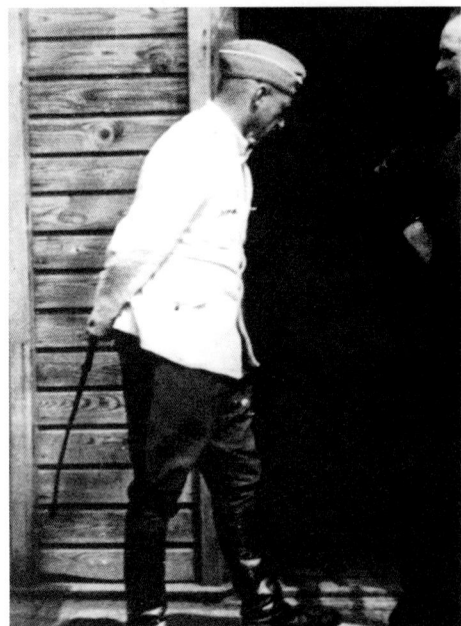

Top left: SS-Untersturmführer Kurt Franz, the last commandant of Treblinka II during Operation Reinhard. A sadist even by the standards of his fellow SS officers, he trained his dog, a St Bernard, to attack and maul Jewish prisoners. *(© Archive PL/Alamy)*

Top right: The gas ovens in the crematorium at Majdanek, photographed after the camp's liberation by the Red Army in July 1944. *(© Everett Collection/Shutterstock)*

Below left: SS-Sturmbannführer Christian Wirth, who helped develop the concentration camps selected for Operation Reinhard into instruments of mass extermination. *(© CBW/Alamy)*

Below right: Yet another Austrian SS officer: Hauptsturmführer Franz Stangl, photographed wearing a summer tunic, possibly at Sobibor. After the prisoners' break-out at Treblinka II in August 1942, Globočnik, Wirth and Stangl decided not to reopen the camp, since by then the Auschwitz-Birkenau complex was large enough to handle all extermination operations. *(© Yad Vashem)*

departed from Bremen on the same day: 'Concerning evacuation of Jews, transport train DO56 has left Bremen destination Minsk with 971 Jews on 18.11.1941 . . . '[71]

At the same time that Beaumanor and the other intercept stations were picking up SS and German police signals sent from eastern Europe, Bletchley Park's cryptanalysts were simultaneously decrypting the encoding settings used on the German Enigma machine and on some of their other encipherment systems. Out in the Battle of the Atlantic, the cracking of the Kriegsmarine's Enigma setting, codenamed 'Triton' or 'Shark', meant that the Royal Navy could sometimes have advance warning of where U-boats might be lying in wait for Allied convoys. Nigel de Grey and his colleagues in the Naval Section, as well as senior officers in the Admiralty, were increasingly aware of a huge threat to the security of British signals intelligence. It was an electronic elephant in the living room. As the British and Americans were working to decrypt German, Japanese and Italian codes, so of course the Germans and Russians and Italians would be doing the same thing in reverse.[vii] The British had lost key diplomatic and merchant navy codebooks in the chaotic evacuation from Norway in 1940; the situation worsened when the Royal Navy lost vital codebooks off Crete in April 1941, after Italian explosive motorboats sank the cruiser HMS *York*. The potential compromise of naval and merchant navy codes could spell disaster for the British in the Battle of the Atlantic: the cryptanalytical war was a two-sided one, and the British were extremely careful to keep their signals intelligence successes, and failures, secret, often from their own senior officers and ministers.

---

vii Across the English Channel from Bletchley Park, German cryptanalysts were, in turn, working for the Kriegsmarine's signals intelligence service, called the Beobachtungsdienst ('observation service'), or B-Dienst. Since 1936, they had been trying, and by 1939 and 1940 succeeding, in making entries into the three main codes used by the Royal Navy, the Submarine Service and the Merchant Navy. As the war progressed, so did their urgent, secret and highly confidential work.

Churchill was continually worried about what he saw as a wide circulation of Ultra material. He wrote to Stewart Menzies in September 1941 and to his chiefs of staff about the dissemination of Ultra signals intelligence regarding a convoy of German tankers crossing the Mediterranean:

> Surely this is a dangerously large circulation. Why should anyone be told but the 3 C-in-Cs. They can give orders without giving reasons. Why should such messages go to subsidiary HQs in the Western Desert.[72]

Although the SS and German police units on the Eastern Front had changed their codes, the British cryptanalysts were reading into the new Einsatzkommando encipherments within a month. Then two of de Grey's leading cryptanalysts began to make a stunning, and vital breakthrough. One of the cryptologists was the veteran Greek scholar, Dillwyn Knox, the other Oliver Strachey, who was the son of administrator in India. He went to Eton, joined the Foreign Office, and in the First World War worked for British Military Intelligence. He was at GC&CS between the wars, and worked on breaking into the code of the Japanese naval attaché, leading him to make further compromises of other Japanese naval cipher settings. This vital work was partly shared with and based upon cooperation with the Americans, who at the same time were making successful decryptions of the Japanese diplomatic code, which they had codenamed 'Purple'. This name was derived from a mix of the two colours of the covers of other Japanese codebooks, which were blue and red. By 1941 Strachey was in charge of a section that worked on decrypting German signals from the Wehrmacht's military intelligence agency, the Abwehr. These messages were at first codenamed 'Pear', but then ISOS, for 'Illicit Services Oliver Strachey'.

British intercept stations were now picking up German signals encrypted in a new Enigma setting, that de Grey named 'Orange 1'. Twice a day these Morse code transmissions were sent from a series of dispatch stations across Germany and Occupied Poland, containing identical messages every day, each encrypted signal consisting only of multiple lines of figures. De Grey thought the code could be uncrackable, but then a tiny error of repetition, made on a daily basis by an SS radio clerk somewhere in a signals hut in Poland or Germany, gave Bletchley Park a breakthrough. The SS were using Code Orange to send signals from right inside the concentration camp system. The breakthrough into Code Orange told the British something newer, and bigger. It held a huge and more urgent secret: German signals sent in this cipher included daily administrative reports, containing rosters of new arrivals, escapees, living inmates and those who had died or been killed, from some of the Third Reich's largest concentration camp networks. These included Auschwitz, Mauthausen, Oranienburg and Dachau. Cryptanalysts noticed that the SS camp messages made frequent reference to detaining prisoners, but no mention of killing them. The more signals were decrypted, the clearer it became that Orange I was an administration key, of how the camps were actually run.

The breaking of Code Orange

Due to the volume and nature of the messages which they were intercepting and decrypting, the British estimated that Germany was expanding its operations to persecute the Jews. As Einsatzkommando operations continued on the Eastern Front into winter 1941, the ATS clerks at Beaumanor also began to intercept a new type of message that appeared to be coming from a series of dispatch stations across Germany and Occupied Poland. A number of German units, headquarters and bases were sending identical messages twice a day, at exactly the same time. Once decrypted, the messages contained almost no words, just rows of figures. To begin with, the staff in Huts 5 and 6 could not work out what these messages were, where they came from, or what information they contained. They were encrypted in an Enigma Code that Hut 6 at Bletchley Park first decrypted, and then, similarly to 'Pear', codenamed after a fruit. Other SS signals were already called Quince, or Grapefruit or Pear, and so this new Enigma encipherment was given the name '4152 Orange'.

> The contents of 4152 Orange dealt with some of the concentration camps . . . Auschwitz, Dachau, Oranienburg, and the next sensational advance connected with SS cryptography was connected with this frequency. For several months a number of messages had been sent out from some six to seven stations early in the morning . . . in fact between 7am to 8am. The messages, known as HOR-HUG reports, from two frequently occurring code groups were short, consisting of about ten groups of letters, followed by a few more or less invariable code groups.
>
> In the message proper the number of letters in any group never exceeded four, and on any one day only ten different letters were used. The last point strongly suggested a figure code, and on this hypothesis one day's traffic was broken ...[73]

Through cryptanalysis, the British were about to decrypt messages describing the logistical workings of the next phase of Germany's persecution of the Jews, the one that led entropically onwards from the mass executions on the Eastern Front. For the messages in Code Orange came from some of the concentration camps themselves, most of them clearly labour camps. What was being decrypted from Auschwitz and Dachau was not the electronic records of extermination. So where were the Jews from the Polish ghettos being taken? Was there another huge camp system that Allied codebreakers were not yet aware of?

The information about the killings of the Jews was like a huge picture, it seemed to de Grey, and although Bletchley Park and London had a great deal of information, the problem was putting it all together into a coherent whole. Code Orange was gradually giving up the secrets of a network of concentration camps, like Auschwitz and Dachau, but not of mass killings. Signals detailing executions on the Eastern front had by November 1941 trickled to a standstill; de Grey knew the bulk of the massacres were going on somewhere – he suspected in Poland – but he could not provide concrete details. Without this, it was proving impossible for Churchill to persuade a sceptical war cabinet, and Washington, of the need for urgent action.

Information, much of it unverifiable, was pouring out of occupied Europe, and from neutral capitals such as Lisbon, Berne and Stockholm, hubs for desperate Jews trying to escape to Britain and the United States. A handful of Polish Jews had escaped from camps and ghettos with witness testimonies of starvation, torture and mass killings: but British government officials around the Prime Minister were increasingly sceptical – one was to describe the reports of mass executions of Jews in Ukraine as 'products of the Slavic imagination'.[74] In the United States, President Franklin D. Roosevelt was preoccupied in mobilising his country, and launching a vast amphibious campaign in the Pacific. His State Department was reluctant to even increase the quota of immigration visas available to Jews. Publishers in London and New York issued *The Polish White Book* and *The Black Book of Poland* in late 1941 and early 1942, based on official documents, including first-hand reports, eyewitness testimonies, even photographs, all authenticated, collected by the Polish government-in-exile. The former recorded the deaths of 400,000 Jews in Poland, before the invasion of the Soviet Union had even been launched.

British and American codebreakers were now also trying to break into ciphers used by the Vatican. The Holy See was receiving regular letters and signals from the worldwide network of Apostolic Delegates – the Vatican's de facto ambassadors, spread across the world's capitals - all about the persecution of the Jews. They in turn disseminated a limited version of this information to British, Swiss and American diplomats in the Vatican, who then signalled it back to their own capitals. The Government Code and Cypher School had, by now, also succeeded in decrypting the diplomatic codes of a number of neutral and enemy countries, meaning that the British could gain information at second hand on German, Italian and Japanese operations and intentions through the reports of diplomats of other countries. The diplomatic decrypts from one week in late 1941 and early 1942 gave an idea of the breadth of this information.

On 31 December, the Irish ambassador in Rome reported on food shortages in the Italian capital, while on the same day the French air attaché in Ankara reported back to his foreign ministry in Vichy that according to the German air attaché in Ankara, who in turn had just returned from the Russian front, the situation on the Eastern Front was preoccupying the Reich to the extent that there could be no question of any military action against Turkey. The German ambassador in Ankara, Franz von Papen, had given this assurance personally to the President of the Turkish Republic. On 3 January 1942, the Japanese foreign ministry in Tokyo reported to its embassy in Madrid that the Italian ambassador to Japan had, in turn, reported that the Pope had instructed all Catholic organisations in South American countries to make efforts so that these countries should not join the war. On the same day, the Turkish ambassador in London signalled about German withdrawals in Russia, while on 5 January, the Turkish ministry of foreign affairs in Ankara said to its ambassador in Vichy that Hitler had taken command of all the Reich's armed forces, after SS divisions in Rostov attacked prematurely. Finally, on 8 January, the Belgian ambassador in New York reported to the Belgian foreign ministry in London about food relief in the Low Countries. All of these diplomats would soon be signalling about what they knew of the persecution of Europe's Jews, and for the British and Americans, this would be a further way of obtaining information about the progress of the Holocaust.[75]

CHAPTER VI

KEEPING THE SECRETS OF LUBLIN AND WARSAW

The General Government and Warsaw, Poland, spring 1942

On 20 January 1942, Reinhard Heydrich, commanding officer of the RSHA, convened a meeting of senior SS officers and government officials from Nazi Germany at a villa on the Wannsee, a lake in a suburb of Berlin. Heydrich outlined his plans for what he called 'the Final Solution to the Jewish Question'. Jews from occupied Europe, as well as those already in ghettos in Poland, Ukraine and Byelorussia, would be taken to camps in the General Government and be exterminated. The SS would have complete operational control and primacy of the programme of institutionalised mass murder. The conference attendees included the head of the Gestapo, Heinrich Müller, Otto Hoffman, who ran the SS Race and Settlement Main Office, and Adolf Eichmann, from the Jewish Affairs Department of the RSHA. He acted as the recording secretary. SS-Sturmbannführer Rudolf Lange, who ran the SD in Latvia and was the head of Einsatzkommando 2, explained how mass executions had reduced the number of Jews in Latvia to only 3,500. Estonia had reached the desired target of being *Judenfrei*, or Jew-free. There were state secretaries from the Foreign, Justice and Interior Ministries present too, as well as officials from the General Government.

Eichmann had prepared a briefing document. It laid out how many Jews remained in Europe in German-occupied or controlled territories: this was his List A. List B counted the Jews in Allied and neutral states, as well as those at war with Nazi Germany. There were 2,284,000 in the General Government alone, 700,000 in unoccupied France, 160,000 in occupied French territory, nearly 161,000 in the Netherlands, 400,000 in Bialystok, and nearly 70,000 in Greece. The list contained sixteen countries, occupied territories or parts thereof. The total came to 4,536,500. At the end of the meeting, Heydrich told Eichmann what to put in the official minutes. The proceedings were to be kept absolutely secret, and no explicit instructions to be included in the account of the conference. 'How shall I put it? – certain over-plain talk and jargon expressions had to be rendered into office language by me,' Eichmann was to say.[76]

The SS would now have overall responsibility across the Reich for the arrests, deportation and 'special handling' of Europe's Jewish population. In Poland, Operation Reinhard, under the command of Odilo Globočnik, with Hermann Höfle as his operations and administration officer, would begin the operations without delay.[77] Nobody, but nobody, inside or outside a very closed circle within the SS and Nazi Party could be allowed to know what was going on. Secrecy was paramount.

So, at the beginning of February Hermann Höfle and Globočnik received the top-secret and urgent orders. They followed those received after meetings the general had had with Himmler in October. Previous to February, Höfle had been assistant chief-of-staff at the Higher SS and Police Leader's base, also taking responsible for the building of SS and Police posts in the General Government. The base in Lublin at the Julius Schreck barracks on Litauer Strasse was now to be the headquarters of Aktion (Operation) Reinhard. Overseen and commanded by the ruthless, criminally inclined Globočnik, the primary objective of Höfle and his SS colleagues would be the forcible evacuation of all Jews from the ghettos in Warsaw, Krakow, Bialystok, Minsk and Lublin, their transfer by rail to five camps in the General Government, and then their *Sonderbehandlung*, their 'special handling'. This would be accompanied by the arrival of deportation trains carrying convoys of Jews from other European countries. The operation was to be carried out in complete secrecy. Communications security was paramount. Nobody outside of the upper echelons of the SS could find out what was taking place. The operation had to be kept secret from most of the German governmental administration, from the OKW, or Wehrmacht High Command, and even parts of the SS itself. Spreading outwards, the web of secrecy would hopefully ensure that the British, French and Americans did not discover what was going on, either through decrypted radio signals or through information relayed by personal Polish couriers. It was vital to try to keep it secret from the Jews and the Poles in the ghettos too: if they discovered they were being gathered in ghettos to facilitate a German operation of extermination, they could flee, riot or try to stage a desperate armed insurrection against the SS and their Ukrainian auxiliaries.

Höfle and Ernst Lerch were to be in charge of all communications, budgets, administrations, and ensuring strict confidentiality. As a start, Hermann Höfle made all of his SS subordinates sign a written declaration agreeing to adhere to a policy of complete secrecy about what they were about to do:

I may not under any circumstances pass on any form of information, verbally or in writing, on the progress, procedure or incidents in the evacuation of Jews to any person outside the circle of Einsatz Reinhard staff. That the process of the evacuation of Jews is a subject that comes under 'Secret Reich Document' . . . and that there is an absolute prohibition on photography in the camps of Einsatz Reinhard . . .[78]

Five of the camps for 'special handling' were either already operating, or being set up, and the first experimental camp was at Chelmno. The second and third were south-east of Lublin, and north of Warsaw respectively. They were called Belzec and Treblinka. There was one more at Sobibor, while at Majdanek a forced labour camp was reconfigured to accommodate gassing facilities. The former was in a forest outside the village of Żłobek Duży, within the District of Lublin, while the second was in the suburbs of the city itself. A separate extermination operation would be based on the camp complex at Auschwitz-Birkenau, near Oświęcim in the southern General Government, although this was not part of the Reinhard administrative operation. Höfle and Globočnik wanted their camps fully operational as soon as possible, and building work on the camps, the gas chambers, the killing facilities and the railway disembarkation points had to be finished by April, even though preliminary activities in Belzec and Majdanek were already under way.

Erwin Lambert, an SS corporal, formerly a master mason and building trade foreman in civilian life, would oversee the design and installation of the gas chambers at Sobibor and Treblinka; SS-Hauptsturmführer Richard Thomalla, another of Höfle's SS colleagues, would manage the camp construction, following his successful completion of Belzec, the first of the Reinhard camps to be built. In command of Sobibor would be an Austrian SS major called Franz Stangl. Chelmno, thirty miles north of Łódź in central Poland, had been carrying out experiments with gassing operations since the end of the previous year. An SS captain called Herbert Lange was in charge. Belzec sat just next to a spur of railway line near the village of the same name, itself within Lublin District. SS-Sturmbannführer Christian Wirth commanded. Treblinka was divided into two camps: Treblinka I, a forced labour camp, and Treblinka II, whose operations focused exclusively on extermination. SS-Obersturmführer Irmfried Eberl would take charge. Majdanek would be under the control of SS-Standartenführer Karl-Otto Koch, who would bring his expertise gained running the concentration camps at Sachsenhausen and Buchenwald.

The guards at all of the camps would be provided by former Soviet prisoners of war who had volunteered or been forcibly recruited to serve with the Germans. Often this was their only alternative to starving to death or dying of disease in one of the primitive, ad hoc POW camps the Germans established as Operation Barbarossa swept across the Soviet Union. The SS trained 2,500 of these men at a base set up at Trawniki outside Lublin. They became known as 'Trawniki men' or Hiwis, a shortened version of the German word *Hilfswilliger*, meaning 'those willing to help'. Simultaneously, while the SS, German Police and the Einsatzgruppen were executing tens of thousands of Jews, embarking on a camp building and extermination programme in Poland, behind the lines they were fighting partisan groups made up Ukrainians, Russians and Poles, some of them Jews. Hermann Höfle and his colleagues would be busy. His group of Austrian SS colleagues had increased in size, with the arrival of SS-Untersturmführer Amon Göth, originally from Vienna, Albert Susitti from Carinthia, and Höfle's colleague and now deputy, Helmut Pohl, who was from Klagenfurt.

In March 1942, prior to the forcible evacuation of some Jews from the Podzamcze ghetto in Lublin, Höfle held a meeting with

German civilian officials and SS and SD personnel in Lublin. Fritz Reuter, a civilian government official in the Lublin District offices, kept a note of the meeting, and of what Höfle said.

> It would be appropriate to divide transports of Jews arriving in the Lublin district already at the departure station into the fit and unfit for labour [wrote Reuter]. If it is not possible to make this separation at the departure station, it would be advisable to divide the transports in Lublin according to this principle. All Jews unfit for labour are to be transported to Belzec, the farthest border station of the Zamosc county. Haupsturmführer Höfle intends to build a large camp where the Jews that are fit for labour will be registered according to their professions, and where the demand for them can be made [referring to the Majdanek camp]. He concluded by declaring that he could receive 4–5 transports of 1,000 Jews a day, directed to the Bełzec station. These Jews, having crossed the border, would never return to the General Government.[79]

Höfle was relieved, worried, and perplexed. Relieved because he was not being transferred to the Russian front, like so many colleagues. In December the previous year, 1941, Operation Typhoon, the Wehrmacht assault on Moscow, had stalled eleven miles outside the capital, as temperatures plummeted to thirty degrees below zero. He was worried for his wife and four children, especially his twin daughters: at least they were in Lublin, and not in Berlin, or Vienna or Hamburg, which British bombers were pounding with nighttime air raids. He was deeply suspicious of any SS or Wehrmacht personnel from outside the small, tightly knit gang of mostly Austrian SS officers and men, like himself, that Globočnik had assembled. By early 1942 there were some forty of these SS officers and senior NCOs in Lublin, before any count was made of the separate teams of SS men who operated the five camps. Many of the team in Lublin had, like Höfle, been members of the Austrian Nazi Party in the early 1930s, before the Anschluss, when it was still illegal. They had come a long way. The secretaries for the Reinhard operation were mostly Austrian too, often married or in relationships with the SS men, and they could be relied upon to keep silent. One of Höfle's colleagues in Lublin was Hans-Gustav Maubach, who initially worked as Globočnik's aide de camp and civilian liaison officer. He assisted him on the myriad labour, construction, base-building, economic and settler-related activities and responsibilities he had taken charge of. Maubach's secretary Irmgard Rickheim, who before the war had worked as a secretary in the Hitler Youth headquarters in Berlin, was now in a relationship with Globočnik, and Lerch, being close to the general from Trieste, was selected as the SS man who would do the honourable thing, and ask Fräulein Rickheim if she would consider taking Odilo Globočnik's hand in marriage. In a manner of speaking, it would be a reciprocation, since Globočnik had acted as best man when Lerch himself married Gertrude Ferchner, a Gestapo officer from Klagenfurt.[80]

Höfle knew that secrecy meant ensuring the security of transmission of electronic signals, and the ways in which information was otherwise carried or sent, by courier, post, or dispatch. Fundamentally, it meant ensuring that people kept secrets too, and did not talk about or record what they were doing or seeing. Forever worried about security, he was obsessive that any outsiders should not know what was happening in his camps, in his office, his zone of operations. In the middle of this he would also be responsible for sending updates required to the SS Jewish Affairs Office at the RSHA in Berlin about the progress of the 'special handling'. He was also responsible, as head of administration for Operation Reinhard, for sending economic updates to the SS Main Economic and Administrative Office, where SS-Obergruppenführer Oswald Pohl[viii] was in charge. This meant not just the financial affairs, the budgets, the books of the administration of the Reinhard camps, but the huge economic profit being made by the SS from the wholesale looting of valuables of all kinds from Jewish prisoners. From the beginning of March 1942, the administration of all camps had come under Pohl's jurisdiction.

Additionally, on the list of senior SS officers to whom Höfle was answerable, came the head of the SS Personnel Main Office: this was, first, General Walter Schmitt, and then, Maximilian von Herff. They oversaw everything to do with the functioning and performance of the people who ran and were involved with the camps, such as Höfle himself, Eichmann, Stangl, Wirth. This was the SS people-handling department. Höfle was well aware that everything had to be done to avoid being called back to Berlin to explain oneself to these men. The stop after them was standing to attention in front of Himmler's desk. SS men were routinely far more frightened of their own superiors than anything an enemy might deliver.

Controlling and limiting to almost zero the flow of radio transmissions would now take a great deal of electronic cunning. Instilling a sense of rigid secrecy into the idiosyncratic, brutalised, tough and sometimes ill-disciplined officers who ran the five camps was going to be hard, even though they were SS men, had sworn an oath, and did as they were told. Each of them, in his own way, presented Höfle with a different set of problems.

The case of SS-Standartenführer Karl-Otto Koch epitomised one of these problems. Now serving in Höfle's area of operations as the commandant of Majdanek, Koch was an opportunist criminal. He had served a prison term in 1930 for embezzlement and

---

viii   Not to be confused with Höfle's SS colleague from Salzburg, called Helmut Ortwin Pohl.

forgery, before joining the SS. He served as the adjutant at Dachau, and then commanded both Sachsenhausen and Buchenwald concentration camps. He was currently under investigation by an SS general on suspicion of corruption, murder, embezzlement and substantial theft of gold, silver, gems and other prisoners' valuables while working at Buchenwald. The SS was merciless to those it disapproved of, disliked, considered dangerous, or, simply put, had orders to kill. Yet it was also ruthlessly strict to those within its own ranks. Stealing prisoners' valuables was tantamount to stealing property which belonged to the SS, and was punishable by death.

Karl-Otto Koch was married to a woman called Ilse Koch, with whom he had three children. His wife was now a concentration camp guard, earning the nickname *die Hexe von Buchenwald*, 'the witch of Buchenwald'. The couple had been caught out by accident. In April 1941, an aristocratic SS general was looking through the death-list from Buchenwald. Obergruppenführer Josias was the hereditary Prince of Waldeck and Pyrmont, and had been one of Himmler's first adjutants. As Höfle stood in Lublin a year later, the prince was by now High Commissioner for the Order Police in German-occupied France. On the Buchenwald death list he had spotted the name of a prisoner he recognised, a hospital orderly who had treated him in the past. Investigating further, it transpired that Koch had had him, and two other prisoners shot on trumped-up charges as political prisoners, because they had treated Koch for syphilis. Josias then ordered an investigation led by SS Judge Georg Konrad Morgen, who worked in the SS Court Main office. The case was ongoing. Koch was transferred to Majdanek as Josias and Morgen's men continued their work, while his wife continued to live in the Buchenwald commander's house.

Höfle knew that Colonel Koch's case was by no means an isolated one. Jews deported to concentration camps – and now to extermination camps – were ordered to bring money and valuables with them. They did. Huge quantities of small gold ingots, sterling silver bars, loose diamonds and emeralds, rings, jewellery, gold fob watches, American dollars, German Reichsmarks, British pounds, Swiss francs, silver propelling pencils, religious icons and every kind of small, transportable item of value arrived with them on the trains into the camps. The SS relieved them of it all. Höfle was well-aware, of course, of the rumours and reports around Globočnik. Considered a sadist even by the standards of cruelty of the SS, the embittered officer, bullied at school by Italian Catholics on account of his rural Slovenian accent, had already been demoted once by Himmler. He was reduced to the rank of corporal when Himmler caught him embezzling foreign currency in Vienna in 1939, but later re-promoted to SS-Brigadeführer. It was now suspected that he was embarking on his own plan of personal enrichment through the looting of gold, precious stones and valuables from Jews. Rather than shipping it all back to the SS Economic Administration in Berlin, Globočnik and fellow officers were going to take their own, highly unauthorised cut. They would not only be hiding the Final Solution from the Allies and the outside world, they would also be hiding their criminal activities from Heinrich Himmler himself, and by extension from an SS hangman.

Was Koch also complicit in Globočnik's illicit scheme of personal enrichment? The SS Economic Office asked for regular audits of prisoner valuables sent back to Berlin. If Globočnik, and/or Koch and any other officers were stealing from prisoners – and hence from the SS – they would also be involved in falsifying the accounting for the gold, jewels and valuables looted from the camp's inmates. It was one thing to be worrying about Allied bombing, the enemy's decryption of your secret codes, lethal partisan attacks, a transfer to the Russian front, the safety of your wife and children, to oversee the arrests and killings of hundreds of thousands of human beings, but being caught in the middle of a group of ruthless colleagues up to their eyes in a monumental programme of theft from the SS itself, was another thing entirely, a very different form of danger. And every German and Austrian soldier knew that everybody in the SS was expendable, especially from their own organisation.

Then came Höfle's colleagues like Christian Wirth, loathed by colleagues and subordinates, a man who ruled by fear and violence. The Trawniki guards, themselves no strangers to extreme brutality and violence, were terrified that if they made mistakes or were guilty of disciplinary offences, Wirth would kill them. A man cut out to be the commander of an extermination camp, perhaps, Wirth was one of the earliest recruits to the Nazi Party, a policeman from Stuttgart who had risen to be the criminal commissioner of the city, thrice decorated for bravery on the Western Front. His behaviour towards prisoners under his charge in SS institutions resided in the centre of a Venn diagram of personality traits whose component circles were sadism, psychosis, extreme sociopathy and psychopathy. Wirth had been involved in the so-called Aktion T4 at the Hartheim killing centre, a castle near Linz, in Austria, where at the beginning of 1940, carbon monoxide gas was trialled on a small group of German mental patients. The idea to eventually disguise gas chambers as showers sprang out of these experiments on the mentally ill and the disabled: by the middle of that year Wirth oversaw twelve killing centres across German and Austrian territory. When the German Church condemned the T4 euthanasia programme, Globočnik recruited Wirth and made him commandant of the new camp of Belzec in December 1941.

Viktor Brack, from the Führer's Chancellery in Berlin, had been one of the organisers of the T4 operation. Once it had been terminated, Globočnik and he discussed whether the officers and NCOs who had worked on the programme could now be transferred to Lublin, as they had experience of how to run large-scale gassing operations. He wrote to Himmler about it:

On the recommendation of Reichsleiter [Philipp] Bouhler, I put my men at Brigadeführer Globočnik's disposal for the execution of his special tasks. Having received a further request from him I sent him more people. Brigadeführer Globočnik has stated that the campaign against the Jews should be carried out as quickly as possible, as unforeseen difficulties might stop the campaign altogether and then we should be stuck in the middle of the road. You yourself, Reichsführer, some time ago drew my attention to the necessity of finishing this work quickly, if for no other reason than the necessity to mask it. In view of my own experience I now regard both attitudes, which after all have one and the same end in view, as all the more justified.

The Reich's Propaganda Minister Joseph Goebbels, had made a note of the operation in his diary:

Starting with Lublin, the Jews are today deported from the General Government towards the east. The procedure utilised is completely barbaric and it does not do to go into details. Not much is left of the Jews themselves. Overall, we have to admit that 60% should be liquidated, while only 40% are useful for labour. The former Gauleiter of Vienna [Globočnik], who is in charge of the operation is proceeding very carefully, and meticulously, and making sure not to attract attention . . . The ghettos of the General Government which are emptied are now going to be filled with Jews deported from the Reich and after a certain amount of time, the same process will repeat itself.[81]

One of the staff also working at Hartheim was an Austrian Gestapo officer from Innsbruck called Franz Stangl. He too had been a member of the Nazi Party while it was still illegal in Austria. He joined the SS in 1938, reaching the rank of Hauptsturmführer, captain, and worked for the Jewish Affairs Office in Linz. Eager to escape a superior officer he disliked, he accepted a position at Hartheim. Wirth was his supervising officer. Stangl loathed him. 'Wirth was a gross and florid man,' said Stangl . . .

. . . My heart sank when I met him. He stayed at Hartheim for several days that time and often came back. Whenever he was there he addressed us daily at lunch. And here it was again this awful verbal crudity: when he spoke about the necessity of this euthanasia operation, he was not speaking in humane or scientific terms, the way Dr Werner at T4 had described it to me. He laughed. He spoke of 'doing away with useless mouths', and that 'sentimental slobber' about such people made him 'puke'.[82]

In March 1942, Stangl accepted an offer to go and work in Lublin; it was that, or back to the Linz Gestapo, and his hated former boss. Franz Stangl joined Operation Reinhard. Teutonic efficiency had not, however, allowed for the human fallibility of its staff. The next key member of staff was SS-Obersturmführer Irmfried Eberl. He was, Höfle knew, going to be incompetent. The exigencies of running an extermination camp were to be beyond him. A psychiatrist from Bregenz in Austria, he had worked enthusiastically for the T4 euthanasia programme. When he arrived in Lublin, Höfle had initially posted him to Chelmno, but Eberl's ambition and repeated requests to command his own camp led Globočnik to transfer him to run Treblinka II in June 1942 as its first commander.

Höfle had no room for manoeuvre in communication. He was boxed in by the rigid secrecy rulings of SS signals transmissions, particularly those concerning executions and special duties. Yet he was beset by Berlin's constant demands for information about the progress of the operation. What could he do? Like all senior officials, particularly signals officers, he was convinced the German Enigma system was unbreakable, if used correctly, changing the rotor settings as often as prescribed. The new Double Square hand-held encryption system ('Double Playfair' to the British cryptanalysts) was solid, too – if it was not, then why did the Reichsführer use it to communicate with his senior officers on the Eastern Front? There were constant concerns about signals security: yet, if the British had compromised Enigma, ran logical German thinking, then surely their operational behaviour in the Atlantic, in North Africa, would betray their knowledge of the Third Reich's secrets? Surely there would have been an inadvertent security slip in one, just one, of their tens of thousands of messages that would have contained information that could only have come from a German navy, army, Luftwaffe message, thus showing that their signals experts had compromised German codes? Apparently not. The Operation Reinhard staff in Lublin had received the warning about signals security from SS-Obergruppenführer Daluege in September 1941, like everybody else in the General Government, in occupied Polish areas and on the Eastern Front. Ernst Lerch had made the necessary changes to the encoding procedure. Signals between Berlin and Lublin, between the headquarters of the various Higher SS and Police leaders, flowed normally. Yet despite Daluege's explicit instructions in September, the SS and the Order Police were still reporting executions and 'Jew-actions' across the radio net. On 26 May, the SS commanding officer in Kamenez, in western Ukraine, sent a report saying that in cooperation with the Security Service a Jew-action was carried out at Stara Utschitza and Studenica, 60 kilometres south-west of Kamenez. '700, being incapable of work, were shot.'[83]

Arrangements for the funeral of Höfle's almost-supreme leader, Reinhard Heydrich, who died on 4 June 1942, were also being broadcast across the radio net.[84] Everybody had heard the news after 26 May: assassinated in Prague by a team of Czech resistance agents. Appropriate reprisals, Höfle knew, had been taken. Kurt Daluege, by then promoted to SS-Oberst-Gruppenführer und Generaloberst der Waffen-SS, had taken charge. The home village which had helped harbour the assassins was liquidated: the men executed, the women and children put on trains. Two dozen of the Czech women had arrived in his fiefdom, at Chelmno.

The secrecy clause which he had ordered his staff to sign covered all the operations of the Reinhard office: nobody within the circle of officers involved would send any radio messages to Berlin or elsewhere without Höfle or Lerch or Globočnik knowing about it. In theory, they would not need to, anyway. That was the business of headquarters. The RSHA would be demanding updates, audits, figures, information, as they always did. Yet if any transmissions about the nature of the five camps, the total numbers of Jews arriving and being handled, and logistical arrangements, such as gas, could be a kept to a minimum, or zero, Höfle estimated that Lublin would be in the clear. He knew that Obergruppenführer Pohl's accountants from the Main Economic Office would turn up, sooner or later. If secrecy could be arranged around a series of concentric circles of security, word should not get out. If none of the SS officers or NCOs within the camps themselves talked about what was happening, then those in Lublin could keep their mouths shut too. The difficulty was going to be reconciling the ongoing looting of Jewish valuables with the accounts sent back to Berlin. Yet Höfle knew there was no means by which the RSHA could discover quite how much treasure existed in the first place, before Globočnik or Koch or anybody else took their cut. The auditing of humans and money was going to be crucial, and Höfle and his colleagues were determined to keep as much as possible of the communications about it off the radio net.

His priority concerns, as the eastern European spring of 1942 turned into a blazing hot summer, was the huge upcoming operations to empty the ghettos, particularly the largest one, in Warsaw. Then the SS had to ensure sure that the new gas chambers and gassing vans in each camp worked as efficiently as possible, and that the supply of Zyklon B pesticide and ammunition used could be maintained. If Berlin could keep the train transports arriving, he could keep handling them. Christian Wirth had realised – not surprisingly, given his nature – that if the Jews could be kept moving fast, terrified, disoriented, from the moment they arrived on the trains to the moment they died, the momentum of order could be kept up. Hermann Höfle was keen to fulfil his orders, to kill all the Jews from the Polish ghettos, give Berlin a full and secret reporting of it, and then destroy the camps, and get out of the General Government, with his wife and children, before the Russians arrived. For now, this last seemed to be long in the future: the SS and Wehrmacht's star was still in its ascendancy, despite heavy fighting. At the top of the list of priorities for the Austrian Sturmbannführer was the Warsaw Ghetto: empty it, and transfer as many of its occupants as possible to Treblinka.

The Warsaw Ghetto and the start of the 'Grossaktion Warschau'

There was a running total of approximately 420,000 Jews in the Warsaw ghetto, Höfle knew, although exact numbers were hard to establish. Since its establishment in November 1940, some 85,000 people had died of hunger, disease or been shot within its confines.

It was only slightly larger than a mile square, and was divided into three parts. There was the Little Ghetto, where people with money and influence lived, where life, largely based on the black-market and bribery of German, Polish and Jewish officials, was comfortable for most occupants. The Big Ghetto, where most Jews were sequestrated, was hell. Starvation, murder, extortion, betrayal and constant attacks by the SS and Gestapo was the routine. The third ghetto was a place of work: an industrial area where Jews performed forced labour, under the brutal and watchful eyes not just of the Germans but of Jewish Ghetto Police, chosen by the SS, and employed to keep order. It was in the Little Ghetto that two of Hermann Höfle's key Jewish contacts lived and operated. One was his dermatologist, the other his barber. He suffered from a skin condition, exacerbated by dirt, dust and the duty of war. Dr Edward Reicher, a Polish Jew, was a dermatologist who originally came from Łódź. He treated Höfle when he was in Warsaw. The Pole did not have any choice – the Gestapo had made it clear that he would minister to selected German officers or he and his wife and children would be shot. One day Reicher went to a Sabbath meal in the ghetto, in the home of a Jewish barber who said that he worked for a well-connected German official.

Leon Kac, said Reicher, had a very large apartment and the meal was superb. Food they had not had for years. Herring, sardines, hard-boiled eggs with mayonnaise, gefilte fish, consommé, chicken, vegetables, and a bottle of genuine Carmel wine from Palestine. Then followed coffee and cake and good cognac. The following day Reicher went back to Leon and listened as the barber told him how he had managed to procure such excellent food, in a ghetto where most people were almost starving. He said he had been appointed 'Höfle's court barber'. He had been given soldiers and a lorry and told to find a proper salon, so he took everything he needed from unoccupied hairdressing salons – furniture, mirrors and instruments – and set himself up in business. The German SS officers, including Höfle, whose hair he cut, would ask about the addresses of rich Jews. After those Jews had been arrested, the Germans would search the apartments; Leon confessed he knew some addresses, so the SS gave him a wheeled cart, and two Ukrainian guards. They loaded their plunder from looted and robbed apartments, and gave the SS officers wristwatches, gold cigarette cases, cufflinks, pins studded with precious stones, things, Leon said to Reicher, they could easily hide and sell.[85]

The smugglers were the people who made the most money, and profited from the misery of most of the ghetto. Everything possible was smuggled in from the Polish side. Every day, truckloads of food arrived. Cows, geese, chickens, flour, sugar, chocolate, wine, vodka, and even flowers. Smuggling was punishable by death, but business thrived, and the Germans, Poles and Jews all took a cut.[86] Höfle knew the Germans had divided the ghettos into three categories in 1940, and knew that life and death in all of them was defined by access to food, favours and freedom. Who could eat, who could provide services for the SS and German, Jewish and Polish officials and black-marketeering businessmen, and who just slowly starved or was worked to death. In the Litle Ghetto, there were concerts, cafés, and restaurants, full of food, drink, entertainment, prostitutes, music and dancing for those who could pay in Polish zlotys, or, preferably, in treasured foreign currencies or even gold.

Hermann Höfle wanted to empty the ghetto of its Jews, and also try to control the flow of information both within and without the ghetto about the mass executions carried out by the Einsatzkommandos the previous year, and the gassing operations at the five Reinhard camps which were beginning. His concerns were that the Jews would report both sets of atrocities not just in their illegal underground presses, but also on their illegally manufactured citizen's band radio sets. He knew the Gestapo worked furiously and brutally to stamp out both, but it was vital that no news about the ongoing killings could reach the outside world, either through escapees from camps, Polish resistance workers, or broadcasts from inside the ghettos.

So, in the early morning of 22 July 1942, Hermann Höfle arrived with several of his SS staff outside the office of the Jewish administration of the Warsaw Ghetto. Alongside him was SS-Untersturmführer Wilhelm Brandt, head of the SS Jewish Affairs office in the ghetto. The group of men walked up the stairs to the office, where they found several members of the ghetto's administration sitting nervously around a table. Three days previously, Himmler had told Friedrich-Wilhelm Kruger, the SS official in charge of the General Government, that he wanted all Jews in the region relocated by 31 December that year. Kruger ordered Höfle to begin the relocation of the estimated 400,000 Jews from the Warsaw Ghetto, by then the largest in Nazi-occupied Europe.

'So, gentlemen,' said Höfle. 'The time has come to displace the Jews from Warsaw. Please record the following order.'

He then dictated an order which he had written out that morning. All the 'unproductive' people in the Jewish district were to be relocated to the east. The following persons only could stay behind: employees of procurement units, employees of workshops operating on behalf of the German army, members of the Ordnungsdienst (the Jewish ghetto police) and indispensable officials of the Judenrat with their families. Everybody else was subject to displacement. The 'evictees' were to be allowed to take luggage with them weighing up to fifteen kilos, and they were allowed to carry valuables and money. There was one other instruction: all those being deported from the ghetto were to bring with them a box or crate, measuring 150 by 170 centimetres, for storing what Höfle called 'necessary items'.

Later that morning Höfle looked at his watch. The displacement operation would begin in a minute, he said, that is, at 11.00 sharp. Six thousand people would be delivered to the station square by the end of the day. That number would be repeated every day from then on, until the ghetto was empty. Before leaving, Höfle took the head of the Jewish Council into his office. He told Adam Czerniakow clearly that his wife was, at that moment, free. However, if the deportation failed, she would be the first to be shot as a hostage.[87]

The Warsaw Ghetto Jews were now en route to Treblinka. In July 1942, Franz Stangl visited the camp while Eberl was still in command:

I drove there with an SS driver . . . We could smell it kilometres away. The road ran alongside the railway tracks. As we got nearer Treblinka but still perhaps fifteen, twenty minutes' drive away, we began to see corpses next to the rails, first just two or three, then more and as we drove into what was Treblinka station, there were hundreds of them – just lying there – they'd obviously been there for days, in the heat. In the station was a train full of Jews, some dead, some still alive – it looked as if it had been there for days. When I entered the camp and got out of the car on the square I stepped knee-deep into money; I didn't know which way to turn, where to go. I waded in notes, currency, precious stones, jewellery, clothes ...

The smell was indescribable; the hundreds, no, the thousands of bodies everywhere, decomposing, putrefying. Across the square in the woods, just a few hundred yards away on the other side of the barbed-wire fence and all around the perimeter of the camp, there were tents and open fires with groups of Ukrainian guards and girls: whores from Warsaw

I found out later; weaving, drunk, dancing, singing, playing music. Dr Eberl, the Kommandant, showed me around the camp, there was shooting everywhere ...[88]

One of the SS NCOs who worked in the camp described Eberl's combination of ambition and poor management. SS-Unterscharführer Willi Mentz, called 'Frankenstein' by his colleagues, said that:

He was very ambitious. It was said that he ordered more transports than could be 'processed' in the camp. That meant that trains had to wait outside the camp because the occupants of the previous transport had not yet all been killed. At the time it was very hot and as a result of the long wait inside the transport trains in the intense heat many people died. At that time whole mountains of bodies lay on the platform. Then Hauptsturmführer Christian Wirth came to Treblinka and kicked up a terrific row. And then one day Dr Eberl was no longer there . . .[89]

CHAPTER VII

THE RIEGNER TELEGRAM AND THE MESSAGE FROM AUSCHWITZ

Bletchley Park, Washington DC and Rome

On 11 August 1942, Nigel de Grey received a copy of a telegram that had just been sent to the British Foreign Office in London from their embassy in Berne. The Foreign Office was circulating the telegram to a group of staff members, to Bletchley Park and to the Joint Intelligence Committee. A Jewish group in Geneva had passed on the information contained in the telegram, urging the British diplomats in Switzerland to forward it to London.

The report, transmitted from Berne in the Foreign Office Departmental Cypher No.1, was stark and straightforward.

By July 1942, Germany was fighting an aggressive war on four fronts. As the Red Army in the Crimea collapsed, the Wehrmacht captured the port of Sevastopol; on the Volga, the Germans were ready to attack Stalingrad. In North Africa Generalfeldmarschall Rommel stood before El Alamein, while in the Atlantic, Admiral Karl Dönitz's U-boats were battling an increasingly effective American convoy system. The Final Solution was being implemented at full speed: the SS were now rounding up Jews in Athens, Paris and Yugoslavia. On 17 and 18 July, Heinrich Himmler visited the concentration camp system at Auschwitz-Birkenau. He inspected a construction site in the satellite complex named Auschwitz III, and the expanded part of the extermination and labour camp at Auschwitz II. Camp commandant Rudolf Höss showed Himmler what he described as 'the area of interest' in the complex – the crematoria, the gas chambers, the workshops – and then the Reichsführer-SS watched the arrival of a train transport of Polish Jews. He witnessed the unloading of the prisoners, the selection on the railway ramp, and then watched as they were forced into gas chambers, and their bodies buried in pits.

On the evening of the second day of his visit, the owners of a German industrial company called Giesche gave a dinner for Himmler, which they held at a villa they owned near Auschwitz, in the small neighbouring town of Monowice. It was close to the site of a new industrial plant which the IG Farben company was building, to manufacture synthetic oil and rubber for the German war effort. At dinner, Himmler described what he had seen that day, and discussed his visit with the other guests. One of these was the company's managing director, a man called Eduard Schulte, who had conversations with SS officers about what they and Himmler had seen and done in the Auschwitz camp complex. Schulte was a prominent industrialist from the aristocratic von Giesche family, a man whose passion in life was excelling at bureaucracy. In the First World War he had been the civil servant responsible for overseeing soap production in Germany.

Before 1939, the Giesche family's industrial sites in southern Poland were co-owned by an American consortium, but the Germans confiscated the company assets after their invasion of the country in 1939. Schulte then set up another consortium in Switzerland, and tried to buy out the American-owned part of the company, but failed. A committed anti-Nazi, he had made contact in Switzerland with Allen W. Dulles, the country's director of the American Office of Strategic Services. Through him, Schulte had also met Hans-Bernd Gisevius, an Abwehr intelligence officer, who used his position as the German Vice-Consul in Zurich as a cover for his covert activities on behalf of the anti-Hitler resistance. After Himmler's visit to Auschwitz, Schulte wanted to pass on the crucial information about what the head of the SS had said, both at dinner and during his inspection tour of the camp. Schulte wanted to give it to French and Polish intelligence, but was most concerned to pass it on to Jewish organisations in Switzerland who could perhaps ensure the information arrived in the United States, and even reached the President. He realised that if it was to have any hope of reaching the Allies in London or Washington, it had to reach either the Vatican in Rome, the American OSS and Jewish groups in Switzerland, the neutral Swedish government in Stockholm, or one of its European embassies. Passing information along these three routes had the highest likelihood of it reaching London or Washington.

On 29 July, Eduard Schulte arrived in Zurich from Breslau, the largest city in Silesia, the region where the Auschwitz-Birkenau complex was situated. This area was now part of the German-occupied General Government. Looking for contacts within the Jewish community, he met up with a Swiss Jewish investment banker called Isidor Koppelmann, and told him what he had heard at Auschwitz. The banker then contacted Benjamin Sagalowitz, a Russian Jewish journalist who ran the press centre for the umbrella organisation that represented all the Jewish groups in Switzerland. Koppelmann passed on Schulte's story. Sagalowitz, in turn, then gave it to a German Jew in Geneva called Gerhart Riegner. He had been a judge in Berlin until 1933, when the Nazi Law for the Restoration of the Professional Civil

Service forced him out of his position. By 1934 he had fled to Geneva, where he was studying international law, working for the League of Nations, and collecting intelligence that would help Europe's Jews. He had also met officials from the World Jewish Congress, and by 1942 was their representative in Switzerland. On Sagalowitz's recommendation, he took Schulte's information, and passed back the message that he would keep Schulte's identity completely secret. Then, on 8 and 10 August, Riegner visited both the American and British consulates in Geneva. At both diplomatic missions, he dictated an identical text of a telegram. He gave it first to the United States Vice-Consul, Howard Elting, who forwarded it to the US Legation in the Swiss capital, Berne. Two days later he gave it to the British.

At 4.48 p.m. on the 10th, the duty officer in the British Embassy in Berne encrypted the text that he had just been sent in a telegram from Whitehall's consul in Geneva; he used the Foreign Office's Departmental Cypher Number 1, and then dispatched it to London. In Berlin, Ursula Hagen at the Pers-Z cryptanalytical section of the foreign office was looking out for intercepts of American and British diplomatic messages from Switzerland: these would have been picked up by the German radio intercept station at Lauf, on the western edge of the Black Forest in Baden-Württemberg.[ix] The German foreign office wanted to find out if the International Committee of the Red Cross in Geneva intended to make any form of statement about the Holocaust. The Germans began to break into American diplomatic codes by spring 1943, and decrypted signals from the United States minister for Switzerland, Leland Harrison, were often shown round in German meetings. However, the German

---

ix   The German Wehrmacht High Command signals intelligence agency was called OKW/Chi, an abbreviated version of a longer title. The Foreign Ministry codebreakers worked in the agency called Pers-Z, again an abbreviation

cryptanalytical agencies do not appear to have broken into the Berne embassy's signals in summer 1942.

Transmitting confidential information from Switzerland to Britain in summer 1942, with the war at its height, meant using one of four methods of communications. The most reliable and fastest was an enciphered telegram from a government embassy to a government ministry – in this case the Foreign Office. The second was by radio; the third by mail; the fourth was by human courier. Knowledge could not travel any faster than this. If something that existed in the human mind or on paper, in Geneva, could not be transmitted by these methods, then it stayed where it was, and did not become known. Although the development of radio technology had made the worldwide transmission of information by telegram, radio and telephone, accessible and possible, most information did not travel. Word was slow to get out. Newspapers and the radio carried the news. Secrets, covert information, and knowledge of events were thus much easier to hide than in a more modern era of mass communication, and it was simpler to limit their dissemination. Yet the words from Gerhart Riegner, paraphrased by the British consular official, travelled to London as fast as it was possible.

Following from His Majesty's Consul General at Geneva No. 174 (Begins).

Following for Mr. S.S. Silverman M.P., Chairman of British Section, World Jewish Congress London from Mr. Gerhart Riegner Secretary of World Jewish Congress, Geneva. (Begins).

Received alarming report stating that, in the Fuehrer's Headquarters, a plan has been discussed, and is under consideration, according to which all Jews in countries occupied or controlled by Germany numbering 3½ to 4 millions should, after deportation and concentration in the East, be at one blow exterminated, in order to resolve, once and for all the Jewish question in Europe. Action is reported to be planned for the autumn. Ways of execution are still being discussed including the use of prussic acid.[x] We transmit this information with all the necessary reservation, as exactitude cannot be confirmed by us. Our informant is reported to have close connexions with the highest German authorities, and his reports are generally reliable. Please inform and consult New York.[90]

The Foreign Office officials left their remarks and comments on the text of the decrypted signal:[91]

Pt. Submitted.
A. David 11/8: We have no confirmation of this report from other sources, although we have of course received numerous reports of large scale massacres of Jews, particularly in Poland: see The Polish report in C 7843/957/55, marked passage on pages 7 and 8.

Mr Law asks what we know of Riegner. Main Index can produce only C 3208/3208/62 of 1940 which does not help much. Can Refugee Dept. or Eastern Dept. provide any information? D. Allen 14/8

Refugee Dept Eastern Dept And b.u. (?) 16 Aug I have no information. Sir H. Emerson[xi] might be consulted.

A. Walker 14/8 We have never heard of Dr Riegner, but

---

x   Prussic acid is a solution of hydrogen cyanide in water: it was the main active component of Zyklon B, the pesticide used in gas chambers

xi   The League of Nations High Commissioner for Refugees, Sir Herbert Emerson.

will consult Sir H. Emerson and the Zionists (Mr Namiar) informally. AWR 14/8 Transcript 3: FO 371/30917

Sir H Emerson is away, + the Jewish Agency have no information. A. Walker 15/8 Eastern Dept. have no knowledge of Mr Riegner. (?)

15/8 N. Grey; [*marked only with a tick in fountain pen, and no comments]

I do not see how we can hold up this message much longer, although I fear it may provoke embarrassing repercussions. Naturally we have no information bearing on this story.

F Roberts[xii] 15/8

The message from Switzerland became known as the Riegner Telegram. Via a series of encrypted messages, de Grey and colleagues at the American State Department asked the Vatican if they could help verify the information in the report. The Holy See had the wherewithal to do so, but hesitated. One of the reasons for their reluctance to provide specific information to Washington was because they feared – rightly – that the Americans and possibly the British were trying to decipher their codes. What they didn't know was that they were correct in this concern. In January 1942, the analysts in Hut 5 had started work on breaking into the Vatican's diplomatic ciphers, along with the diplomatic codes of other countries. Yet it was to take the British and American cryptanalysts more time to be decrypt the Vatican's ciphers than, say, the Turkish or Japanese or Italian diplomatic codes.

The British consular official in Berne had added instructions that the information should be passed to Samuel Sydney Silverman, the Labour Member of Parliament for the Liverpool constituency

---

xii Sir Frank Roberts was a British diplomat who served on the Eastern Europe Desk and Central Desk of the Foreign Office before being posted to Moscow – he served as Winston Churchill's adviser at the 1945 Yalta Conference

of Nelson and Colne. Born and brought up in Liverpool, Silverman was the son of a poor Jewish draper who had fled to Britain from Iaşi in north-eastern Romania. During the First World War Silverman was a conscientious objector and was imprisoned three times for his refusal to wear uniform or to fight. By 1942, he was the Chairman of the British Section of the World Jewish Congress, and was a vocal supporter of a permanent Jewish homeland in the then-territory of Mandatory Palestine. When the Germans started persecuting the Jews, he altered his stance on pacifism, and voted to support Britain's entry into the war. He fiercely resisted the idea of repatriating Jewish refugees, saying to Churchill that:

> It would be difficult to conceive of a more cruel procedure than to take people who have lost everything they have – their homes, their relatives, their children, all the things that make life decent and possible – and compel them to go against their will, to go back to the scene of those crimes.[92]

Howard Elting, at the American Consulate in Geneva, had meanwhile suggested to his consular colleagues in Berne that the information in the telegram from Riegner bore an element of truth, but the American Consul in Berne, Leland Harrison, did not believe it. He dismissed it as a 'war rumour, inspired by fear'. He did however forward the message to the State Department in Washington DC where it was received with the same scepticism. Riegner, knowing the urgency of the message, and the reliability of its source, had been adamant that the message be passed on to Chief Rabbi Stephen Wise, Roosevelt's friend and contact, and the President of the World Jewish Council. But officials in the State Department refused to forward it.

The British, in turn, were wondering what to do with the message, Sir Frank Roberts, as cited above, being worried about 'embarrassing repercussions' if the British general public were to hear about it. But, hesitantly, they decided that Roberts's advice, as written in the original minutes to the telegram, was the best way forward, and they passed the cable on to the Labour MP. He, in turn, had been directed in the telegram to 'consult New York', so he sent it on to Stephen Wise, who received it on 29 August. This was a month after Eduard Schulte had arrived in Switzerland from Silesia. Astonishingly, and partly on the advice of Under-Secretary of State Sumner Welles, Wise decided not to publicise the information he had received. We should wait for State Department officials to confirm the information, counselled Welles. It transpired that Riegner, in introducing the cautious caveats he had written into his signal, about 'exactitude,' and 'reservations,' had unwittingly but effectively made sure the information stalled. The Holocaust was then at its height, but generating a sense of urgency in transmitting secret information about it proved extremely challenging.

Although some of the factual information that had come from Schulte was wrong – the mass murder of the Jews was not planned for the autumn of 1942, but had actually already begun that year – Welles's primary reservations came from the fact that the information was fourth-hand. Schulte had reported the conversations of SS officers, described them to another man, who passed them as remembered to Benjamin Sagalowitz, who in turn repeated the conversations to Riegner. In fact, it was allegedly his superior in the World Jewish Congress in Geneva, Paul Guggenheim, who instructed Riegner to introduce the caveats in the telegrams.[93]

Sumner Welles then proceeded to try to verify the information himself. As has been written, the Americans and the British had, by this stage of the war, been receiving information about the ongoing Holocaust from a wide variety of sources. From the media, from reports published by the Polish government-in-exile, testimonies of camp escapees and investigators such as Witold Pilecki and Jan Karski, from intelligence networks, from decrypting German signals, from books like Peter Wallner's *By Order of the Gestapo*, and from the reports from The Jewish Agency and other groups and refugee organisations. Although the Poles, as well as German Jewish refugees, had told the Allies about the physical locations of camps such as Dachau, Auschwitz and Buchenwald, the British and Americans wanted more detail. If they were ever to be able to take effective military or political action, they needed to know where the camps were, their transport links, and how many inmates there were, guarded by how many SS men, and in what security conditions. The decrypts of the Code Orange signals did not mention the numbers of prisoners whom the Germans were murdering, nor of the means they were using to do it, but they did mention, in precise detail, the number of guards in some of the main camps in the camp network, their armaments, health and morale. Were the British or Americans ever to stage a direct assault on any of the camp networks, this information would be vital.

Did the information in the telegram from Switzerland corroborate or further existing knowledge? Welles needed to know, and what would it enable the Allies to do, in terms of making a declaration about the Holocaust, or taking action to try to impede the progress of the Final Solution? To find out more, the American State Department then sent an encrypted signal to Myron Taylor, their diplomatic envoy to the Holy See in Rome. What reports had the Vatican Secretariat of State received recently? they asked Taylor, what knowledge did they have about the ongoing persecution of the Jews and plans for their mass murder?

The Riegner telegram and the Vatican

Myron Taylor wrote:

> Vatican City, 26th August, 1942
>
> My dear Cardinal Maglione,
>
> I have the honour to bring to the attention of your eminence the following memorandum which has been received from my government. The following was received from the Jewish Office for Palestine in a letter dated August 30th 1942. That office received the report from two reliable eye-witnesses.
>
> (1) Liquidation of the Warsaw Ghetto is taking place. Without any distinction, all Jews, irrespective of age and sex, are being removed from the ghetto in groups and shot. Their corpses are utilised for the making of fats and their bones for the manufacture of fertiliser. Corpses are even being exhumed for this purpose.
>
> (2) These mass executions take place not in Warsaw, but in specially prepared camps for the purpose, one of which is stated to be in Belzec. About 50,000 Jews have been massacred on the spot in Lemberg . . . . . . 100,000 have been massacred in Warsaw . . .

Taylor went on to summarise in two pages the contents not just of the Riegner telegram, but of reports received from the Polish government-in-exile, and the World Jewish Congress.

> (3) Jews deported from Germany, France, Belgium, Holland and Slovakia are sent to be butchered . . .
>
> (4) . . . During the last few weeks a large part of the Jewish population deported to Lithuania and Lublin has already been

executed ... caravans of [such] deportees being transported in cattle cars are often seen . . .

I should much appreciate it if your Eminence could inform me whether the Vatican has any information that would tend to confirm reports contained in this memorandum. If so, I should like to know whether the Holy Father has any suggestions as to any practical manner in which the forces of civilized public opinion could be utilized in order to prevent a continuation of these barbarities . . . [94]

Myron Taylor, like his British counterpart D'Arcy Osborne, lived within the walls of the Vatican City. So, on 27 September he walked to see Cardinal Giovanni Montini,[95] taking with him the five-page diplomatic pro-memoria.[96] Having not received a reply from the Vatican by 1 October, he asked Montini if he had any news. He knew how important it was to pass accurate, reliable information about the persecution of the Jews to the Allies – they could take far more effective military, economic and judicial action than could the Vatican. But Montini hesitated, and decided to keep his response broad and imprecise. In the internal memo in which the cardinal mentioned Taylor's request for a reply, he noted that for the moment, he would tell the United States envoy that the Vatican had received much information about the harsh treatment of the Jews, but could not substantiate all of it. They were, however, taking what action they could in response to each piece of news that arrived. Montini also noted that they were aware that Taylor had received telegraphic instructions from his government to obtain information from the Pope himself.[97] So to find out more, the cardinals working in the Vatican's Secretariat of State decided to send an encrypted telegram to their papal nuncio, or chargé d'affaires, in Berlin. What they were unaware of, again, was that the British and Americans were in the process of trying to intercept and decrypt their signals.

Cardinal Cesare Orsenigo had been the Apostolic Nuncio to Germany since 1930. A right-wing Italian, he was a believer in Benito Mussolini's Fascist state, and openly advocated a policy of compromise and conciliation with Hitler's government and the Nazi Party. Orsenigo's passive approach had infuriated senior figures in the Catholic Church – as early as 1939, the Archbishop of Vienna, Theodor Innitzer, had written to Cardinal Luigi Maglione at the Vatican's Secretariat of State urging him to replace Orsenigo, whom he described as timid and ineffectual. Montini wanted to know what Orsenigo would find out from talking to the government in Berlin, but based on past experience, he expected little. On 7 October, he sent a message to Orsenigo. Aware that the Germans, Italians, Americans and British might be trying to intercept and decipher the Vatican's coded signals, Montini did not tell Orsenigo about three specific pieces of information he had received in the preceding six weeks, that would back up his request. The Vatican cardinal's response to Myron Taylor and the State Department might well have been more precise and detailed, if he had thought the Americans and British were not trying to decipher his private messages, and those of the Papal Secretary of State, Cardinal Maglione, and Pope Pius XII himself.

Montini's fears about communications security were well-grounded. In 1941, the Italian SIM, or Military Intelligence Service, had used a series of safecrackers and break-in experts to steal codebooks from the Vatican. As the SIM cooperated with the Gestapo and the SS intelligence service, the Italians passed on copies of the codes to them. Knowing what the Vatican was doing, or what plans it was making, benefited the Italians as much as the Germans. The codebooks that SIM obtained contained four primary encipherment systems, one of which the Germans named STA/PCZ 3858, and one other Code II-441.[98] In Berlin, the Foreign Ministry's cryptanalytical department was, as written, known as Pers Z for short. The deputy chief of the Italian language desk there, who was responsible for trying to decipher the Vatican's codes, was a former classical archaeologist who had worked in Rome in 1935 and 1936. He was called Dr Ottfried Deubner [99] By the summer of 1942, he estimated that the cryptanalytical work that he had done enabled him to read just twenty percent of only one of the Vatican's codes, which it used on occasions to communicate with foreign diplomats.

It was thus statistically unlikely that he would have been able to read Montini's message to Berlin, nor, if he had been able to, would he have discovered anything. The unwitting betrayal of trust between the Vatican and the Americans, at exactly the moment when both Allies most needed the other to share precise and detailed information as fast as they received it, was compromised over the perceived need to run a cryptanalytical intelligence operation, which in reality yielded little. American cryptanalysts at Arlington Hall in Virginia, and the British at Bletchley Park, could also read only a percentage of the three main Vatican ciphers, which they had named KIA-Red, KIB-Yellow and KIC-Green, partly after the colours of the codebooks' leather covers. Yet the British had made some crucial recent progress forward.

There was a strong element of domestic politics to the American desire to keep their codebreaking operations against the Vatican as covert as possible. One reason that the Americans at Arlington Hall did not want the Vatican to know that they and the British were decrypting some of coded Vatican transmissions was because of the negative effects it could have on political support for their war effort. The US intelligence community had thus introduced an extra level of domestic secrecy to its codebreaking efforts of Vatican ciphers. There were millions of Catholics in America, and these included Catholic voters, Catholic congressmen and senators, and Catholic constituencies: if they were to discover that their own government was trying to read the private messages of the Pope, it could easily alienate them. So American intelligence chiefs decided that the word 'Vatican' should not appear in any documents or messages or governmental or military correspondence, to do with codebreaking.

The department at their codebreaking headquarters that handled the decryption of the Vatican's codes was called 'Gold Section'. If one of the American analysts was decrypting the codes of other countries, such as Greece or Turkey or Spain, the cryptosystem the particular analyst was deciphering would be referred to by what was known as a trigraph, or series of three letters. The first two of these, for instance GR, TU, or SP, indicated the country of origin of the code, and the last letter where the extract of coded text came from in any given message.

Messages coming from the Vatican, however, could not be given the formal digraph, or two-letter indicator of VA, so they were called KI, which bore no resemblance to any known country. Hence the three main Vatican ciphers (and the colours of the codebook covers) led to the names KIA-Red, KIB-Yellow and KIC-Green. The first was a straightforward code used for low-level Vatican communications: movements of clerical staff between apostolic delegations, logistics, diplomatic conferences, feeding arrangements for visiting bishops at seminaries in Lisbon. The Red code simply consisted of 12,000 groups of three letters, each representing a word in Italian. The British, Americans and Germans had cracked this code, only to discover that the most confidential message intercepted concerned the bedding and accommodation arrangements for a group of Vatican delegates visiting Madrid.

KIB-Yellow was much more complicated. It was based on a combination of a codebook and a Vigenère cipher, an encryption device that was more than four hundred years old, having been invented by an Italian cryptologist in 1553. It had resisted almost all efforts to break it. KIC-Green was considered uncrackable, and it was in this code that Montini wrote to Orsenigo. In this cipher, 17,500 permutations of three letters represented different words. The message thus encoded was then further enciphered with twenty-five code 'keys', which were a collection of letters, chosen from substitution tables of randomly mixed alphabets which only the sender and recipient possessed. Each papal nuncio's office anywhere in the world had a unique set of sixteen of these twenty-five keys and would use them on particular, pre-assigned days of the month. A Vatican nuncio might begin a telegram in the assigned key for the day but then shift, as many as eight times, to other keys in the course of the message.

As Montini's coded message was dispatched to Berlin, he received another report from the front line of the Final Solution. This one was delivered in person to the Holy City by a priest who was a personal friend of Pope Pius XII. Don Pirro Scavizzi was a fifty-eight-year-old Roman Catholic clergyman from the medieval town of Gubbio, in east-central Italy. In 1940, while working for the Italian Association of the Sovereign Order of the Knights of Malta, he was assigned as a military chaplain to an Italian infantry division. This unit was sent to fight in Russia. Operating on the left flank of the German Army Group B, the Italians fought alongside both Hungarian and Romanian units. It was the killings of Jews and Soviet POWs and NKVD officials by the Einsatzgruppe and SS units that formed some of the body of Scavizzi's reports to the Vatican. Between September 1941 and February 1942, for example, Einsatzkommando 5 of Einsatzgruppe C murdered approximately 20,000 Jews in and around the city of Dniepropetrowsk, on the Dnieper river. Scavizzi was present in the town on two occasions during this time.

Alongside the Einsatzkommandos, as Scavizzi knew, there were other nationalities of men fighting as volunteers in the SS units.

To the frequent embarrassment of some of their own governments, Finns, Norwegians, Dutchmen, Swedes and Danes served alongside Germans in the ranks of the 5th SS Panzer Division 'Wiking', which deployed into Ukraine as soon as Operation Barbarossa began on 22 June 1941. The division not only witnessed numerous mass killings committed by Einsatzgruppe C, but was involved in committing atrocities itself.[100] Some of these took place in the city of Lemberg, or Lvov, which lay on the same train route the Italian chaplain took as he travelled eastwards on his respective trips. Einsatzgruppe C had entered the city, on the Polish-Ukrainian border, on 1 July 1941, and one of its NCOs, SS-Hauptscharführer Felix Landau noted in his diary that the Einsatzkommando C had arrived in Lemberg on 1 July, that 133 Jews were killed on the 2nd, and then another 800 on the 3rd, and recorded what he saw:

There were hundreds of Jews walking along the street (in Lemberg) with blood pouring down their faces, holes in their heads, their hands broken and their eyes hanging out of their sockets. They were covered in blood.[101]

Similar descriptions were repeated many times by other men from German Einsatzkommandos or SS units, and Scavizzi recorded some of them.

Between October 1941 and October 1942, Scavizzi made a total of five trips on hospital trains to Poland and Ukraine, including to Krakow and Dniepropetrowsk, when the implementation of the Final Solution was at its height. He wrote four reports on what he saw there and was told by SS and Wehrmacht officers, Red Army POWs, wounded German servicemen, and Ukrainian civilians. Hungarian and Romanian officers were also sending reports back to Bucharest and Budapest about the Einsatzkommando atrocities they were witnessing, and Scavizzi heard about these as well.

At the end of each trip, he passed this information by hand directly to Cardinal Montini, and on two occasions during private meetings, to the Pope himself. The information from the Finnish soldiers made its way back to their country's military intelligence agency: trading intelligence with the Japanese for money, and with the Americans for weapons, the news of the Ukraine executions was passed to both by the Finns.

On 3 October, the Polish Ambassador to the Holy See also wrote a report and gave it to Cardinal Montini. Kazimierz Papee was his country's diplomatic envoy to the Vatican, as well as the de facto unofficial representative of its government-in-exile. The killing of Jews in Poland had by then become a matter of public knowledge, he said in his summary, and each day a group of 1,000 Jews was taken from the Warsaw Ghetto, and by railway from Lublin towards the east. He quoted in his message[102] 'a source from an Axis country who says the Jews were put in a camp where they were subsequently put to death'. The Warsaw Ghetto was being methodically emptied, and in the next months it was expected that 300,000 Jews from the ghetto would be sent into the camp system.

Scavizzi's report of 7 October went further. The killing of Jews in massacres was now almost all-encompassing, he wrote, right down to breastfeeding babies. Before being sent to their deaths, Jewish adults and teenagers were being made to work as forced labourers. There were reports that around two million Jews had already been killed. Some hid in the ghettoes, but Polish houses in the General Government were raided and emptied systematically every day by the SS in their hunt for Jews.[103]

On 19 October, Cardinal Orsenigo wrote back to the Pope's Secretary of State, Cardinal Maglione. His reply from Germany was firmly in keeping with the reputation the Berlin nuncio had established for himself.[104]

When the nuncio [Orsenigo] was directed by the Holy See to discuss incidents concerning Jewish victims with Nazi officials, he did so timidly and with embarrassment.[105]

Orsenigo said in his message that he was replying to the request from the Vatican of 7 October, and that to discover more information, he had met the German Foreign Minister, Joachim von Ribbentrop. As always, von Ribbentrop had told him that the question of the Jews concerned non-Aryan people, and so 'there's nothing that can be done'. Orsenigo then wrote that the diplomatic corps in Berlin regarded the anti-Semitic deportations as an element of (German) internal politics. 'However hard the Holy See tries,' he wrote, 'or however many times [the message about the Jews] is repeated, it always gets rebuffed, diverted or distracted.'

It was by now 19 October, nine weeks since Eduard Schulte had arrived in Switzerland. Neither the American State Department nor Rabbi Stephen Wise were any closer to verifying the contents of the Riegner telegram. Official communications between individuals in two or three countries in wartime were slow, whether by letter, telegram or in person. Often a government committee or group decision was needed to authorise a reply, meaning that weeks could elapse as information was passed, checked, filtered and read. Schulte's information about Himmler at Auschwitz, Scavizzi's selection of first-hand testimonies from the Eastern Front, the Polish ambassador's information received from the Polish Free Army in Warsaw was dissipated, disbelieved, diverted, or just blocked. Crucial intelligence that could have gone straight to decision-makers in London and Washington was diluted along the way – partly because of key officials' distrust of the means of conveying the information. The Pope and Cardinal Montini feared that the Americans, Germans and Italians were trying to read their coded messages, while the State Department was cautious about disseminating fourth-hand information. Yet sometimes none of these things were an influencing factor, as was to be the case with the next covert, insider's report about the Holocaust that was to reach Cardinal Orsenigo. This one, a firsthand eyewitness account by a key SS officer who had visited Belzec and Treblinka, would arrive at his office through an extraordinary combination of luck and coincidence.[106]

The progress of the Riegner Telegram

The verification trail of the Riegner telegram continued. The United Nations Commission for the Investigation of War Crimes had asked the British Foreign Office for information from the decryption of the German Police Codes. They had opened investigations and were assembling indictments against the senior leaders of the SS and Nazi Party in preparation for war crimes trials. They needed any information that could be used as evidence in their investigations against the Germans. The senior official at the Foreign Office who was given the task of responding was Sir Victor Cavendish-Bentinck, the Chairman of the Joint Intelligence Committee. For Bletchley Park, this was a crucial time in their development from a decryption and analysis centre to a war-winning intelligence asset. This was a point when the Code and Cypher School could expand into something more than that, be a greater weapon of war, where cryptanalysis could become a tool of international justice as well.

Unfortunately, Cavendish-Bentinck was a sceptic whose aversion to so-called 'atrocity stories' was partly a product of the anti-German propaganda stories of corpses and soap from the First World War that Stewart Menzies had fought against at the time. In messages Bentinck also displayed a virulent anti-Eastern European bent. Was this a blinkered, insular prejudice?

Was it linked to the fact that his wife, who was Hungarian, had left him on the first day of the war, taking their two children? When he received news about the massacres of some 33,000 Ukrainian Jews at the Babi Yar ravine outside Kiev in September 1941, Cavendish-Bentinck had dismissed it as 'products of the Slavic imagination'.[107] Asked by the UN Commission whether the Domino decrypts contained material that could provide evidence of war crimes, he showed a mild disinterest, writing that they 'contained accounts of wholesale executions etc'.[108]

On the task of provision of evidence to support war crimes prosecutions, he worked with a colleague from the Foreign Office, a lawyer called Howard Allen. He too had read the Riegner report, responding that:

> . . . we have also received plenty of reports that Jews deported from other parts of Europe have been concentrated in the Government-General, and that also that once there Jews are being so badly treated that very large numbers have perished: either as a result of lack of food or of evil conditions e.g. as in the Warsaw ghetto, or as a consequence of mass deportations or executions. Such stories do provide a basis for Mr Riegner's report, but they do not of course amount to 'extermination at one blow'. The German policy seems rather to eliminate 'unuseful mouths' but to use able-bodied Jews as slave labourers.

The telegram finally reached its intended recipient, the British Member of Parliament Sydney Silverman, who, accompanied by Alexander Easterman of the World Jewish Congress, took it in person to the Home Office on 26 November. There he met with the Home Secretary in Churchill's cabinet, Herbert Stanley Morrison. He took with him a four-page declaration which the World Jewish Congress had just released.

'Mr Silverman and Mr Easterman called on me this morning,' wrote Morrison in an internal memo . . .

. . . about the extermination of the Jews in Europe. Mr Easterman left with me the attached document, which was handed to him last night by a member of the Polish Government. It is his only copy and I promised to have it copied and returned to him. Mr Silverman said that it was now clear that whatever our view might be, the State Department accepted the substantial truth of these stories. I said that I did not think the State Department had any more evidence than we had, and that probably on their knowledge of the German character and of Nazi ideology it seemed to them that there was nothing intrinsically improbably [sic] about the story. I said that we had had no more evidence, that Mr Norton had seen M. Reigner, but had been unable to get from him the facts upon which his evidence was based.

Mr Silverman said that we might take the view that there was nothing that could be usefully done at the moment. If that was our view, it meant that nothing in fact could ever be done. He said that we would be in an impossible position unless we took some steps to try and prevent this happening even if we thought that the steps would be ineffective. He asked first of all that a Four-Power Declaration should be made to the effect that the United Nations had been informed of this plan, that if it was carried out the perpetrators of it would be held responsible and would receive their due punishment, and that the German people could not escape responsibility for the acts of their government. He also suggested that some use should be made of broadcasting, not to threaten the Germans, but to encourage the Jews and to encourage those non-Jews who might be willing to give the Jews their protection. He pointed out that the deportation of Jews from France had had a good effect upon the general resistance of the French against the Germans and that apart from anything else, such a broadcast of encouragement might be an important weapon of general political warfare.

I should be glad if the department [Home Office and Foreign Office] could consider this as a matter of urgency since I promised Mr Silverman that I would let him have our general view at the House next week. I doubt very much whether his proposals, if we were able to carry them out, would do very much good, and I think Mr Silverman agrees. *On the other hand I think that we would be in an appalling position if these stories should prove to have been true and we have done nothing about them. Silverman and his friends have been very forbearing on the whole, but I am afraid that unless we can make them some kind of gesture they will cause a lot of trouble.* [Author's italics]
26th November, 1942[109]

(The reference to Mr Silverman and 'his friends' is the Foreign and Home Offices' polite shorthand of the time for British Jews.)

The four-page declaration from the World Jewish Congress, which Silverman took to the Home Secretary, read as follows:

December 1st, 1942

WORLD JEWISH CONGRESS
(BRITISH SECTION).

———

ANNIHILATION OF EUROPEAN JEWRY.

HITLER'S POLICY OF TOTAL DESTRUCTION.

The Jews of Europe are being exterminated by the Nazis. It is not merely that atrocities are being committed against the

Jews. They are being quite literally slaughtered in masses, in pursuance of a systematic plan and in accordance with a deliberate policy.

This is Hitler's 'final solution of the Jewish problem of Europe'. He has openly proclaimed his design. He is now executing his policy with a diabolical fiendishness unknown in the whole history of human savagery.

2,000,000 is the barest minimum number of Jews murdered, tortured and deliberately starved to death in Eastern Europe. The number is probably much greater.

It is now clear that the mass deportation of Jews from France, Belgium, Holland and other Western European countries, has been for the purpose of concentrating all the Jews of Nazi occupied Europe chiefly in Poland for the purpose of facilitating their mass massacre.

On the 27th November 1942, it was stated at the Polish National Council in London that at the beginning of last September about 1½ million Jews have been murdered in an organised way. About half a million were deported to the U.S.S.R. in 1940, and of the rest of the peace-time Jewish population of Poland, several hundred thousand Jews have died of starvation, disease and frightful living conditions imposed by the Nazis.

Several hundred thousand Jews have been murdered in the Nazi occupied areas of the U.S.S.R. and in the Ukraine.

Almost the entire Jewish population of the Baltic States have been exterminated.

Hundreds of thousands of Jews of Roumania have been deported to Transdniestria and there massacred.

In addition, scores of thousands of German, French, Belgian, Dutch, Czechoslovak and Yugoslav Jews have been deported to Poland and the occupied areas of the U.S.S.R. for mass slaughter.

Many transports of Jewish deportees from Western Europe do not reach their destination. The victims, crammed into closed cattle-trucks, either die of suffocation or disease on the way or are done to death by their captors.

It is known that at the beginning of last August train-loads of Jewish deportees reached Germany from Belgium, Holland and France. The compartments were filled with dead and living Jews crowded together.

Poland has become the Nazi slaughter-house for the Jews of Europe.

Massacres of Jews have been going on from the first say of the German occupation. The holocaust took on a formal design, under an explicit policy, in March 1942. Himmler then gave orders for the extermination of 50% of the Jewish population of the so-called Government-General. The extermination was to be completed by the end of 1942.

Not satisfied with the speed and extent of the mass massacres, Himmler, in July last, decreed the total destruction of all the Jews concentrated in Poland.

It is from approximately this date that the large-scale deportations of Jews from Western Europe began. The massacres started on July 21st 1942, when German Police cars invaded the Ghettoes, shooting the inhabitants indiscriminately and at sight. On that date all the Jewish members of the Jewish Council of Warsaw were arrested on bloc as hostages.

On July 22nd 1942, the Nazis ordered the deportation to Eastern Poland and the Ukraine of all Jews irrespective of the age and sex. The daily quota of deportees was fixed at 6,000. Later this quota was increased to 10,000. Victims were dragged from their homes or seized in the streets in organised manhunts.

Jews were congregated in the squares. Old people and invalids were driven to cemeteries and shot in droves. Others were loaded into trucks, 150 persons being crowded into the space normally holding a maximum of 40. The trucks were then driven off. Hundreds died of suffocation.

This process is now going on continuously. The floors of the trucks are covered with a thick layer of lime and chlorine sprinkled with water. The doors are locked. Often the trains remain on a siding for a day or two or longer. The fumes of lime and chlorine, the lack of air, water and food, cause hundreds of deaths, with the result that dead and living remain packed side by side.

On arrival at their destination, 50% of the deportees were found dead. The remainder were taken to the special camps of Treblinka, Belzec and Selibor [sic], where they were shot. Neither children nor babies were spared. By the end of September 1942, 250,000 Jews had been thus exterminated.

The deportations are described by the Nazis as 'the re-settlement of the Jews'. The 're-settlement' is a final one in the sense that few, if any, of the 're-settled' Jews remain alive.

THE WARSAW GHETTO:

In March 1942, according to official German statistics, there were 433,000 Jews packed into the Ghetto – the area walled off by the Nazis which formerly contained about 200,000 Jews.

According to 'Arbeitsamt' – the official Nazi Labour journal – only 40,000 Jews are to be left in the Warsaw Ghetto. These are the highly-skilled workers whom the Nazis require for their war industry.

For September 1942, the Nazis distributed 120,000 ration cards for the Warsaw Ghetto. In October, the number issued was only 40,000. The same process of elimination and massacre is going on in all the other Ghettoes of Poland. The reports state that the Ghetto of Lodz which formerly contained about 250,000 Jews has been entirely cleared of Jews.

NAZI METHODS OF EXTERMINATION:

Besides the Firing Squads, the Nazis are now facilitating mass executions by the use of electrocution and lethal gas chambers in which Jews are crowded and 'eliminated'.

An electrocution station has been installed at the Belzec Camp. Transports of deportees are de-trained near the execution place, stripped naked, ostensibly for bathing. They are then led to sheds with a metal plated floor. The sheds are then locked and an electrical current passed through the metal plates. Death is almost instantaneous.

A large digging machine for mass graves has been recently installed at Treblinka.

In Chelm, 10,000 Jews have been gassed recently.

The Germans have organised special Extermination Squads – Vernichtungskolonne – whose task is to round up and kill Jews on sight. The Squads fire indiscriminately into windows of Jewish houses.

The above summary takes no account of suicides, the insanities of mothers whose children are seized or murdered, and the innumerable outrages and atrocities resulting in the deaths of many thousands of Jewish men and women.

The next document the British government received was the so-called Third Karski report, name after a Polish ex-soldier who now travelled between Poland and France and Britain, working as an undercover investigator. He had interviewed survivors and escapees of a variety of camps and ghettoes:

The persecution of the Jews in Poland, which has been in progress from the very first day of the German occupation, has taken on extremely acute forms since March 1942, when Himmler ordered the extermination of 50% of the Jewish population in the Government General, to be carried out by the end of 1942.

Though the German assassins had started this work with extraordinary gusto, the results apparently did not satisfy Himmler, for during his visit to the General Gouvernement [*sic*] in July 1942 he ordered new decrees personally, aiming at the total destruction of Polish Jewry.

The persecutions in Warsaw started on July 21st 1942, when German police cars suddenly drove into the ghettos. The soldiers immediately started rushing into houses, shooting the inhabitants at sight without any explanation. The first victims belonged mostly to the educated classes. On that day almost all the members of the Jewish Municipal Council were arrested and held as hostages.

On July 22nd 1942 the Jewish Council was ordered to proclaim the decree of the German authorities dealing with the resettlement of all the Warsaw Jews, regardless of sex or age, in the Eastern part of Poland, with the sole exception of persons working in German factories or members of the Jewish militia. The daily quota of people to be re-settled was fixed at 6,000 and members of the Jewish Municipal Council were ordered to carry out the order under the pain of death.

By the next day, however, on July 23rd, the German

police again appeared in the Jewish Municipal Council and demanded to see the chairman, Mr Czerniakow. After the police had left, Czerniakow committed suicide. From a note he left for his wife, it became clear that he had received an order to deliver 10,000 people the next day and 7000 daily on the following days, in spite of the fact that the quota had been fixed originally at 6,000. The victims to be delivered to the Germans are either dragged out of their homes or seized in the streets. As the zeal of the Jewish police to perform these duties against their own people was slight and did not give a guarantee of efficiency, the Germans have mobilised temporary security battalions for the man-hunts, consisting of Ukrainians, Latvians, and Lithuanians. These battalions, under the command of SS men, are characterised by their utter ruthlessness, cruelty and inhumanity.

The Jews, when caught, are driven to a square. Old people and cripples are then singled out, taken to the cemetery and there shot. The remaining people are loaded into goods trucks, at the rate of 150 people to a truck with space for 40. The floor of the truck is covered with a thick layer of lime and chlorine sprinkled with water. The doors of the trucks are locked. Sometimes the train starts immediately on being loaded, sometimes it remains on a siding for a day, two days or even longer. The people are packed so tightly that those who die of suffocation remain in the crowd side by side with the still living and those slowly dying from the fumes of lime and chlorine, from lack of air, water and food. Wherever the trains arrive half the people arrive dead. Those surviving are sent to special camps at Treblinka, Belzec and Sobibor. Once there, the so-called 'settlers' are mass murdered.[110]

The Allies condemn the Holocaust

Faced with the evidence from the World Jewish Congress, the intelligence coming from the Polish government-in-exile, Bletchley Park's irrefutable documentation of the killings of Jews on the Eastern Front, and Churchill's determination to make a powerful, international condemnation of the persecution of the Jews, Eden, Morrison and their American counterparts took the decision to make as powerful a statement as possible.

On 17 December, the Joint Foreign Committee of the Board of Deputies and the Anglo-Jewish Association released a report to the press about the Babi Yar massacre, which took place at the end of September 1941 outside Kiev. It stated that the Germans had murdered 52,000 people after they occupied Kiev and was one of the first documented reports in the West about the activities of the Einsatzgruppen in the Soviet Union. The toll from the two of shootings was just over 33,000, but the Committee had exercised numerical leeway and included other mass executions which had taken place around the same time, in the Baltic states and Byelorussia. Meanwhile the British and international media were showing none of the hesitation and caution of the British government.

'More than 700,000 Polish Jews have been slaughtered by the Germans in the greatest massacre in the world's history,' the *Daily Telegraph* reported on 25 June 1942, adding that the Germans had 'embarked on the physical extermination of the Jewish population'. This article not only included mention of the mass shootings after Operation Barbarossa had begun, but, crucially, included details of the gas vans used in the camp at Chelmno. On 30 June The Telegraph ran another article headed 'More than 1,000,000 Jews Killed in Europe,' in which it claimed that the Nazis intended to 'wipe the [Jewish] race from the European Continent'.

The British press had taken an editorial decision, individually and seemingly collectively, that the Third Reich's persecution of the Jews was now an established fact. It would now be up to the British government to act, and not to be seen to hesitate. The increasing publicity for German atrocities in the media would now mean that de Grey and his colleagues would be bound to follow the chain of atrocities as hard as possible, and provide solid intelligence about what the SS were now doing. This would be a very difficult task, but it was incumbent on them. The flow of information about executions encoded in Domino had now slowed considerably, and since there was almost no solid signals intelligence of any executions from any of the network of camps in Poland, GC&CS would now have to try even harder with every conceivable interception and encryption asset they had.

The British newspaper coverage stormed ahead: the *Daily Mail*, the *Evening Standard*, the *Manchester Guardian*, *The Times* and the *News Chronicle* carried almost identical headlines: '1,000,000 Jews Dead.' On 4 December, *The Times* ran an article with the headline 'Deliberate Policy for Extermination'. It alleged that a total of 1,700,000 Jews had been 'liquidated'. It went on to say that 'all other war crimes of Nazism will fail in the end and the defeat of German Fascism is inevitable, but this particular aim, a complete extermination of Jews, is already being enforced.' On 11 December 1942, the Jewish Chronicle ran a headline saying 'Two Million Slaughtered; Most Terrible Massacre of All Time; Appalling Horrors of Nazi Mass Murders.' The page was bordered in black, and listed German atrocities carried out to date.

Great Britain and a number of Allied governments then made the strongest possible statement they could. On behalf of the British Government, the Foreign Secretary, Sir Anthony Eden, stood up in the House of Commons on 17 December 1942, in response to a question from Sydney Silverman.

The statement [was] issued in the name of eleven Allied Governments and the French National Committee and stated that the attention of these governments had been drawn to . . . 85 numerous reports from Europe that the German authorities, not content with denying to persons of Jewish race in all the territories over which their barbarous rule has been extended, the most elementary rights, are now carrying into effect Hitler's oft-repeated intention to exterminate the Jewish People in Europe.

From all the occupied countries Jews are being transported in conditions of appalling horror and brutality to Eastern Europe. In Poland, which has been the principal Nazi slaughterhouse, the ghettos established by the German invader are being systematically emptied of all Jews except a few highly skilled workers required for war industries. None of those taken away are ever heard of again. The able-bodied are slowly worked to death in labour camps. The infirm are left to die of exposure and starvation or are deliberately massacred in mass executions. The number of victims of these bloody cruelties is reckoned in many hundreds of thousands of entirely innocent men, women and children.

The toughest and most decisive ramification of this declaration was that it included a resolution by the Allied governments 'to ensure that those responsible for these crimes shall not escape retribution, and to press on with the practical measures to this end.'

Following the declaration, the British Political Warfare Executive issued a directive for the week beginning 24 December 1942: the persecution of the Jews was to become a central theme in British war propaganda. The Executive was a clandestine government organisation, formerly the propaganda arm of the

Special Operations Executive. Its task was to disseminate both 'black' and 'white' propaganda in countries allied or hostile to Nazi Germany. The organisation then ordered that all leaflets and wireless broadcasts to occupied Europe 'should coldly and factually establish Hitler's plan to exterminate the Jews in Europe'. Again, it would now be incumbent on Nigel de Grey and his colleagues to try to provide intelligence that continued to support this statement. In the midst of the enormity of total war, the task of the cryptanalysts and intelligence officers at Bletchley Park was now even more complex, even more urgent.

In the aftermath of declaration, Anthony Eden's Foreign Office and Morrison's Home Office seemed to backtrack, to lose impetus and momentum, to try to dilute the powerful words of the statement with compromise and half-hearted action seemingly designed not to antagonise any party, to please none, and to achieve little. What could now be done in practical terms to help the Jews? Eden replied in Parliament:

Certainly we would like to do all we possibly can. There are, obviously, certain security formalities which have to be considered. [A fear of German spies entering Britain under the guise of refugees was a prevalent and abiding concern of the British Home and Foreign Offices throughout the war.] It would clearly be the desire of the United Nations[xiii] to do everything they could to provide wherever possible an asylum for these people, but the House will understand that there are immense geographical and other difficulties in the matter.

---

xiii Despite the fact that the United Nations organisation per se was not fully established under charter until October 1945, the British and Americans and their allies, both combatant and neutral, took to referring to themselves as the United Nations on occasions. The Allies also referred to the triumvirate of Great Britain, the United States and the Soviet Union.

On 17 December, the government established the Cabinet Committee on the Reception and Accommodation of Jewish Refugees. It held its first meeting on 31 December, chaired by Eden. Also present was Morrison, the Home Secretary, who stated that he could not agree to the admission of more than 1,000 to 2,000 refugees into Britain, and that it had to be borne in mind that most of the 100,000 refugees then in Britain were Jewish. He stipulated that this was contingent upon 'the firm understanding that the United States and the Dominions would accept proportionate numbers'. He also said that he 'deprecated the tendency to regard the United Kingdom as the sole repository for refugees' and warned of an upsurge in domestic anti-Semitism if large numbers of Jews were to be admitted into Britain. Oliver Stanley, the Colonial Secretary, suggested that when referring to the refugee crisis no distinction should be made between Jews and non-Jews, and for this reason the word 'Jewish' was deleted from the name of this committee.

This, helpfully in the government's eyes, blurred the distinction between European Jews fleeing the mainland continent to avoid being put into ovens or gas chambers, or executed by firing squad, and the much lower number of European refugees, such as the French, Spanish, Czech and Polish, most of whom had arrived already in the preceding three years and been granted admission. On 20 January 1943, the Cabinet Committee sent a memorandum to the American State Department: the British government was adamant that they should involve the United States in efforts to deal with what they called 'the refugee crisis'. The first two sentences effectively summarised the British governmental position towards the Jews of Europe:

The refugee problem cannot be treated as though it were a wholly Jewish problem, which could be handled by Jewish agencies or by machinery only adapted for assisting Jews. There are so many non-Jewish refugees and there is so much acute suffering among non-Jews in Allied countries that Allied criticism would probably result if any marked preference were shown in removing Jews from territories in enemy occupation.

In the winter snow, the frozen mud, the bombed cities and grey-skied steppes of Poland, in Germany, and across occupied territories in Europe, the Final Solution was now at its height. The British government, meanwhile, announced they would discuss the refugee situation at a conference to be held in the spring, in Bermuda.

CHAPTER VIII

THE HÖFLE TELEGRAM

Spring 1943 - Poland and Berlin

On the morning of 11 January 1943, in Lublin, Hermann Höfle took some handwritten signals to his radio room. Four of them contained a mix of words, letters and numbers laid out in rows on one sheet of paper. The SS radio man on duty at the Julius Schreck barracks took them for encryption and then transmission. He first took the list of weekly encipherment keys, and then the codebook to encrypt the one-page dispatch in the double square cipher that had replaced the Double Transposition encryption two years before. The security keys for encipherment had a twelve-hour duration, so he chose the one that covered the period from midnight on the 10th up to midday on the 11th. He put on the three-letter signifiers for both recipients, and his own signifier of OMQ for Lublin. Then he sent the first message in Morse code to Adolf Eichmann at Referat IV B4 – the Jewish Affairs and Evacuations Department – at the RSHA in Berlin. The second, third and fourth he sent to the SS commander in Krakow, a lieutenant-colonel called Franz Heim, who was the second most senior SS security officer in the General Government. He ran the SD and the Sipo, and answered to

SS Oberführer Eberhard Schöngarth, who had represented the General Government at the Wannsee Conference.

Höfle could have sent the message to Berlin by personal courier – it would have been the most secure method – but the time necessary for an SS messenger to travel by truck and train across snowbound, frozen Poland meant keeping Heinrich Himmler waiting, and Höfle, who like many of his SS colleagues had no desire to see the Russian front at close hand from a frozen foxhole, discounted that option. There was the possibility of a new Enigma coding the Gestapo had started using, or one of the new machine ciphers, but the Lublin headquarters did not have a Lorenz enciphered teleprinter. So Höfle decided that the double square German Police cipher issued back in summer 1941 might deceive Allied codebreakers, so he sent his telegrams in that. One went to Eichmann, the others to Heim. He then sent at least the second signal to Heim a second time, this time encrypted in the Enigma Code Orange I, the contents exactly the same as the first.[111] This was only one of a handful of signals sent in Orange I by Höfle in Lublin: another had preceded it in December. It said that new camps for Jews were being set up in the General Government, and new guards were being demanded from existing camps.[112] The signals sent to Heim also included something crucial that appears in almost no other message from Operation Reinhard or elsewhere: Hermann Höfle's surname. If the Allies were listening or intercepting, they now had a name for one of the senior officers running the operation in the General Government.

> OMX de OMQ [began the first one]. State Secret! To the Reich Main Security Office, for the attention of SS Obersturmbannführer EICHMANN, BERLIN . . .
>
> OLQ de OMQ. State Secret! To the commander of the Security Police, for the attention of SS Obersturmbannführer HEIM, KRAKOW.

Re: 14-Day report of Operation REINHARD. Reference: radiogram from there. Recorded arrivals until 31 December 42: L 12761, B 0, S 515, T 10335 totalling 23611.

Situation (. . .) 31 December 42, L 24733, B 434508, S 101370, T 71355, totalling 1274166

SS and Police Leader of Lublin, HÖFLE, Sturmbannführer.[113]

What Höfle was transmitting was the total number of arrivals in the four camps designated in the radio transmissions by the letters L, B, S and T, or Lublin-Majdanek, Belzec, Sobibor and Treblinka. The figures covered two periods: the first was a fourteen-day report for the last two weeks of December 1942. The second was an annual summary of figures for the year of 1942.

The figures themselves came both from the *Deutsches Reichsbahn*, the German railway system that transported the Jews, and from the camps themselves. In the fourteen-day total the figures were as follows:

L: 12761
B: 0
S: 515
T: 10335
TOTAL: 23611

The '0' next to the B for Belzec referred to the fact that parts of the camp had been closed two weeks before. The last transport of Jews had arrived at Belzec on 11 December 1942. Globočnik had issued orders, in turn received from Berlin, that the killing operations at the camp were now to be concealed in their entirety. Working parties of Jewish slave labourers had begun exhuming the corpses of those gassed and shot between March and December

1942, and burning the decomposing corpses on open-air pyres, laid out on racks made out of sections of metal railway tracks. The three other camps, Majdanek, Treblinka and Sobibor, still continued to operate.

As Höfle sent the signal from Lublin, a thousand miles to the east on the River Don at Stalingrad, the Wehrmacht's Sixth Army was heading to destruction in one of the most decisive battles on the Eastern Front. Ten entire armies of Army Group B and Army Group Don, 1,600,000 German, Italian, Romanian and Hungarian troops, along with 40,000 Hiwis, had fought to take the strategic industrial city on the Volga river since August the previous year. In November, with temperatures plunging to minus thirty degrees, the Soviets counter-attacked, cutting off the German flanks, and trapping the Sixth Army inside the ruins of the city. Hitler forbade retreat: the Luftwaffe supplied the enclave by air, but everybody knew the end was very close, not just for German strategic hopes of reaching the oilfields of the Caucasus, but for the momentum of Hitler's advance across the Soviet Union.

The shock waves of impending defeat hit the camp extermination programme, and SS-Gruppenführer Globočnik and SS-Sturmbannführer Höfle saw that the tide of victory which had swept across the Soviet Union since the German invasion in June 1941 had now turned. Knowing that the Red Army would counter-attack and eventually reach occupied Poland, the Operation Reinhard killings took on an additional urgency. Berlin was now adamant: exterminate the remainder of the Polish Jews, exhume and burn the bodies where necessary, dismantle the camps, hide the evidence. Signals traffic between Lublin and Berlin about the operation, almost at zero, was effectively to cease.

In the second three signals Höfle sent that day in January, the second series of figures in the messages concerned the total of Jewish arrivals for the previous year:

L: 24733
B: 434508
S: 101370
T: 71355
TOTAL: 1274166

The total number of Jewish deaths at Chelmno was around 160,000, but as the camp operated in parallel with Operation Reinhard, Höfle had not included the figures in his estimates. From the figures and the mathematical addition he sent it was immediately clear that a figure or figures was either missing or wrong, as the list of numbers do not add up to the total. Only by the insertion of an extra '5' into the figure for Treblinka – making it 713555 – does the total become clear. Who, therefore, had been responsible for missing out a figure '5' in Höfle's message? For only by appending it to the Treblinka total of '71355' from Treblinka could the sum total of 1,274,166 be obtained. Was it Höfle himself, copying the numbers down from a list given to him, sitting in the office on a freezing cold January morning in southern Poland, holding a pencil or fountain pen as he laid out the death toll in one year from Operation Reinhard? Did he miss the figure 5? Did the SS signaller? Or when the messages were dispatched, was it some other agency or body?

The identifying code name of 'Reinhart', referring to Globočnik's extermination programme, had also been used in one of the KL messages enquiring about field ovens. The name for Odilo Globočnik's operation was 'Special Order Reinhard', which was written under the list of his various functions in SS personnel files. The first evidence of the cover name 'Reinhard' as a code for the special duties, the killings of Jews, could be found in early June 1942, immediately after the assassination of Reinhard Heydrich in Prague. Höfle knew that the former head of the RSHA wrote his first name at times with a final 'dt, as can be seen from his genealogical table and the SS annual promotion lists. Himmler himself had even pointed out this peculiarity of the first name in a speech. Höfle used an 'Einsatz Reinhart' on the service seal stamp used with the Reich eagle, corresponding to a stamp of his department. Or was 'Reinhart' simply another example of Höfle's poor spelling, as was, perhaps, the missing '5'?

The human accounting of Operation Reinhard

Once Höfle's signals reached Adolf Eichmann in Berlin, the numbers he had reported became part of a statistical analysis that Himmler requested at the beginning of 1943, an accounting of the Final Solution. On 19 July the previous year Himmler had ordered Globočnik that the evacuation – for which read mass murder – of the entire Jewish population of the General Government had to be completed by 31 December. Höfle had ordered the evacuation of the Warsaw Ghetto on 22 July, and on the following day, 6,250 Jewish men, women and children travelled down the railway spur to the extermination camp at Treblinka II. They were gassed immediately. This total was approximately repeated each day until mid-September, with the operation under the command of Franz Stangl, after Irmfried Eberl was replaced. By November, Himmler was requesting an update and an accounting on Operation Reinhard, both human and economic. He asked Adolf Eichmann to prepare a report.

Using figures which he already had in Berlin – Hermann Höfle did not send his telegrams until January – Eichmann put together what he called an 'Activity and Situation Report 1942 on the Final Solution of the European Jewish Question' which was presented to Himmler. He was not pleased. Eichmann was meticulous, and eager to please those who commanded him. He was also astute enough to know that with the war beginning to turn against Germany, with the incipient defeat at Stalingrad, and the British gains in North Africa, Himmler would want to complete the Final Solution as quickly as possible. The US Army Air Force had just joined the British aerial bombing campaign, and their first target in Germany had been the port of Wilhelmshaven. The British had just taken the port of Tripoli. Everybody knew that once they had defeated the Germans in North Africa, Sicily and Italy would be next. There was urgency in the air. The Reichsführer would not be in an accommodating mood. Nobody wanted to find themselves suddenly transferred onto a Junkers Ju-52 transport flying into the frozen reaches of the Eastern Front.

Eichmann's report was as detailed and accurate as he could make it. Yet it did not satisfy the notoriously precise and picky SS general. The RSHA was displeased too. On 18 January, a week after Höfle wrote his signals in Lublin, SS-Oberst-Gruppenführer Daluege wrote to Heinrich Müller at Gestapo headquarters. The head of the Order Police had temporarily replaced Heydrich as the head of the Reich Security Main Office following his assassination. Vienna's Chief of Police, SS-Untersturmführer Ernst Kaltenbrunner would take over the position within a fortnight. Daluege told Müller, who was also Eichmann's de facto commanding officer, that following Himmler's orders the RSHA now had no more statistical work to be done in the field of accounting for Operation Reinhard and the Final Solution. This was because their statistical documents to date lacked professional accuracy. Eichmann was shocked and resentful. To add insult to injury, he was replaced by a man who was barely an SS officer, more of a civilian statistician.

Richard Korherr was from Bavaria, and from 1935 to 1940 had been the head of the Statistical Office in Würzburg. Following the invasion of Poland, Himmler decided that the SS needed a statistical study, a set of figures of how the programme of the resettlement of the Jews was progressing. He brought Korherr to work for the SS in Berlin, making him a Sturmbannführer. Following on from Eichmann's efforts, he instructed the mild-mannered Bavarian Catholic to summarise the total of all those Jews who had been subject to 'special handling' or *Sonderbehandlung* between 1937 and December 1942. The report had to be prepared as soon as possible. Himmler would then give it to the Führer. So Korherr, who by now was using Höfle's newly arrived figures, along with others, prepared a sixteen-page document. To add to the humiliation of being told his work was not satisfactory, Eichmann had also been instructed to provide Korherr with two assistants, and all the documents needed. The number of victims that appeared in his report in the section for the Operation Reinhard total was 1,274, 166, exactly the same as Höfle had calculated. When Korherr used the word *Sonderbehandlung* in the report, he was unexpectedly and sharply criticised, and told he risked disclosing the true nature of the operation. The word must be replaced. The SS told him to use the phrase 'to be smuggled': Jews 'were smuggled through the camps.' Then, on 1 April, Himmler asked for a summary of the report so that he could show it to Hitler.

The title in German was *Endlosung der Judenfrage* or the 'Final Solution to the Jewish Question'. Korherr calculated that the number of Jews in Europe had fallen by four million. Between October 1939 and 31 December 1942, 1,274,166 Jews were 'handled' or 'processed' at the camps in the General Government, and 145,301 at the camps and ghettos in the territory named the Warthegau, which was essentially Greater Poland outside the General Government. Korherr included in his report all other available SS information. He submitted sixteen pages to Himmler on 23 March, which the Reichsführer abridged, including information up until the end of March 1943. In the final version the words 'special handling' had been replaced by 'processed' and 'smuggled through'. The report did not contain all the numbers of Soviet and Baltic Jews executed in Ukraine, Byelorussia or the Baltic States after the beginning of Operation Barbarossa, but Korherr concluded that in the first decade of National Socialist German government, the number of Jews in Europe had essentially been halved.

The economic accounting of Operation Reinhard

It was not just a human accounting of the special handling of the Jews that Himmler and the RSHA wanted. They needed to know how much money the SS Main Economic and Administration Office was making from the camps in the Operation Reinhard complex. Consequently they asked for regular lists of the valuables and other property taken from Jewish prisoners. Höfle, Globočnik and the RSHA were, of course, aware of the ongoing investigation into Karl-Otto Koch, by spring 1943 still at Chelmno. It hung like an unspoken warning over the heads of those men tempted to steal from the SS. Yet the extraordinary quantities of jewellery, gold, currency and silver alone that the extermination and concentration camp staff encountered during their daily operational activities proved overwhelming for many of them.

In December 1942, one of the SS garrison administrators in Lublin, Georg Wippern, was becoming suspicious of potential illicit activities – the looting of Jewish property – and so sent his accounting officer to Belzec to deal with the camp commandant. In a letter written in summer 1942, Globočnik had entrusted Wippern with the handling of the valuables and currency taken from the Jews, while Höfle took stock of clothing and shoes:

To SS-Hauptsturmführer Höfle
To SS-Sturmbannführer Wippern
Lublin

As already discussed orally,

1. A central card catalogue is to be created, in which all the valuables arising from the
resettlement of Jews are recorded and maintained
a) For all valuables, currencies, etc. - Stubaf. Wippern
b) For all clothing, shoes, etc. – H'stuf. Höfle

2. This catalogue to contain an index sheet arranged according to the individual categories, on which the . . . [unclear – counted/numbered?] Input must be listed in the same way as in 4,

Output. Based on this file, a property report must be presented to me on the 1st of each month.

Signed (Odilo) Globčcnik

Brigadeführer und Generalmajor der Polizei

Lublin, July 15, 1942

So that day in December Wippern's accounting officer, Unterscharführer Wilhelm Schwarzkopf arrived and went to see SS-Obersturmführer Gottlieb Hering, who was the second commandant of Belzec, having succeeded Christian Wirth in August 1942. Described by one inmate as a broad-shouldered bully, he terrified both German SS and Ukrainian guards. Like Wirth, Hering was a former police detective and had served on the T4 euthanasia programme. The stationmaster at Belzec, who was Polish and lived in the village, reported that on one occasion Hering tied a Jew to his car with a rope and drove off around the village, while his dog ran behind the car, biting the Jew as he was dragged along.[114] Hering told Schwarzkopf that he did not want any 'snoopers' there, and Wippern's NCO then waited for two weeks in the village of Bełżec, without being able to gain access to the camp, while Wippern himself arrived on several occasions, leaving quickly each time.[115]

Some of the more basic items that the Germans were

confiscating were recycled back to the SS troops at the front: huge quantities of spectacles, for instance, were collected from Jewish inmates; the SS Main Economic and Administrative Office in Berlin had decided these should be repaired by other Jews, and then distributed to SS soldiers. In encrypted messages about other materials, the concentration camps at Flossenburg and Hinzert reported that collected human hair was sent to factories to be turned into brushes and brooms, as well as to a facility for processing salvaged materials at Straubing in Bavaria.[116] One inmate at Treblinka said that he had been told the hair would be used to fill mattresses used by German women.[117]

The gold bullion, coins, gold taken from teeth, silver bars, foreign currency and jewels taken from the Jewish inmates in the four Reinhard camps that Höfle oversaw were transported by train back to Berlin, where the SS had made a deal with the Reichsbank. The gold and silver were melted down both in Lublin, and back in Berlin by the Degussa chemicals company, which specialised in refining precious metals. The proceeds were credited to two SS accounts at the Reichsbank and Dresdener Bank. The cash funds, and gold, amounting to millions of Reichsmarks, were traded on the 'open' gold market operating in neutral Turkey, and then used to buy weapons, vehicles, industrial supplies and food by the SS. Globočnik, who was promoted to SS-Gruppenführer in November, was in charge of providing the accounting from the extermination camps in Poland, which required frequent exchanges of messages between Poland and Berlin. These were sent by personal courier, not dispatched by radio. The economic activities in Lublin centred not just on the Reinhard camps, but on factories and workshops. Himmler and Obergruppenführer Pohl, the head of the camp administration, required detailed, itemised updates. By spring 1943, the stolen valuables which the SS were accumulating – and in several cases stealing parts of – amounted to tons of precious metals and millions of Reichsmarks' worth of jewellery, valuables and foreign currency. The latter was traded on international markets in Switzerland and Turkey. The approximate exchange rate between the US dollar, the British pound sterling and the Reichsmark in 1939 was as follows: 2.48 Reichsmarks to the dollar, and 12.24 Reichsmarks to the pound. It helps in understanding the following, from 3 February 1943, a representative selection of the valuable material collected from Jews within the four Reinhard camps, summarised by Globočnik and his staff. It included the following:[118]

- 1,775 kilograms of gold, 9,639 kilograms of silver in ingots, and 5 kilograms of platinum;
- 67,000 watches, of which 51,000 were sent for repair and to be given to troops;
- 843,802 Reichsmarks-worth of foreign currencies in the form of gold coins;
- 505,000 US dollars;
- 3,822 English pounds;
- 2,894 gold gentlemen's pocket watches, and 7,313 ladies' gold pocket watches;
- 1,675 gold rings with brilliants and diamonds;
- 49 kilograms of pearls;
- 1,974 gold brooches with brilliants and diamonds;
* 1.4 kilograms of coral.

With nearly two tonnes of gold bullion, ten tonnes of silver and half a million American dollars in cash alone, it was not to be surprising that the SS officers and NCOs decided to take their own unauthorised share of these valuables, especially as the news from Stalingrad showed that perhaps the One Thousand-Year Reich would not be lasting quite that long, and the men would need all the money they could lay their hands on.

CHAPTER IX

FROM POLAND, THE VATICAN AND UKRAINE: THE MATRIX OF DECRYPTION

Bletchley Park, the Vatican City and the North Atlantic, March 1943

At the British intercept station at Beaumanor Hall in Leicestershire, the Morse code of Höfle's message was intercepted immediately, and the transcript of the enciphered signal taken to Bletchley Park on the same day. Nigel de Grey and his analysts noted the use of the words 'Einsatz Reinhard' in the signal, and 'Höfle', the same name as an SS officer which had appeared in a German Police decrypt from Ukraine in summer 1941. Yet they could not work out what the figures represented. Their only cross-reference was the encipherment in the Russian cipher of the Domino system – which Bletchley still sometimes called the German Police Code No.3. The second series of messages, to an SS officer called 'Heim', had been sent in a Domino key and in the Enigma Code Orange I. The signals were clearly important. Yet what did they mean? They were included in the distribution summaries on 15 January 1943.

The Polish government-in-exile had supplied reports all through

1942 based upon the testimony of escapees from camps in the Auschwitz-Birkenau complex, which contained the only mention of gas chambers the British had so far received. There were no first-hand testimonies from the Reinhard camps, which seemed to operate outside of the network mentioned in the signals encrypted in Orange I, such as Auschwitz, Dachau and Mauthausen. Höfle's telegram was archived, as de Grey's teams waited for a follow-up signal which they could use as context for the first one. None came.

It was unclear, meanwhile, who had been responsible for missing out a figure '5' in Höfle's message. As mentioned earlier, only by inserting the figure 5 at the end of the number '71355' could the sum total of 1,274,166 be obtained. It could have been Hermann Höfle with his poor spelling, or Ernst Lerch's SS radio operator in Lublin, the transcribing operator at Beaumanor, or a failure by Bletchley Park. The only clue to the message seemed to be the identifying codename of 'Reinhart', which had also been used in one of the KL messages encrypted in the 'Orange' code that Bletchley had already decrypted.

> . . . on 15 Sept. a car is sent from Auschwitz to LITZMANNSTADT to try out the field kitchens for the Aktion REINHARD (237b42).[119]

The coded network of the camps

Each of the ten camps in the KL network, whose signals Hut 6 was decrypting, identified itself with a three-letter radio call-sign. Dachau was OMB, Auschwitz was OMF, Mauthausen was OMC, Buchenwald was OMD, and so forth. The designation letters originated in part from the use of the Enigma system, on which any letter of the alphabet could be encrypted as any other, except for itself. Thus Auschwitz in the three-letter code was not A, nor

Dachau D, and Mauthausen not M. This differed crucially from the letter designators that SS-Sturmbannführer Höfle used in his reports from Lublin, about the five camps under his operational and parallel control. These used L for Lublin-Majdanek, T for Treblinka, S for Sobibor, C for Chelmno, and B for Belzec.

The monthly updates were then grouped under ZIP headings, with monthly indicators of the letters 'OS' and a number designating their chronological order. As the Second World War ground forward, with the Final Solution crashing onwards in a kind of semi-secret, ever-bloodier entropic parallel, the SS administrative messages from their camp system, the KL network, reflected all the startling urgency and ceaseless bureaucracy of the war, but little of the Holocaust. Had the Germans' programme of mass executions ceased in mid-June 1942 in Ukraine? the British intelligence analysts speculated. This was the last date on which a notice of a mass execution, of 700 Jews, was decrypted. Across army Groups North, Centre and South, the intercepted traffic from the Einsatzkommandos, the SS and the Police had simply ceased to mention mass killings.

For four months in autumn 1941 and spring 1942 there had been the increased euphemisation of large-scale atrocities, with the use of such terms as 'special duties', and 'actions according to the usages of war'. By early 1943, these were no longer used. The message from 'Höfle' obviously referred to camps or a network or actions involving numbers of humans, but precisely what it meant was hard to decipher. Had the Germans stopped killing Jews? Were they doing it somewhere else, with another method than execution, and, most importantly, not reporting the actions on a radio network? However many camp messages the British intercepted and decrypted encoded in Orange I, they did not make any mention of mass killings. Prisoner numbers, deaths by suicide, illness, shooting, the transfer of people – these were the daily signals of work camps, not camps where the SS was killing Jews in large quantities. So where, thought the intelligence analysts, were they doing this?

The contents of the concentration camp messages decrypted from Orange I were set against the flailing losses and swift, harsh victories of the Waffen-SS, overlaid with a predictable, repetitive German order, bureaucracy and respect for protocol. They were the electronic administrative messages from a genocide, and a nation at total war with half the world. In October 1942, said one message, at Sachsenhausen Camp north of Berlin a visiting labour commission came to carry out an inspection. This was a form of German wartime trade union that came to assess whether the camp guards and civilian staff had the requisite working conditions. A signal picked up by the British intercept station at Beaumanor in Leicestershire, and then decrypted by Hut 6, showed the SS concerns about this visit, of how they were trying to hide the conditions in concentration camps from their own administrative officials.

> Some light on conditions in concentration camps is shown by the instruction that a visiting labour commission is not to be shown either 'special quarters', or, if it can be avoided, 'prisoners shot when escaping'.[120]

Meanwhile, the numbers of confirmed inmates in Buchenwald at the beginning of September was 9,888, and at the end, 10,075. During this month 183 prisoners, referred to in one signal as 'anti-social, political, criminal, homos, Poles, Jews, Russians, civilians' had died a 'natural' death.[121] The daily camp rosters in other parts of the messages showed the numbers of prisoners who on certain dates and days had not died a natural death.

In one of the camps of Auschwitz, the number of inmates

dropped from 22,355 on 1 September 1942, to 17,365 on 30 September, and then to 16,966 on 20 October. Among these the number of Jews fell from 11,837 on 1 September to 6,475 on 22 September – these were counted, and registered inmates, and 5,000 disappeared, died, or departed unexplainedly, and as the signal says, it was not always clear exactly how or why. [122] The fog of disinformation was palpable in some of the messages. Prisoners, particularly those who were even remotely capable of working, and those who had some residual trade skills, were constantly being transferred between camps in the KL system. Certain SS camp commanders were almost obsessive in their desire to record, document and transmit the daily ebb-and-flow of their operation. Nobody, but nobody in the SS hierarchy wanted to be caught out by Berlin: every day in every message there was mention of camp guards being needed for transfer to the Russian Front. Within the daily HOR-HUG reports (as Hut 6 still called the signals, after the two oft-repeating trigraphs), the shape of the forced labour plan of the SS Main Economic and Administrative Office was clear. There was a constant revolving transfer of prisoners, both Jews and non-Jews, between ten different camp systems, to be used for forced labour, until they died or were murdered. The interactions between other camp commanders, such as those from other camps like Chelmno, Treblinka and Sobibor, were not mentioned in the message exchange between camp complexes like Dachau and Auschwitz and Mauthausen. These, with their dozens of sub-camps, comprised a mixture of forced labour, manufacturing work and military instruction.

Some of the concentration camps, Bletchley learnt, were also being used as training centres for SS men, normally those from ethnic German Volksdeutsche communities, Germans who had lived outside their own national territory, in the Balkans or Poland or Hungary. These were the same men who had worked under

Hermann Höfle in Poland in 1939 and 1940, and now came to the camps to be trained before moving to the front with SS divisions which were in action.

'A considerable number of Volksdeutsche from Bosnia are introduced in mid-November [said the radio section from Auschwitz-1]. Apparently as concentration camp guards, and the utmost economy is to be observed in arming them.[123]

The Bosnian SS soldiers were, however, given rifles, and then returned to fight with the 7th SS Volunteer Mountain Division 'Prinz Eugen' in Yugoslavia. As they departed, thousands of Jews at the same time arrived near Auschwitz to start work in the IG Farben synthetic rubber plant, two miles away. Meanwhile the camp of Niederhagen, a satellite camp of Sachsenhausen, sat at the foot of a hill near the north-western German town of Büren. In 1941, the first prisoners in the small camp were Jewish slave labourers, who were repairing parts of the medieval castle of Wewelsburg. In the thousand-year scheme of the Third Reich, Himmler saw this local medieval fortress as being a focal point of the coming Nazi empire, and so wanted to restore it. The Jews died doing the job, and then a crematorium was built at the camp, after which it was designated as a site specifically to be used for executions.

On 21st October the camp asked for a lorry to take corpses to Bochum, as the crematoria at Bielefeld and Dortmund were too hard-pressed to take any more.[124]

New camps for Jews were being set up in the General Government by December 1942, as the SS looked forward to deporting more French, Greek, Danish and Czech Jews; typhus roared through Auschwitz, while the SS guards who were not hit by it were being selected for transfer to the Russian front for a new offensive. The guards spent a lot of time trying to avoid duty in the camps, being absent, sick, on leave, on courses, and on various occasions committing suicide. On the 7 December 1942, there were 754 guards in Buchenwald, of whom 485 had managed not to be physically in the camp, on duty, at all, during the month.

Training at a concentration camp preceded SS service in Russia, Ukraine, or Byelorussia, especially for the Volksdeutsche recruits, and the men knew that if they were going to slip sideways inside the system before they were transferred to a slit trench, under fire from a human-wave Red Army assault, they had to do it while in training at one of the camps. The other fear, besides being transferred into battle against the Russians, was that their erstwhile colleagues in SS combat units sometimes looked down on many occasions with violent contempt on the former concentration camp guards, and made their lives in their front-line units even more difficult than normal.

By the end of December 1942, large numbers of Jews were arriving and departing in the different camps every day. And each week, the bureaucratic mill in Berlin was asking for numbers, for progress, for news, for updates. On 10 December, the central camp headquarters at Auschwitz was requested to provide the numbers of Russian inmates, POWs, civilian workers, men, women, returns of guards present, escaped prisoners, prisoners who had been shot trying to escape, prisoners who had died in other ways while trying to escape, prisoners in protective custody, and even the number of prisoners who had entered the camp in question since 1933. The administration of mass death, of mass slave labour, this constant accounting and documentation of a vast criminal industry produced a huge amount of information transmitted by coded radio links by SS staff, none of whom wanted to be seen to make mistakes. Because the results of that were too often a train trip westwards back to Berlin to face Himmler or one of his staff, or a train trip east to face the Russians.

The numbers in these signals were sub-divided into Jews, and non-Jews, and each nationality of Jews, so a constant tally of them could be kept, in order that the RSHA in Berlin could itself keep track of its progress in solving and answering the 'final solution to the Jewish question'. And the information broadcast from the midst of this blizzard of reporting, of numbers and figures, gave Allied intercept stations a large volume of electronic knowledge which they could potentially intercept and decrypt. And this in turn gave the cryptanalysts of Hut 6 a vast choice of material to decipher, leading to their careful, painstaking construction of the wider picture.

In the camp signals, the mundane, colour detail of daily life and national difference sometimes intervenes: in December 1942, some Dutch deportees, who had previously been described as preferable to Italian POWs in terms of suitability for labour, were now described as 'unwilling, idle, and addicted to sabotage and desertion'.[125]

SS Div. Wiking is still without large amount of supplies requested in September and October. (324d16/17). SS. Kav. Div. repeats request that 600 pairs of felt boots be dropped. This supply by air had been refused by Heeresgruppe Mitte (324d33) cf: 325d43. Oberfuehrer MARTIN, Nachschub Kommandantur Russland Mitte, says the Lettenkomp. Cannot go on duty in present weather conditions owing to lack of footgear and asks for 180 pairs of boots urgently (352d54).??? The falling temperature also causes MARTIN to ask SS. RHA to release 100 O.T stoves as it is no longer possible to hear the huts with the small stoves for dugouts. (360d24)[126]

SS-Obersturmbannführer Arthur Liebehenschel, from the SS Main Economic and Administrative Office, which included the former Concentration Camps Directorate, sent a technical question to both the commanders of Flossenburg and Mauthausen. What was the best way to re-use the fat collected from sewage water from the SS barracks? Hinzert camp, near the border with Luxembourg, meanwhile reported that in December 1942 it had collected two kilograms of human hair. [127] The messages were encrypted in the Orange encipherment range, and others, while the Waffen-SS messages enciphered in Orange II drifted in and out of what Bletchley's teams were breaking. In December, SS divisions were being reformed and re-equipped in France. In the Caucasus the Wiking Division continued to fight, short of clothing and equipment. By 28 February 1943, the Leibstandarte SS Adolf Hitler Division was reported as being 'completely disorganised' on the Russian Front. Wiking had lost most of its tanks. Behind the concentration camp network's veneer of constant bureaucratic order, Germany was fighting a desperate war.

The manpower of slave labour needed to maintain this was being exploited to its maximum within the camps. Typhus hit Dachau again in January 1943, while in the granite quarries and sprawling hut complexes at Mauthausen, the camp's commandant complained that the prisoners he had were not capable of carrying out the back-breaking work. Some of them were 'unfit, eighty years old, and need their physique building up'.[128] And within these bureaucratic reports of forced labour, deaths and disease, there was, as noted previously, mention of Aktion Reinhard just once. The Einsatzgruppen Reinhard were in contact with Auschwitz with a repeated logistical request, this time for field-kitchens. While the mystifying signals in Code Orange continued, some information about the ongoing persecution of Jews, and the operations within the concentration camp system was now also reaching the British government through the Polish government-in-exile, and from crucial messages decrypted at Bletchley Park from other sources.

The coded signals from the Vatican: Red, Yellow, Green and Purple

On 9 March 1943 in Rome, the Japanese special envoy to the Vatican wrote a message to his foreign ministry in Tokyo. Japan and the Holy See had established relations in 1942, and Ken Harada was the first Japanese diplomatic representative appointed to the Vatican. In turn, the Italian archbishop Paolo Murella had been appointed the apostolic delegate, or papal nuncio, to Japan. While Harada constituted Tokyo's diplomatic mission to the Vatican, there was a separate Japanese embassy in Rome, which acted as the formal governmental liaison between Emperor Hirohito and Benito Mussolini. In the first week of March, the Archbishop of New York, Francis Joseph Spellman, had been visiting both Rome and the Vatican while on a four-month-long trip to Europe, North Africa and the Middle East. He was travelling as the personal envoy of President Roosevelt, who thought that as a Catholic Archbishop he would have easier and greater access than a formally accredited diplomat from a country then at war with Germany, Japan, Italy and their allies. It helped that Spellman was also a friend of Eugenio Pacelli, Pope Pius XII, since the time when the two men had known each other in Germany in the late 1920s, while the latter was serving as the apostolic delegate to Berlin.

Like other diplomats accredited to the Holy See, Ken Harada was working hard to find out what the Pope and Spellman had been discussing during a series of private meetings. One of the officials with whom the Japanese diplomat had spoken was Fritz Menhausen. He was one of the counsellors of the German embassy to the Holy See, and along with his foreign ministry in Berlin, had tried to limit the dissemination in Germany of papal encyclicals deemed critical of Hitler and Mussolini. In Francis Spellman he had an adversary: in 1931, the American prelate had been based in Rome, when the then-Pope Pius XI had released an encyclical entitled 'Non abbiamo bisogno' ('We do not need)', which condemned Mussolini and Italian Fascism's 'pagan worship of the state'. Spellman had smuggled a copy of the document out to France and Spain hidden in his luggage, and given it to journalists. Harada signalled his first impressions of Spellman's visit to Rome back to his foreign minister in one of his messages on 9 March 1943:

I send for your reference the following information given to a member of my staff by MENSHAUSEN, the German counsellor . . . owing to the strict secrecy observed with regard to Spellman's mission, and particularly about his conversations with the Pope, it was impossible to get information from a responsible quarter, but his own opinion was that the chief object was propaganda . . .[129]

With this caveat in mind, Harada then details Menshausen's opinions. The German thinks the Americans are making a gesture towards the Catholics of the United States and South America by trying to 'camouflage' the relationship of alliance with Soviet Russia. Spellman reportedly tried to persuade the Pontiff and other officials that after the war there was no danger of communism. A Vatican official had told Menshausen that Americans clearly had 'very simple ideas about Communism'. The two had probably discussed the topic of Allied bombing, which gave the Vatican a lot of anxiety, as well as that of finance. The contributions of American Catholics made up half of the whole world's contributions to the Vatican, but owing to the war, it had been impossible to physically transfer the funds (to the Vatican Bank). Menshausen added to Harada that there was no need to pay much importance to these conversations between the Pope and the American archbishop, and he had signalled as much back to Berlin.

Once he had finished typing out the message, Harada then enciphered it in his Grade 1 Cypher, and sent it. He copied it to the Japanese ambassadors in both Berlin and Madrid, and noted that he had passed on the contents to the ambassador in Rome as well. He took it to the signals office at the embassy building, where a signals clerk transmitted it into the ether, in the Japanese Wabun form of Morse code. In classical Morse, dots and dashes are used to represent Latin letters and numbers, while in Wabun each symbol represents a Japanese 'kana' or syllabary. Summer time in Rome is six hours ahead of Washington DC, seven hours behind Tokyo, while the exigencies of different time zones in wartime meant the Italian capital and Buckinghamshire were the same time that day. By the time the signal was being decrypted in Japan, it had already been intercepted in both the United States and Great Britain, and was on its way for decryption to Hut 7 at Bletchley Park, and to OP-20-G at their new headquarters in a commandeered girls' school at Mount Vernon, Washington DC.

The Japanese ambassador in Berlin, Baron Hiroshi Oshima, was still unaware that the Americans and British were decrypting his government's diplomatic signals encoded in the Purple cipher. His friendship and professional relationship with both Hitler and Ribbentrop had deepened, and the Third Reich's foreign minister now gave him daily intelligence summaries which he signalled to Tokyo. The time difference, and the often slow and disrupted telephone and telex and radio connections between Germany and Japan sometimes meant that the Americans at OP-G-20 read his signals before his colleagues at the foreign ministry in Japan. Oshima's information was precise and normally correct: on 6 June the previous year, for instance, he had signalled to Tokyo that

Operation Barbarossa would begin on 22 June. His thinking on how to fight the war and the best way to treat their mutual enemies matched the Germans. He and Hitler had agreed the previous year that Allied merchant seamen whose ships were torpedoed by U-boats should be taken prisoner if possible, and if not, shot while in the water. In this way, the Germans could reduce the number of valuable seamen, whose training all required time and money, available for duty in the Atlantic. On 10 March Oshima received the message, copied from Ken Harada in Rome, about the visit of Cardinal Spellman.

On the same day, the Turkish Ambassador to Rome also sent a message to his foreign minister in Ankara, with some personal reflections and information he had gathered about the American visit. Turkey was still a neutral country at this point, and would remain so until February 1945, when it entered the war on the side of the Allies.

> The visit of the Archbishop of New York to the Vatican [wrote Huseyin Ragip Baydur] has given rise to a number of rumours about peace overtures. It has even been (reported?) that the American (Catholic?) had a conversation in Rome with Foreign Minister RIBBENTROP. According to the inquiries which have been made, he said in his signal, its decryption transcribed by Bletchley, this is (quite?) incorrect. Some absences in the transcription occurred because some words had not been intercepted fully – these the British put in brackets with question marks. While he was in the Vatican it was suggested to Spellman that a Soviet victory could give rise to an extension of Bolshevism in EUROPE. Spellman is reported to have replied that he did not see any such danger, and even if there were, there (? would be) a remedy. This reply did not please the Vatican officials: one of them, indeed,

said 'SPELLMAN talks not like a (? Catholic) but like an American national . . .'[130]

The ambassador then says that he gathered, from his sources, that the Pope wanted to make the US feel more accommodating [the phrase in the transcribed decrypted signal, with a questioned decrypt, appears as '(?soften) America' in regard] to the Axis, and to try to persuade them not to send aid to Russia. He also felt that the Pope would naturally want to maintain links between himself and an individual (Spellman) who might assist in any forthcoming peace overtures.

This time it was the turn of the ATS 'Listeners' at Beaumanor alone to intercept the signal; because of the time difference, they managed this an hour earlier than when it was picked up by the Turkish military signals intercept station in Ankara. It was not just diplomatic messages from ambassadors to the Vatican that Nigel de Grey's teams could now decrypt: following the initial efforts to break into the codes of the Holy See since January 1942, the diplomatic decryption staff in Hut 6 could now read enciphered messages from the Vatican's network of apostolic delegates and nuncios, sent to and from Luigi Maglione, the Cardinal Secretary of State at the Holy See. By spring 1943 the Vatican had delegates and nuncios in Rome, Vichy France, Berlin, Budapest, Ankara, Berne, Bratislava, Zagreb, Bucharest, London, Washington and Ankara. The delegate in the last was Archbishop Angelo Roncalli, who served as the Vaticans's representative for both Greece and Turkey. These men were in signals contact with each other, and Rome, on a daily basis, all using the same two ciphers, KIC-Yellow and Green. The Vatican's signals protocols specified they should change the different keys they used with each message, but because the archbishops frequently repeated exactly the same messages to each other on the same day in the same key, this meant de Grey's cryptanalysts had a variety of 'depth', or repetitions in messages, which gave them cribs into that day's Vatican key.

Twelve people sending and receiving twelve repetitive message chains over the course of three days, focused on one specific subject to and from one recipient – Cardinal Maglione – gave Hut 6 a large amount of material to work with. As previously written, the Italian Military Intelligence service, SIM, and the German foreign ministry signals intelligence agency, Pers-Z, were both in possession of some of the Holy See's codebooks so Bletchley Park could monitor any information crossover that 'somersaulted' from German and Italian diplomatic messages concerning the Vatican. In the week before the visit of Cardinal Spellman to Rome, British intercept stations and cryptanalysts picked up, and decrypted, a chain of messages to and from the Holy See concerning the urgent fate of some 20,000 Jews in Slovakia. It was full of 'cribs'. There were the same repeated words and numbers in each message which gave the British cryptanalysts several entry points into it, such as Poland, Palestine, Slovakia, Jews, 2,000, deportation, Turkey.

Slovakia, as previously written, was a client state of Nazi Germany, and had declared autonomy from Czech territory when the Germans occupied the Sudetenland in 1938; the nationalist Slovak People's Party took power, under its leader President Jozef Tiso. The party, known as the HSL, saw Jews, Hungarians, Czechs, Romani as an anti-Slovak problem, and along with banning newspapers and opposition parties, the HSL distributed anti-Semitic literature, especially from 1938 onwards when thousands of Austrian Jews arrived on Slovak territory as refugees. The party had its own paramilitary group too: the Hlinka Guard. It had helped the Germans deport 58,000 of Slovakia's estimated 90,000 Jews in spring 1942, even paying the SS 500 reichsmarks per person for the train journeys, the costs of 're-settlement'.

The Slovak Jews were 'resettled' predominantly in Auschwitz, while some were deported to Poland, coming under the authority of Hermann Höfle in Lublin. Only a few hundred survived. By March 1943 there were about 20,000–25,000 Jews left on Slovak territory. The Vatican's delegates in at least five countries set out to help them escape deportation.

On 6 March, the chargé d'affaires at the apostolic delegation in Bratislava tried to seek some form of diplomatic means to prevent the arrest and deportation of the remaining Jews, who included an estimated 2,000 young children. He wrote a message to Maglione at the Vatican on the 11th, saying that deportation was likely.[131] Meanwhile the delegate of the Jewish Agency in Istanbul, Haim Barlas, and the treasurer of the Jewish Agency for Palestine, Eliezer Kaplan, wrote and possibly spoke to Archbishop Roncalli on 11 and 13 March, asking him to try to obtain an intervention by the Pope, and that he should try to speak to, and if necessary against, Jozef Tiso and the HSL government. The Jewish Agency had obtained immigration certificates under the British quota system, and the Turkish government would allow them – in principle – to transit through Turkey to Palestine. Roncalli signalled the Holy See on the 13th, from the Turkish apostolic delegation in Beyoglu, on the European side of the Golden Horn in Istanbul. His message was intercepted, probably at Beaumanor, and the transcription delivered to de Grey's cryptanalysts. Once the plain text was revealed, it was then translated, and by spring 1943 de Grey and his colleagues had this process very precisely established, regardless of the language of the original message. It was the job of men and women at Bletchley Park on the so-called 'Z-Watch':

> A wire tray comes in, laden with decrypts in the form of sheets covered with tapes carrying the printed German (or Italian) text in five-letter groups like those in the original cipher text.

The sorter, often Number 2 of the group, glances at them, quickly identifies those most important for the Admiralty, and hands them to Number 3; who rapidly writes out the German text in word-lengths, staples it to the decrypt , hands it to Number 1; who translates it into English, stamps it with a number (e.g. ZTPG/4793), and passes it to a WAAF girl who teleprints it to the Admiralty, adding the initials of Number 1, e.g. WGE.[132]

The message from Turkey read as follows:

From: Apostolic Delegate, BEYOGLU
To: Cardinal Secretary of State . . .
The Jewish Agency in Palestine through its representative KAPLAN communicates as follows: 'About 20,000 Jews in SLOVAKIA run the risk of being deported to POLAND at the end of March. We supplicate the Holy Father's intervention with the Slovak government to avert the measure (group corrupt)[xiv] or else to obtain that two thousand Jewish children may emigrate to PALESTINE in conformity with the British assurance and may be permitted to cross TURKEY. We would ask (group corrupt) the Slovak government and in due course the Hungarian government to allow the children to stay temporarily during the indispensable preparations. The Jewish agency will provide everything. The need for intervention is urgent.'[133]

Haim Barlas had, in the meantime, sent a similar message to the Apostolic Delegate in the United States, Cardinal Giovanni

---

xiv 'Group corrupt' means that the intercept radio clerk has not been able to make out all the letters or words in a group of words, meaning that the decryption is slightly unclear.

Cicognani. Reportedly ambivalent about the suitability of Palestine as a Jewish homeland, Cicognani did, however, take a strong position about the Jews of Slovakia. He asked for the Holy See to issue a *démarche*, or statement, a public appeal against the persecution of the Jews in Poland. Maglione demurred. The situation in Slovakia was made more difficult for the Vatican because the nationalist Prime Minister Jozef Tiso was not just himself a Catholic, but also a priest.

'The trouble is that the president of Slovakia is a priest,' wrote Cardinal Domenico Tardini. 'That the Holy See cannot manage to get Hitler to do what he should, everybody understands. But that they cannot hold back one priest – who can understand that?'[134]

The Apostolic Delegate in London was William Godfrey, the Archbishop of Westminster, the first papal representative to England since the Reformation. He also acted as chargé d'affaires for the Vatican to the Polish government-in-exile in London: he was thus well placed and well-connected to act on behalf of the Vatican in efforts to save some of Europe's Jews. He signalled Cardinal Maglione on 13 March.

> From: Apostolic Delegate, LONDON
> To: Cardinal Secretary of State, Vatican.
> The ALIYAH organisation for assisting the immigration of Jewish children (states?) that the British government will give permission for Jewish children from all European countries to go to PALESTINE, and implores the help of the Holy See if possible in obtaining visas.[135]

He enciphered the signal in that day's key, in either the KI Yellow or Green ciphers, almost certainly the latter, and had the message sent to Rome by telex from the Catholic Church's headquarters in Westminster. Before the message had arrived in the Vatican City it was intercepted in Britain, and sent for decryption by some of Archbishop Godrey's fellow countrymen.

Cardinal Tardini then noted that the situation in Slovakia was one where the religious concept of humanity was involved, and violated divine right and natural law, and as the Germans' operations to deport and kill the Jews violated humanity, then the Vatican could intervene. Slovakian bishops had already issued a pastoral letter defending the rights of Jews. Cardinal Maglione then made a verbal protest to the Slovakian ambassador to the Vatican, Charles Sidor, imploring him 'not to proceed with deportations of people of the so-called Jewish race'.[136]

On 4 May Maglione sent a message to Roncalli that the Vatican had repeatedly intervened and protested (via the ambassador) on behalf of Slovakia's Jews to the Prime Minister Vojtech Tuka. The deportation convoys of the final Jews were then delayed and postponed, for the time being at least.

Breaking back into Shark, and the international matrix of decryption

The decryption of the diplomatic codes of the Vatican now formed part of an interlinked, international matrix of decipherment, involving Japanese, Turkish, Italian, British, American, German, Finnish, Swiss, Hungarian and Romanian ciphers, as well as cryptanalysts from Britain, the United States and Italy. While the Vatican and its Catholic emissaries had been working on behalf of the Slovakian Jews, in Britain the Church of England had condemned the persecution of Europe's Jews.

In March 1943, the Archbishop of Canterbury, William Temple, gave a passionate speech to the House of Lords in London: Britain, he urged, had to take immediate action to save Europe's Jews. He presented evidence about what was happening from Britain, Poland,

Germany and Sweden, some of it based on de Grey's cryptanalysis that had been presented to him in a series of reports. We're doing as much as we can, rebuffed one of Churchill's ministers, and accepting as many Jewish refugees as the country can handle. As per the Home Office's recommendations in December, this now amounted to no more than one or two thousand extra to the Jews already in Britain.

Temple urged that the British government had to take some kind of action, instantly, without procrastination; as the head of the Church of England, he was the most senior clergyman in England.

We know that Hitler near the beginning of the war declared that this war must lead to the extermination of either the Jewish people or the German people, and it should not be the Germans. He is now putting that threat into effect, and we are no doubt to a very large extent powerless to stop him. We are told that the only real solution is rapid victory. No doubt it is true that if we could win the war in the course of a few weeks, we could still deliver multitudes of those who are now doomed to death.

Temple then proceeded to summarise what had taken place since the United Nations Declaration was issued in December the preceding year:

My chief protest is against procrastination of any kind. It was three months ago that the solemn Declaration of the United Nations was made, and we are now confronted with a proposal for an exploratory conference in Ottawa. That sounds as if it involves much more delay: it took five weeks from December 17th for our government to approach the United States, and then six weeks for the Government of the United States to reply, and when they did reply they suggested a meeting of representatives of the government for preliminary exploration.

The Jews are being slaughtered at the rate of tens of thousands a day on many days, but there is a proposal for a preliminary exploration to be made . . . my Lords, let us at least urge that when the conference meets, it should meet not only for exploration, but for decision. We know that what we can do is small compared with the magnitude of the problem, but we cannot rest so long as there is any sense among us that we are not doing all that might be done.[137]

In his speech, Temple made reference to the sources of some of his information, which in turn illustrate how part of the flow of human intelligence about the Holocaust was then reaching London. He said that a recent BBC report had mentioned that Jews in Bohemia and Moravia had their ration cards removed, were forbidden to buy unrationed food, and so were effectively being sentenced to death. The World Jewish Congress in London had passed reports to Temple from Warsaw, which said that in one district of Poland alone, 6,000 Jews were being killed every day. The Board of Deputies of British Jews gave him the report that came from Poland, via Istanbul, which said that the complete extermination of the ghettos in Poland was going on, and that 'in accordance' with this information only 250,000 Jews remained in Poland. Information from Stockholm told him that the Romanian government had agreed to deport 60,000 Jews to Poland. The World Jewish Congress in London had also received a cable saying that between 26 February and 2 March 1943, 15,000 Jews from Berlin were taken away in trucks.[138]

Having described the reports that had reached him, Temple then made a strong, closely argued further statement about the need for Britain's embassies abroad to issue more visas, more compassionately, faster, to many more Jews trying to flee Europe. He also urged that the British government's restrictions on immigration to Mandated Palestine either be relaxed, or lifted completely. As Archbishop of Canterbury, Temple would not, of course, have been on the strictly controlled distribution list for the Bletchley Park Code Orange, and German Police decrypts, but he was a principal conduit of other information to the British Houses of Parliament, and British government ministers.

But one of the ministers in Churchill's War Cabinet disagreed with parts of what Temple had said. Robert Gascoyne-Cecil, Viscount Cranbourne, was the Leader of the House of Lords in 1943, and he insisted that the question of the reception of Jewish refugees was being dealt with by an about-to-be-formed inter-governmental refugee committee, which the governments of Great Britain and the United States had said they would establish when they convened at a conference in Bermuda in April. His reply confirmed Temple's fears.

As Temple urged stronger, faster action by the British government, Nigel de Grey was writing an internal summary of what the Government Code and Cypher School had achieved to date. In the Battle of the Atlantic, Bletchley Park had realised a reassuring success: they had managed to break back into the German naval Enigma cipher codenamed Shark, after eleven desperate months where they were 'locked out' of it. The sudden inability to read the U-boat signals, and thus provide the Admiralty with information about the wolf packs' whereabouts, had a direct impact on the tonnage of merchant shipping sunk:

GC&CS first broke into naval Enigma in March 1941, and by December Bletchley had read some 25,000 naval messages. Shipping losses between March and June 1941 were around 282,000 tons, and then 120,000 from July to December. When Bletchley went 'blind to Shark', the Germans damaged, sank or captured 1,179 ships. In the following nine months, when Shark was compromised again, this figure dropped to 556. During the 'blind' period, the Admiralty made their feelings apparent, the Admiralty's Operational Intelligence Centre sending a memorandum to Bletchley Park stating that the Battle of the Atlantic was 'the one campaign which Bletchley Park are not influencing to any marked extent – and it is the only one in which the war can be lost unless BP do help.'[139]

Shaun Wylie, a Bletchley Park cryptanalyst in Hut 8, described their feelings of frustration:

> We were dismayed when the fourth wheel [the fourth rotor on the naval Enigma] appeared. We knew it was coming. But it was a grim time. We were very much frustrated, the things we hoped to use went bad on us. We realised that our work meant lives ... We did what we could, of course, and we got on with what there was but we kept an eye out for any possibility on Shark that might present itself. There was a lot of pressure and we were trying all we could but we didn't have many opportunities.'[140]

'Now it happens,' de Grey then wrote in his summary, 'that Bletchley Park has been successful – so successful that it has supplied information on every conceivable subject from the movement of a single mine sweeper to the strategy of a campaign and the Christian name of a wireless operator to the introduction of a secret weapon.'

There was no mention in his memo of Domino, or the Final Solution.[141]

CHAPTER X

GETTING AWAY WITH MURDER?

Lublin, Warsaw and Berlin, April–November 1943

On 7 April 1943, Adolf Hitler and Benito Mussolini held a meeting in the city of Salzburg. The two Axis leaders tried to bolster Mussolini's optimism and sense of purpose; the Italian dictator knew that an Allied invasion of Sicily and the Italian mainland was only a matter of months away. That same day American and British forces had linked up in North Africa, near Gafsa in Tunisia. The US II Corps had advanced from the east, following their amphibious landings on Operation Torch the previous November. The British Eighth Army had pushed westwards from El Alamein, while the Luftwaffe launched an operation to rescue German troops trapped in between the two approaching armies. On the Eastern Front, following the capitulation at Stalingrad, the Germans in Army Group Centre had briefly forced back the Red Army at the Third Battle of Kharkov, as both sides prepared for a brutal and vast showdown of armour on the summer plains of central Ukraine. In Operation Watchtower, American Marines had just taken and held the key territory of Guadalcanal in the Solomon Islands, the most significant US land victory to date in their war against Imperial Japan. It marked the decisive transition from defensive to offensive operations in the Allies' war in the Pacific.

Hermann Höfle was nowhere near his home city of Salzburg when the two Axis leaders met. He was seven hundred miles to the north-east, on duty as the second-in-command of SS and German police forces deployed to the Warsaw Ghetto, where the remaining 65,000 Jews who had escaped deportation to Treblinka were now launching an armed uprising. Himmler had ordered that the ghetto, and its occupants, should be eradicated. Yet just before the operation, on 13 April the Reichssender broadcasting network in Berlin made a dramatic announcement. In an international broadcast, it said that Wehrmacht soldiers near Smolensk had discovered a vast mass grave in the forest of Katyn.

'A ditch . . . twenty-eight metres long and sixteen metres wide, in which the bodies of three thousand Polish officers were piled up in twelve layers,'[142] said the broadcast.

German radio and newspapers then reported that this was only the first part of the exhumation of the bodies of an estimated 12,000 Polish officers whom the Russian NKVD had executed after capturing them in March and April 1940. Every serviceman on the Eastern Front could have heard the news, as Propaganda Minister Joseph Goebbels took maximum advantage of it to highlight the horrors of Soviet Bolshevism. It came just as the war appeared to be turning against Nazi Germany. The Allies and the United Nations had condemned the persecution of the Jews, while newspapers and radio stations across the free world along with the Polish government-in-exile kept focusing strident attention on the German massacres of Jews. The latest nail hammered into the coffin appeared to be the deportations from the Warsaw Ghetto, and the uprising that had now exploded in its ruins. The discovery in the dark pine woods at Katyn was of surprise, macabre benefit to the Nazi Party, and its ministers and SS officials intended to maximise its propaganda potential.

Höfle had left his wife and four children behind in Lublin, and with a group of other SS officers and NCOs had taken his steel helmet and MP 40 machine-pistol and driven north-west to Warsaw. The ghetto was blazing, the smoke and flames of burning urban combat rising into the spring sky. 60,000 Poles and Polish Jews, men, women, children, who refused to be deported to their deaths in cattle cars were making a last stand against the SS. For Poland, for freedom and as a monumental and explosive statement against the world, the Western Allies and Russia included, who would not come to their assistance. Dug in to bunkers hollowed out under the cobbles, filling Molotov cocktails in the sewers, knee-deep in stinking water, poised high in the ruins of apartment blocks with Mauser rifles taken from German soldiers they had already killed. The SS went in, backed up by Order Police battalions and Trawniki auxiliaries. Except this time they found a tougher enemy, harder fighting, real combat, very different from emptying villages and enclaves of old people, women and children with rifle butts and whips. The Poles and the Jews fought to the death, and by the end of the first week of fighting, Hermann Höfle, and his SS colleagues, knew they would have to burn or bomb them out, and destroy the whole city. At the beginning of the operation, the Higher SS and Police Leader for the Warsaw Zone had led the fight. SS-Brigadeführer Ferdinand von Sammern-Frankenegg was a fellow Austrian, Höfle knew, an old-schooler, a member of a duelling fraternity, who had fought in the trenches of the Western Front. Yet by 19 April, when the first week of fighting failed to dislodge the defenders, Himmler removed him from command and then court-martialled him on the 24th. His offence? Incompetence. Defending Jews. Himmler and his terrifying deputy in the SS Personnel department,

Maximilian von Herff, banished the disgraced Austrian brigadier to fight partisans in Croatia, a guerrilla war they considered of no real strategic importance, fought against a foe who were just more subhuman Slavs.

His replacement at the head of the SS operation was a different man entirely. The son of a rigid monarchist police officer father, and a devout Roman Catholic mother who beat him as a child, Jürgen Stroop was wounded in 1914 fighting in France. Following the war, he rejected his strict upbringing, embracing a hardline form of neo-paganism, that was to prove popular with many Nazis, that blamed the failings of Christianity on a Jewish conspiracy to weaken mankind. He rose through the ranks of the SS in the 1930s, meanwhile attending his sect's funerals and marriages with their altars devoted to the worship of the pagan Norse god, Wotan. He felt at home in the SS, and in 1939, like Hermann Höfle, he led a Volksdeutsche self-defence unit in Poland. Decorated for bravery on the Eastern Front in summer 1941, by spring 1943 he was an SS-Gruppenführer. When he arrived in Warsaw the ghetto was on fire, every house burning, the skyline blacked out by smoke and the orange lick of flame, while the defenders scurried desperately through the ruins. The Germans had to destroy each house and apartment building one by one.

Jürgen Stroop was very keenly aware of what had befallen his predecessor, and was earnestly trying to ingratiate himself with Himmler. So on every day of the operation, he sent a detailed and lengthy update back to the supreme SS leader in Poland, SS-Obergruppenführer Friedrich-Wilhelm Krüger in Krakow. He in turn forwarded it to Himmler; Stroop was also preparing a bound album of his operational dispatches, with an embossed leather cover and photographs with captions written in fountain pen to accompany them. Stroop's desire to impress Himmler led him to override any consideration for signals security, and as he was not part of the rank structure of Operation Reinhard, he was not bound by Hermann Höfle's secrecy clause. This despite the fact that the Warsaw uprising was intricately involved with Treblinka, the camp to which the SS were deporting the captured Jews whom they did not execute on the spot. Stroop was not sending his very lengthy daily reports by radio, either, or by using hand-held devices, such as codebooks. He was using the latest piece of technology, which the SS and Wehrmacht now used to communicate between its senior officers in the field, and Hitler, Himmler's and Kaltenbrunner's headquarters in Berlin.

It was an enciphering attachment to a regular teleprinter, called the Lorenz Schlüssel-Zusatz, or 'cipher attachment'. This encrypted the messages before their transmission over radio-teletype, rather than fixed telephone lines, or via radio waves. Messages were encrypted by the sender, then decrypted by the recipient, using a selection of daily keys. It was based on a system named after its inventor, an American telephone research engineer called Gilbert Vernam. He designed the Vernam cipher, a symmetric-key algorithm, where the same key was used to encipher the sent plain text and decipher the text received. With an unenciphered teleprinter, the plain text was typed on a keyboard, the machine converted these letters to a series of dots on a paper tape which was then electronically transmitted down a radio-teletype line as a series of impulses. The recipient's machine took this tape, translated it into normal plain readable text, and printed it out on a paper roll at the top of the machine. If a Lorenz SZ40, 42 or 42A encipherment device was attached to the teleprinter, the message left and arrived enciphered, and the machine deciphered it for the recipient. The Germans considered it much more secure than their hand-held codebook systems, like the Double Square, and Double Transposition, and as secure, if not more so, as the four-rotor Enigma system which had been adopted by the Kriegsmarine in February 1942. The Lorenz SZ encryption system was based on twelve wheels, or rotors, rather than four, which all moved forward in one of four ways after each letter of a message had been enciphered. The number of permutations for the twelve different wheels was sixteen billion billion. It is not surprising the Germans considered it unbreakable. There were also two other variations of enciphered teleprinter that the Germans used less frequently, including the Siemens and Halske. Stroop did not mention in any reports which teleprinter system he used to send his messages to Krakow.

Using this enciphered teleprinter, Jürgen Stroop proceeded to send updates which made repeated mention of the words 'Treblinka' (abbreviated as 'TII'), 'liquidation', 'extermination', 'Jews', 'deportation' and 'evacuations'. Were an Allied codebreaker to be intercepting, listening to and reading the messages, the daily progress of one part of the persecution of the Jews in the ghetto would become readily apparent, as would by extension the nature of operations in the camp or camps to which they were being evacuated. Stroop provided daily updates and reports on what he called a 'third resettlement', which began in April 1943: this was an operation to kill or capture the remaining Jews of Warsaw and deport them to Treblinka or Majdanek. He prefaced his overall report with a few introductory lines, and then gave the daily detailed updates:

The first large resettlement action took place in the period from 22 July to 3 October 1942. In this action 310,322 Jews were removed. In January 1943 a second resettlement action was carried out by which altogether 6,500 Jews were affected. In April 1943 another began . . [143]

. . . The number of Jews forcibly taken out of the buildings and arrested was relatively small during the first few days. It transpired that the Jews had taken to hiding in the sewers and in specially erected dug-outs. Whereas we had assumed during the first days that there were only scattered dug-outs, we learned in the course of the large-scale action that the whole Ghetto was systematically equipped with cellars, dug-outs, and passages. In every case these passages and dug-outs were connected with the sewer system . . .

19th April

When we invaded the Ghetto for the first time, the Jews and the Polish bandits succeeded in repelling the participating units, including tanks and armoured cars, by a well-prepared concentration of fire. When I ordered a second attack, about 0800 hours, I distributed the units, separated from each other by indicated lines, and charged them with combing out the whole of the Ghetto, each unit for a certain part. Although firing commenced again, we now succeeded in combing out the blocks according to plan. The enemy was forced to retire from the roofs and elevated bases to the basements, dug-outs, and sewers. During the large-scale action we succeeded in catching some Jews who had already been evacuated and resettled in Lublin or Treblinka, but had broken out from there and returned to the Ghetto, equipped with arms and ammunition.

Progress of Ghetto Operation on 21st April 1943

Supplementing the report which I made today about 1400 hours by telephone. [When not using the Lorenz cipher system, Stroop used a landline telephone.]

23rd April

During this armed resistance the women belonging to the battle groups were equipped the same as the men; some were members of the Chaluzim movement. Not infrequently, these women fired pistols with both hands. It happened time and again that these women had pistols or hand grenades (Polish 'pineapple' hand grenades) concealed in their underwear up to the last moment to use against the men of the Waffen SS, Police, or Wehrmacht.

The resistance put up by the Jews and bandits could be broken only by relentlessly using all our force and energy by day and night. On 23 April 1918 the Reichsführer SS issued through the higher SS and Police Führer East at Cracow his order to complete the combing out of the Warsaw Ghetto with the greatest severity and relentless tenacity. I therefore decided to destroy the entire Jewish residential area by setting every block on fire, including the blocks of residential buildings near the armament works. One concern after the other was systematically evacuated and subsequently destroyed by fire.

The Jews then emerged from their hiding places and dug-outs in almost every case. Not infrequently, the Jews stayed in the burning buildings until, because of the heat and the fear of being burned alive they preferred to jump down from the upper stories after having thrown mattresses and other upholstered articles into the street from the burning buildings. With their bones broken, they still tried to crawl across the street into blocks of buildings which had not yet been set on fire or were only partly in flames.

Considering that the greater part of the men of the Waffen-SS had only been trained for three to four weeks before being assigned to this action, high credit should be given for the pluck, courage, and devotion to duty which they showed. It must be stated that the Wehrmacht Engineers, too, executed the blowing up of dug-outs, sewers, and concrete buildings with indefatigability and great devotion to duty. Officers and men of the Police, a large part of whom had already been at the front, again excelled by their dashing spirit. Only through the continuous and untiring work of all involved did we succeed in catching a total of 56,065 Jews whose extermination can be proved. To this should be added the number of Jews who lost their lives in explosions or fires but whose numbers could not be ascertained.

The Polish population for the most part approved the measures taken against the Jews. Shortly before the end of the large-scale operation, the Governor issued a special proclamation which he submitted to the undersigned for approval before publication, to the Polish population; in it he informed them of the reasons for destroying the former Jewish Ghetto by mentioning the assassinations carried out lately in the Warsaw area and the mass graves found in Catyn; at the same time they were asked to assist us in our fight against Communist agents and Jews (see enclosed poster). The large-scale action was terminated on 16 May 1943 with the blowing up of the Warsaw synagogue at 2015 hours.

Copy[xv]
Teletype message
From the SS and Police Führer in the District of Warsaw
Warsaw, 23 April 1943.
Ref. No.: I ab/St/Gr-16 07-Journal No. 538/43 secret.
Re: Ghetto Operation.
To: The Higher SS and Police Führer East, SS-Obergruppen-führer and General of Police Krüger or deputy. Cracow
Progress of Ghetto Operation on 23 April 1943. Start: 0700 hours.

---

xv This word just acted as an indicator that a message would follow

Today 3,500 Jews were caught who are to be evacuated from the factories. A total of 19,450 Jews have been caught for resettlement or already evacuated up to today. Of these about 2,500 Jews are still to be loaded. The next train will start on 24 April 1943.

Copy
Teletype message
From: The SS and Police Führer in the District of Warsaw
Warsaw, 25 April 1943
Ref. No. I ab/St/Wdt-16 07-Journal No. 549/43 secret.
Re: Ghetto operation.
To: The Higher SS and Police Führer East, SS-Obergruppen-führer and General of Police Krüger or deputy. Cracow

274 Jews were killed. As in the preceding days, uncounted Jews were buried in blown up dug-outs and, as can be observed time and again, burned with this bag of Jews today. We have, in my opinion, caught a very considerable part of the bandits and lowest elements of the Ghetto. Intervening darkness prevented immediate liquidation. I am going to try to obtain a train for T II [Treblinka II] tomorrow. Otherwise liquidation will be carried out tomorrow. Today also, some armed resistance was encountered; in a dug-out three pistols and some explosives were captured. Furthermore, considerable amounts of paper money, foreign currency, gold coins, and jewellery were seized today.

The Jews still have considerable property. While last night a glare of fire could be seen above the former Ghetto, today one can observe a giant sea of flames. Since we continue to discover great numbers of Jews whenever we search and comb out, the operation will be continued on 26 April 1943. Start:

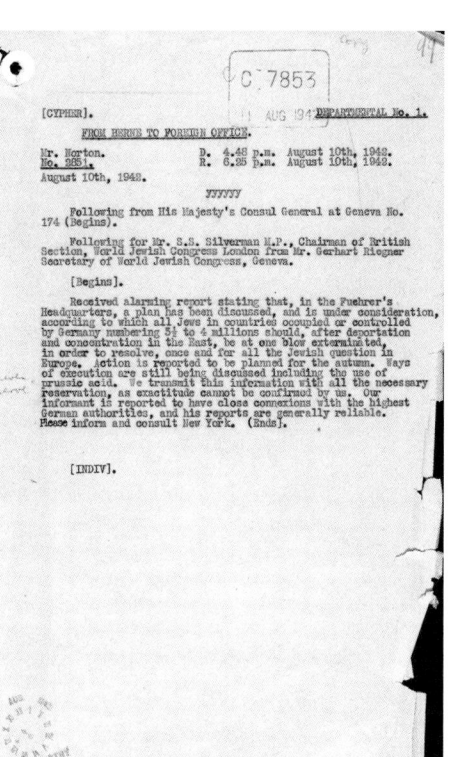

Left: The Riegner Telegram of 10 August 1942. This is the message from the British Consul-General in Geneva to the Foreign Office, with the text of the telegram, outlining the Nazis' plans for the mass extermination of Jews. A Jew who fled Germany for Switzerland, Gerhard Riegner was the secretary of the World Jewish Congress in Geneva, and sent the message to the organisation's London and New York offices. *(© The National Archives [TNA FO 371/30917])*

Below: Bletchley's decrypt of the Höfle Telegram of 11 January 1943, in which the numbers of Jews killed during Operation Reinhard the previous year are listed. The second paragraph (lighter background) gives the number by the initial of each camp: L – Lublin (i.e. Majdanek); B – Belzec; S – Sobibor; T – Treblinka.
(© The National Archives [TNA HW 16/23])

```
                                          GPDD 355a      2.

  12. OMX de OMQ              1000            89 ? ?
      Geheime Reichssache! An das Reichssicherheitshauptamt, zu
      Händen SS Obersturmbannführer EICHMANN, BERLIN ...rest missed..

13/15. OLQ de OMQ             1005            83 234 250
      Geheime Reichssache! An den Befehlshaber der Sicherheitspol.,
      zu Händen SS Obersturmbannführer HEIM, KRAKAU.
      Betr: 14-tägige Meldung Einsatz REINHART.  Bezug: dort.
      Fs. Zugang bis 31.12.42, L 12761,B 0, S 515, T 10335 zusammen
      23611. Stand... 31.12.42, L 24733, B 434508, S 101370,
      T 71355, zusammen 1274166.
      SS und Pol.führer LUBLIN, HOEFLE, Sturmbannführer.

  16. ? de ?                  1010            140
      SS Obersturmführer LOHRENGEL, Willi, befindet sich seit
      20.12.42 bei der Abt. als Zugführer.
      Gez. KORFF, SS Hauptsturmführer und Abt.

17/18. ? de ?                 1030            159 111
      Fs. 10? vom 11.1.43. An Sturmgeschützabt., SS Pz.Gr.Div. T.
      Verladung der Bekleidung erfolgt per Waggon.  Es ist ein
      Begleitkdo. nach hier zu senden, Stärke 2 Mann.  Eintreffen am
      16.1.43 vormittags TWL der Waffen SS, WARSCHAU ..2 groups
      corrupt... Gez. GERLACH, SS Oberscharführer.

  19. Dud.

20/21. OMX de OLG             1100            197 139
      An SS Wirtschaftsverwaltungshauptamt, Chef des Pers.amtes.
      Zu dort. Fs. 9. Jan: SS Oberscharführer PECH sollte, gemäss
      Verfügung vom 27 Nov. 1942, durch 6. Stabsabt. in Marsch
      gesetzt werden. Dies ist bislang nicht geschehen.  Sofortige
      Inmarschsetzung zum SS O.A. Weichsel wird nunmehr von hier
      veranlasst.
      Der Leiter der Verwaltung des SS O.A. Warthe, gez. DITTJEN,
      SS Oberführer.
```

Right: Sir Anthony Eden with Churchill in Paris, February 1945. As Foreign Secretary, Eden chaired the Cabinet Committee on Jewish refugees in December 1942, although 'Jewish' was dropped from the committee's title, and the government decided that discussions could wait until a conference the following spring – in Bermuda.

(© Nixon/Mirrorpix/Getty Images)

Left: Victor Cavendish-Bentinck, photographed long after the war. As chairman of the Joint Intelligence Committee, he regarded reports of the Nazi massacres of Jews as 'products of the Slavic imagination' – despite the evidence from Bletchley Park.

(© Allan Warren/Wikimedia Commons)

Right: Herbert Morrison looking at bomb damage in London, 1944. As Home Secretary, Morrison was opposed to admitting more than 1,000–2,000 Jewish refugees into Britain.

(© Keystone-France/Gamma-Rapho/Getty Images)

Left: Dr William Temple, Archbishop of Canterbury, with Churchill at Downing Street, probably in 1943. Temple argued passionately in the House of Lords and elsewhere that Britain should take immediate action to save Europe's Jews. *(© Print Collector/Getty Images)*

Right: The American industrialist and diplomat Myron C. Taylor, the US envoy to the Holy See in Rome, seen here with his wife in 1941. He alerted the Vatican to the persecution of Jews by the Nazis, offering evidence that included the Riegner Telegram. *(© Fox Photos/Getty Images)*

Left: Don Pirro Scavizzi, the priest who served with an Italian infantry regiment on the Eastern Front, and sent a report documenting German atrocities against Jews and others to the Pope, a personal friend. *(from an unnamed religious pamphlet)*

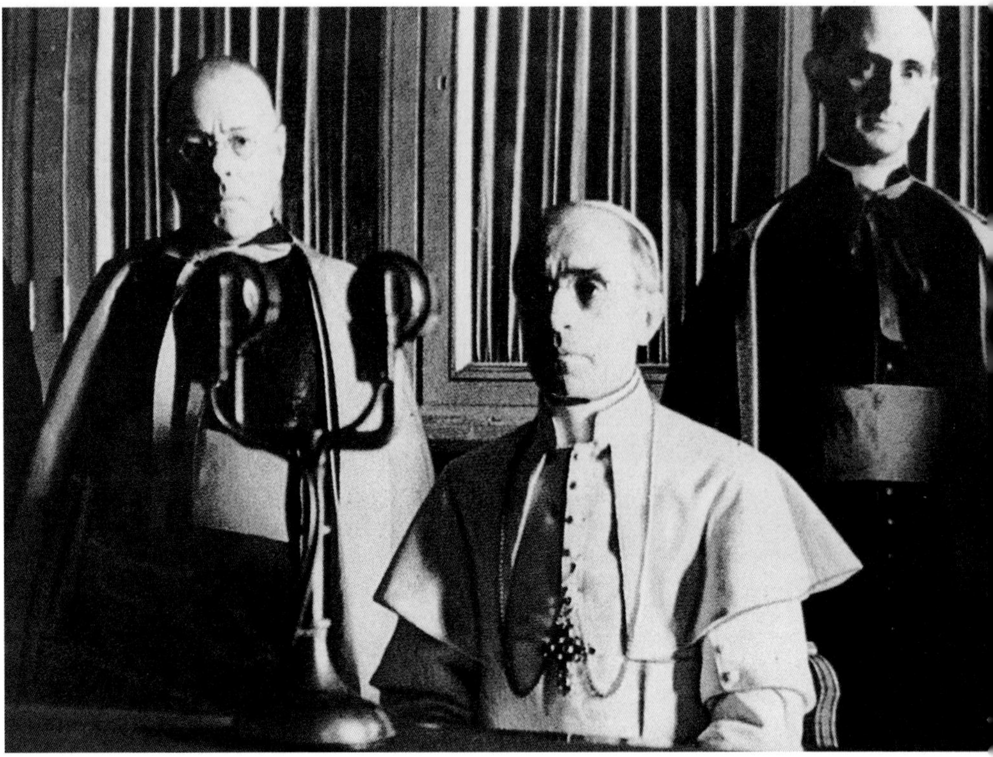

Above: Pope Pius XII in 1939 with, at right, Cardinal Giovanni Montini, later elected Pope Paul VI. It was to Montini that Taylor directed much of his evidence about the Holocaust, while Bletchley's ability to decipher and read the Vatican's signals proved invaluable. *(© Universal History Archive/Universal Images Group/Getty Images)*

Below left: Major Hermann Höfle (right) with General Odilo Globočnik (centre) at the SS training centre at Trawniki, Poland, 31 December 1942. Globočnik and his gang of Austrian SS officers between them stand accountable for the murders of millions of Jews, Poles, Russians, Ukrainians and others. *(© US Holocaust Memorial Museum [USHMM])*

Below right: Edward Reicher, the Jewish dermatologist who treated Höfle in Warsaw. He judged the SS officer a sophisticated sadist who never kept his word. *(© Yad Vashem)*

Above: Newly promoted Gruppenführer Jürgen Stroop created an album of his reports to Himmler, with photographs, detailing his achievements in clearing the Warsaw Ghetto of the 'Jews, bandits and criminals' who attempted – even in the knowledge they were doomed – to resist the deportations from the Warsaw Ghetto. The 'third resettlement' commenced in April 1943, marking the start of the main act of Jewish resistance; here, Jewish families are being marched to the railway station, bound for Majdanek and Treblinka (TII) camps. Behind them billow clouds of smoke from the burning ghetto.

(© US National Archives and Records Administration [NARA])

Below: The resistance groups and their families hid in dugouts in basements and among the ruined buildings. Captioned by Stroop 'Forcibly pulled out of the dugouts', this photograph of a young boy, arms raised in surrender, has become an iconic image of the Warsaw Ghetto Uprising and its tragic outcome. He and the other Jews, mostly women and children, in the photograph were sent to either Majdanek or Treblinka, there to be exterminated. *(© NARA)*

Those who resisted – captioned by Stroop 'Bandits destroyed in battle.'
(© NARA)

The destruction of the Warsaw Ghetto: trapped in a burning block of flats, in desperation, some people tried to escape through the windows – or, as Stroop wrote in his caption, 'These bandits are trying to escape arrest by jumping down.'
(© NARA)

Stroop (centre) with his men, admiring the burning buildings of the Warsaw Ghetto. He took pains to report that 'high credit should be given for the pluck, courage, and devotion to duty' of his men, including the Wehrmacht engineers who demolished the ghetto. 'The large-scale action,' he reported, 'was terminated at 2015 hours [on 16 May 1943] by blowing up the Warsaw Synagogue. ... Total number of Jews dealt with 56,065.' *(© NARA)*

Above: On 26 May 1944 Christian Wirth was killed in an ambush by Slovenian partisans, and accorded a funeral with full military honours in a German cemetery in Italy, near the Slovenian border. There were no such obsequies for the numberless victims of Wirth and his kind, only cremation or the burial pit. *(© Yad Vashem)*

Left: This famous photograph shows a Jewish man kneeling before a mass grave as a member of Einsatzgruppe D prepares to shoot him, at or near Vinnitsa, Ukraine, July 1941. According to some sources, the back of the original photograph bore the legend *'Der letzte Jude in Winniza'* – 'The last Jew in Vinnitsa'. *(© CBW/Alamy)*

Left: SS-Untersturmführer Kurt Gerstein, who passed details of the massacres of Jews to Swedish and Swiss diplomats and to the Catholic Church authorities from 1942–5. After surrendering to the Allies in April 1945, he was eventually sent to a French military prison in Paris where, on 22 July, he was found dead, apparently a suicide.

(© ullstein bild/Getty Images)

Right: Austrian police photograph of Hermann Höfle taken after his arrest in Salzburg on 31 January 1961. On 26 August 1962, the evening before his trial was to start, he hanged himself in his cell.

(© Yad Vashem)

Left: Nigel de Grey, CMG, OBE, watching a game of his beloved cricket at Canterbury at some time after the war. In only one respect did Höfle ever best his nemesis – he outlived him by more than ten years. *(courtesy of and © the de Grey family)*

1000 hours. Including today, a total of 27,464 Jews of the former Warsaw Ghetto, have been captured.

The SS and Police Führer in the District of Warsaw.

Signed: Stroop

SS-Brigadeführer and Major General of Police.

Certified copy:

SS-Sturmbannführer. [This is probably Hermann Höfle as the senior representative of Operation Reinhard present.]

Warsaw, 26 April 1943.

Ref. Nr.: I ab/St/Wdt-16 07 Journal Nr. 551/43 secret.

During today's operation several blocks of buildings were burned down. This is the only and final method which forces this trash and subhumanity to the surface.

Result of today's operation:

30 Jews evacuated, 1,330 Jews pulled out of dug-outs and immediately destroyed, 362 Jews killed in battle. Caught today altogether: 1,722 Jews. This brings the total of Jews caught to 29,186. Moreover, it is very probable that numerous Jews have perished in the 13 dug-outs blown up today and in the conflagrations. At the time of writing not one-of the Jews caught still remains within Warsaw. The scheduled transport to T. II had no success.

Teletype message

From: The SS and Police Führer in the District of Warsaw

Warsaw, 29 April 1943.

fief. Nr. I ab/St/Gr-16 07-Journal Nr. 566/43 secret

Total caught or destroyed: 35,760.

Copy

Teletype message

From: The SS and Police Führer in the District of Warsaw
Warsaw, 12 May 1943

Ref. No.: I ab-St/Gr-16 07-Journal No. 637/43 secret.

Re: Large-scale Ghetto Operation.

To: The Higher SS and Police Führer East, SS-Obergruppenführer and General of Police Krüger or deputy. Cracow

Progress of large-scale operation on 12 May 1943, start 0930
hours.

When the raiding parties combed out the area for remaining
dug-outs in which Jews were hiding, they succeeded in
discovering 30 dug-outs. 663 Jews were pulled out of them
and 133 Jews were shot. The sum total of Jews caught has
risen to 54,463.

The transports of Jews leaving here will be directed to T.II
beginning today.

Copy

Teletype message

From: The SS and Police Führer in the District of Warsaw
Warsaw, 13 May, 1943.

Ref. No.: I ate/ St/Gr 16 07 Journal No. 641/43 secret.

After part of the inmates of the dug-out had been caught
and were about to be searched, one of the females as quick as
lightning put her hand under her shirt, as many others had
done, and fetched from her underwear a 'pineapple' hand
grenade, drew the safety-catch, threw the grenade among the
men who were searching her, and jumped quickly to cover.
It is only thanks to the presence of mind of the men that no
casualties ensued.

The few Jews and criminals still staying in the Ghetto have for the last few days been using the hideouts they can still find among the ruins, retiring at night into the dug-outs whose location is known to them, to eat and get provisions for the next day. Lately we have been unable to extract information on the whereabouts of further dug-outs from the captured Jews. The remainder of the inmates of that dug-out where the skirmish took place were destroyed by using heavier explosive charges. From a Wehrmacht concern we evacuated 327 Jews today. The Jews we catch now are sent to T.II. The total of Jews caught has risen to 55,179.

Copy
Teletype message
From: The SS and Police Führer in the District of Warsaw
Warsaw, May 16th, 1943.
Ref. No.: I ab-St/Gr 16 07 Journal Nr. 652/43 secret.
Re: Large-scale Ghetto Operation.
To: The Higher SS and Police Führer East, SS-Obergruppen-führer and General of Police Krüger or deputy. Cracow

Progress of large-scale operation on 16 May 1943, start 1000 hours.

180 Jews, bandits, and subhumans were destroyed. The former Jewish quarter of Warsaw is no longer in existence. The large-scale action was terminated at 2015 hours by blowing up the Warsaw Synagogue. The measures to be taken with regard to the established banned areas were handed over to the commander of police battalion III/23, whom I instructed carefully.

Total number of Jews dealt with 56,065, including both Jews caught and Jews whose extermination can be proved.

No losses today.

I will submit a final report to the Conference of SS Police Führer on 18 May 1943.

Copy

Teletype message

From: The SS and Police Führer in the District of Warsaw Warsaw, 24 May 1943.

Ref. No.: I ab-St/Gr 16 07 Journal Nr. 663/43 secret.

Re: Large-scale Ghetto Operation.

Ref: Your teletype message Nr. 946 or 21 May 1943.

To: The Higher SS and Police Führer East, SS-Obergruppen-führer and General of Police Krüger or deputy. Cracow

I beg to reply to the above teletype message: No. 1:

Of the total of 56,065 caught, about 7,000 were destroyed in the former Ghetto during large-scale operation. 6,929 Jews were destroyed by transporting them to T.II; the sum total of Jews destroyed is therefore 13,929. Beyond the number of 56,065 an estimated number of 5 to 6,000 Jews were destroyed by being blown up or by perishing in the flames.

By mid-May, the battle was over. Of the 56,000 defenders, the SS put 7,000 of them on trains to Treblinka, and 37,000 to Majdanek. The rest were killed in action, half of them burnt to death or suffocated by smoke. One of the survivors who managed to escape with his family was the dermatologist Edward Reicher who had treated Hermann Höfle, a man whom he described as a sophisticated sadist, who never kept his word.

The SS had, by now, nearly fulfilled Himmler's order of the previous year to evacuate the Jews of Poland. Before the ghetto uprising, from 25 July 1942 until 5 September, the SS, Order

Police and their Trawniki auxiliaries deported around 265,000 Jews from the Warsaw Ghetto to Treblinka II. By November, an additional 380,000 Polish Jews from Radom and Lublin districts had joined them. In August, Franz Stangl had replaced Irmfried Eberl as commanding officer, and had re-organised the manner in which executions were carried out, and built new gas chambers. In October, the SS deported 8,000 Jews from the Theresienstadt ghetto in the German Protectorate of Bohemia and Moravia to Treblinka II, and, by mid-February 1943, 110,000 Jews from the Bialystok District had joined them. On 11 March, the Bulgarian authorities, acting under an agreement with the RSHA and the logistical help of the SS, deported 11,350 Jews from Macedonia and Thrace to Treblinka. The SS had, by this point, shot and gassed around 780,000 Jews and others in the camp.

Reporting the Final Solution in radio silence

Yet if the deportations and killings of Operation Reinhard were proceeding largely according to plan, the remainder of Himmler's vision of a thousand-year Reich, with huge settlements of newly Germanised territory in the east, was not. Fearing a Russian offensive westwards in summer 1943, the SS began to draw down extermination operations in the Reinhard camps, in the lead-up to destroying them, and the bodies of the victims, as soon as possible. It seemed so different from the spirit of optimism of the previous autumn. In September 1942, before the debacle at Stalingrad, the Reichsführer-SS had visited an area of planned German settlements near the Ukrainian town of Zhytomyr, sixty miles west of Kiev. When the Einsatzkommandos following behind Army Group Centre had arrived in the town in October 1941, there were 50,000 Jews living there. Within weeks, there were 6,000. A year later, on 16 September 1942, Himmler had called a meeting of various SS and German civilian administrative staff at an ad hoc headquarters in a wheatfield outside the town. The programme to settle the area with Aryanised peoples had proceeded according to plan, and the group met outside Hegewald, a name given to twenty-seven villages repopulated with German settlers as a Volksdeutsche colony. It was made up of ethnic Germans of Polish, Croatian and Ukrainian citizenship who had been forcibly resettled from their own homes, after the original Ukrainian and Ukrainian Jewish owners had been evicted or executed. The villages in the new settlement were given German names, such as Reichstreu, Pfenningstadt and Heinrichsfeld.

> Who would have dreamed ten years ago [said Himmler to the gathered SS leaders], that we would be holding an SS meeting in a village named Hegewald near the Jewish-Russian city of Shitomir . . . this Germanic East extending as far as the Urals must be cultivated like a hothouse of Germanic blood . . . the next generation of Germans and history will not remember how it was done, but rather the goal.[144]

Three weeks later, on 7 October, Himmler celebrated his forty-second birthday. The Third Reich's operations in Russia were still in their ascendancy. He proposed, over the German Police and SS radio net, that he would send all officers in the SS a copy of a novel.[145] It was published in 1933, and written by Josef Baptist 'Batti' Dohm, a German geologist and palaeontologist. Called *Stielauge der Urkrebs* ('Stalk-Eye the Primeval Crab'), the book tells the story of a fictional trilobite. It is focused around the cosmological concept, popular with Hitler and Himmler, of *Welteislehre*, or World Ice Theory. Conceived by Hans Horbiger, an Austrian engineer, this idea argued that ice was the basis of all cosmic processes, and had been instrumental in forming moons and planets. The Nazis approved of it because it promoted a contradictory stance to natural science, which they regarded as essentially Jewish. While he was proposing this book as a gift for his officers, Himmler also received birthday wishes over the radio net from all SS ranks under the command of SS-General Gerret Korsemann, who had been leading the SS attack towards the Caucasus. SS and Police messages sent around the same time showed that Einsatzgruppe B, with SD and Sipo units was in Smolensk, a unit of the SD with an Einsatzkommando in Rostov-on-Don, and Einsatzgruppe C, with its SD and Security Police units, was in the Ukrainian capital, Kiev. Of executions, special duties, actions according to the usages of war, evacuations, there was no mention.[146]

So how had the SS and German Police reported, and continued to report, the ongoing executions and mass killings of the Final Solution, while still respecting the rigid edict of radio silence laid down by SS-Obergruppenführer Daluege in autumn 1941? Senior officers in command headquarters increasingly used the Lorenz teleprinter, while other units used letters and personally couriered reports, particularly for sensitive and secret messages such as those involving executions. If the various Einsatzkommandos, SS units and Police Battalions had been sending radio reports of executions carried out post-Barbarossa because Gestapo Gruppenführer Heinrich Müller had ordered them to, then the instructions of Kurt Daluege in September would have countermanded this. So units would have kept records of their executions in diaries, and in couriered letters and reports from the Eastern Front back to Germany. An example of such a letter was the following: 'During the course of extensive discussions with SS-Brigadeführer Zenner and the very competent Leiter of the SD, SS Obersturmbannführer Dr Strauch, it was established that we have liquidated about 55,000 Jews in the past ten weeks.' Wilhelm Kube, General

Commissar for White Russia, was writing to Hinrich Lohse, the
Reich Kommissar for Ostland, which comprised the territories of
Estonia, Latvia, Lithuania and parts of Byelorussia. He continued:

> Naturally the SD and I would prefer to eliminate the Jews in
> the Generalbezirk of White Russia [Byelorussia] once and for
> all as soon as the Jews are no longer needed by the Wehrmacht
> for economic reasons. For the time being the Wehrmacht's
> requirements, as the principal employer of Jewish labour, are
> being taken into account.'[147]

A personal report from Himmler to Hitler about mass executions
in the east in 1942 read as follows:

	August	September	October	November
Prisoners executed after interrogation	2100	1400	1596	2731
Accomplices of guerrillas and guerrilla suspects executed	1198	3020	6333	3706
Jews executed:	31246	165282	95735	70948
Villages or localities burned down or destroyed	35	12	20	92[148]

On 31 January 1942, SS-Brigadeführer Franz-Walter Stahlecker,
commander of Einsatzgruppe A in the Baltics, wrote to Reinhard
Heydrich.[149]

> The complete removal of Jewry from the eastern territories
> has been substantially attained, with the exception of White

Russia, as a result of the execution up to the present time of 229,052 Jews. [The final total would be 249,420.]

On 25 October 1941, the Einsatzgruppen across the three Army Group areas stated in a daily situation report that 'special treatment [was applied] to 812 men and women, all without interest from the racial and intellectual point of view.[150]

Two days after the mass executions at the Babi Yar ravine outside Kiev, Einsatzgruppe C said in their Ereignismeldung No.101, or Daily Situation Report 101, that 'in collaboration with the group staff and two Kommandos of Police Regiment South, on 29 and 30 September 1941, Sonderkommando 4a executed 33,771 Jews in Kiev.'[151]

Each of the four Einsatzgruppen, or groups, kept daily operational logs. As previously written, Groups A, B and C were respectively attached to Army Groups North, Centre and South, while D operated with the Eleventh Army, part of the latter Army Group. By late October 1942, all four groups were spread across Ukraine and Byelorussia, with B and C being in Smolensk and Kiev. As the Baltic states and parts of Byelorussia had been largely emptied of Jews by Franz Walter Stahlecker's operations, so Group A was now south-west of Leningrad. Russian partisans had fatally wounded Stahlecker in a firefight south-west of the city in March 1942, and leadership had been handed over to three new SS officials. By spring 1943, all the groups were still under the overall command of the new head of the RSHA, the senior general in the Austrian SS cadre, Ernst Kaltenbrunner. He was now embarking on a programme to increase internal security within the Third Reich, and to speed up the two different, but now concurrent phases of the Final Solution – Reinhard and Auschwitz-Birkenau. On the Eastern Front, individual Police and SS units had, as recorded, been sending encrypted radio situation reports of their mass executions between July and October 1941, which had largely ceased following Daluege's radio security edict of September. The Einsatzgruppen had simultaneously each been compiling similar reports, but dispatching them by courier to Berlin. When Einsatzgruppe C reported that it had executed 33,771 Jews (at Babi Yar) outside Kiev on 29 and 30 September 1941, this was their 101st Daily Situation Report, implying that daily reporting had begun at least in July.

So when Jürgen Stroop and Hermann Höfle finally overcame the last major resistance in the Warsaw Ghetto uprising in late May 1943, their reports back to Kaltenbrunner and Himmler were not sent in the same set of radio encryptions that much of the SS and Police infrastructure, up to and including Himmler's office, were still using. The final phases of Operation Reinhard, which was to include the gassing of the last Polish, Slovakian, Ukrainian and Byelorussian Jews, the destruction of the camps and the attempted elimination of the forensic evidence, was not going to be reported by radio. The RSHA's orders process, however, continued to be predominantly transmitted in the signals encipherment keys – the Double Square system – that the SS and the Police had been using since September 1941. By 1943, parts of the RSHA infrastructure now used the Enigma encipherment system, a combination of One Time hand-held ciphers and, between senior officers, the Lorenz enciphered teleprinter system. One main transmission system was codenamed Sagefisch, or Sawfish.

For Hermann Höfle, the signals reporting system about his duties on Operation Reinhard was much simpler: essentially, he did not send any. Since January that year, when he had dispatched his personal coded telegrams to Krakow and back to Berlin, he had sent no new updates about the operations in Treblinka, Majdanek, Belzec, Sobibor or Chelmno. Himmler and Kaltenbrunner were largely satisfied with the speed of operations in the camps. Yet the

Reichsführer's confident, far-reaching optimism of the previous autumn, when he had stood at Zhytomyr, and thought about celebrating his birthday with the best kind of scientific reading matter for his SS officers, was evaporating. He might have been approving of the efficient and synchronised manner in which Gruppenführer Globočnik, Sturmbannführer Stangl, Wirth, Höfle and the other SS staff were killing Jews, but he appeared not to be satisfied with other economic and personnel-related matters linked to Operation Reinhard. He thought a small, inside cadre of his subordinates was defrauding the SS and stealing from the Reich's Main Economic Office. His court-martial proceedings against SS-Brigadeführer Sammern-Frankenegg epitomised his rigid, disciplinary thinking: if you were guilty of complacency or incompetence in your handling of an attack on a Jewish ghetto, you were guilty of defending Jews. Ergo, you were not with the SS, you were against it. If you were stealing SS property for your own enrichment, Jewish gold or silver, or jewels that could go towards submachine-pistol ammunition or antibiotics or socks for the SS men in the foxholes at the front, you were an enemy of the SS, and every man in it. The only punishment could be death, or to be posted to an active operational area where you could serve the SS until killed, thus providing the maximum amount of manpower extractable from each member of the organisation. In the middle of May 1943, the Warsaw operation was done, and with the brick-dust of the ghetto still clinging to the men's equipment, the roasted, bonfire smell of smoke and burning buildings in every fibre of their uniforms, the faecal barbecue stench of burning humans in their nostrils, they pulled out of Warsaw. Höfle and colleagues returned to Lublin. There they were told by Globočnik that SS-Brigadeführer und Generalmajor der Waffen-SS von Herff, the head of the SS Personnel department, was on his way for an inspection visit.

The SS Personnel Office and the investigation in Lublin

Maximilian von Herff was a doctor's son from Hanover who had fought in the First World War, and then remained in the German Army until war was declared in 1939. He was a lieutenant-colonel in the Wehrmacht by 1939, and fought in North Africa where he won the Knights Cross of the Iron Cross. He had not joined the SS until 1942, when Himmler suggested he should transfer from the German Heer. On 1 October the Reichsführer appointed von Herff to the position of head of the SS Personnel Main Office. Crop-haired, bull-necked and with glaring eyes, his job was to ensure that all personnel in the Waffen and Algemeine SS were executing their assigned missions, and behaving in accordance with the organisation's strict regulations. Investigating and punishing corruption and internal disciplinary and financial matters were part of his mandate. His cousin, Eberhard Herf, was an Order Police officer who had commanded a regiment in Minsk in the early days of Operation Barbarossa, supervising mass executions of Jews from the Minsk ghetto.

On 4 May 1943, Maximilian von Herff, accompanied by SS staff officers and assistants, embarked on a twelve-day inspection visit to Poland. One of his aides-de-camp, SS-Sturmbannführer Alfred Franke-Gricksch, wrote a report about their mission.[152] Flying from Tempelhof airfield outside Berlin, they arrived in Krakow, where they immediately travelled to the Auschwitz camp complex, and met with the commander, SS-Obersturmbannführer Rudolf Höss. He drove the group around the 18,000 hectares of the camp complex, and showed them the farms, fish-farming ponds, pheasant-rearing units, tanneries and land reclaimed from swamps. The SS party heard about the camp orchestra, and the inmates, described as Jews, Poles, gypsies and women. Jewish women from the Sorbonne university in Paris work in the chemical plants.

Large industrial plants nearby manufacture synthetic rubber. No mention was made of gas chambers or executions, or prisoner totals. After a visit to Krakow to meet SS officers, an evening party in the city's castle, the group returned to Berlin, where von Herff attended the funeral of another SS officer. On the 8th the group flew back to Krakow, visited Lvov and Dębica, and arrived in Lublin on 12 May. First was a visit to the Trawniki training camp, and then the city itself, where Odilo Globočnik, Hermann Höfle and Ernst Lerch had their headquarters. Von Herff and his officers saw the warehouses where the possessions of Jews, gathered from the Operation Reinhard camps, were stored.

From Trawniki we travelled back to Lublin to inspect the 'special enterprise REINHARD'. This branch has had the task of realising all mobile Jewish property in the Governorate of Poland. It is astonishing what immense fortunes the Jews have collected in their ghetto and even ragged and vermin infested dirty little Jews who look like beggars, carry with them, when you strip their clothes off them, foreign currency, pieces of gold, diamonds and other valuables. We wandered through the cellars of this 'special enterprise' and we were reminded of the fairy tales of the 'Arabian Nights'.

Whole boxes full of genuine pearls, cases full of diamonds, a basket full of pieces of gold and many hundredweight of silver coins, besides jewellery of every kind. In order to carry out a better realisation of all these valuables, the gold and silver are melted into bars. We inspected the melting process in the garden of the house. There is a small foundry where gold and silver are melted and then formed into bars and then delivered to the German National Bank on certain days. 'Special enterprise REINHARD' has so far delivered 2,500 kilos of gold, 20,000 kilos of silver and six and a half kilos of platinum,

60,000 Reichsmarks in currency, 800,000 dollars in money and 144,000 dollars in gold. The huge quantity of diamonds and pearls can hardly be evaluated. The best proof of the repercussion this enterprise has on the international market is the quotations on the Swiss Stock Exchange and the effects on the international market in diamonds and brilliants. The prices have all gone down and Switzerland could not absorb any more diamonds, because our enterprise has swamped the market.

In this respect alone, the 'Special enterprise REINHARD' gives us the means for our political struggle and would have a decisive effect on the world market. Apart from other valuables there are 60,000 watches, most of them double-cased watches of high value, very often decorated with diamonds, 800,000 wrist watches and a huge quantity of other small valuables from tobacco and cigarette cases and gold fountain pens and silver bracelets etc. In special workshops all these treasures are sorted out and examined by specially trained Jews, jewellers, bank clerks and goldsmiths. If necessary the diamonds are broken out in order to separate them and use the metal in a different way. The wrist watches will be repaired, if necessary and will be handed out to front-line troops.

When one goes through the cellar of this special branch it appears like a secret treasure and you get a very different idea of all the things for which people have sacrificed their lives and forgotten, through them the real issues. You get the right distance from these false values and, even if our eye is delighted by the shine of thousands of brilliants, some of them the size of a pea, for which the old world has paid hundreds of thousands, one recognises a people which saw its whole existence in the heaping up of such treasures. It is a pleasure to see with what indifference the Oberscharführer registers these valuables as if they were bits of coal or other things of everyday life. The real values of our life which carry us as human beings and as a nation become very clear and more precious still.

The treasure of these people of parasites prove that the age of the power of gold is over and a new time, which has new values, has begun.[153]

The accounting of the property appropriated by Operation Reinhard showed immediate discrepancies between the figures Odilo Globočnik sent to Berlin, and those which Reinhard staff reported to von Herff and his entourage. In some instances, the amounts of gold and silver and American dollars that Globočnik said had been transmitted back to Berlin were between 50 and 60 per cent of what the Reinhard staff in Lublin told von Herff. The party then visited the area around Lublin, and then the Poniatowa work camp, where Major Franke-Gricksche observed large parties of Jews who had been deported from Warsaw:

Walking through this camp and watching these people in their servile attitude, one is bound to notice that again and again they try to make the best of every situation without any dignity and self-respect and one realises the alternative with which we are faced: either This generation of ours succeeds in clearing up the Jewish problem completely and to its last consequences or, if their liquidation is not completely achieved, the Jewish people will rise again after this wave of oppression. Some individual cases may appear hard or even brutal but seeing these people in large masses and knowing how dangerous their passive attitude is to the life of the nations, one comes to the conclusion that this problem has to be cleared up completely to free the world once and for all this pestilence.[154]

Maximilian von Herff's group then drove to Warsaw, and watched the operations being carried out by Jürgen Stroop and Hermann Höfle's units to empty the ghetto. Afterwards the SS Personnel chief met his various subordinates in Warsaw, and on the evening of the 15th took a train back to Berlin. Within days, the meetings that von Herff held, and the deductions he made from the various sites he visited, were to have an effect. On returning to Berlin, he gave an immediate report to Himmler of what he had seen and done. For Hermann Höfle, Ernst Lerch and their SS colleagues, the tempo of operations in Lublin, already storming along, gathered urgency and momentum. By the end of May and the beginning of June, Höfle saw troops being moved from the Russian front to Italy, where the Allies staged their first amphibious landings on the islands of Pantelleria and Lampedusa, between Sicily and North Africa. Bombings of the Reich increased. In the deadly fighting against Marshal Tito's partisans in Yugoslavia, the SS and the Wehrmacht launched a fifth offensive as the spring of 1943 turned into summer. The mountains and valleys of Bosnia and Croatia, along with the Dalmatian coast, took on a new strategic importance as the Americans and British prepared to invade Sicily and the Italian mainland. Yugoslavia now represented a southern back door into the Reich, through Austria and Slovenia.

Then, on 12 July, near the small railway station of Prokhorovka in central Ukraine, Höfle's colleagues from the Leibstandarte Adolf Hitler, Totenkopf and Das Reich SS Panzer divisions – the three elite armoured units of the Waffen-SS – went head-to-head with the Soviet's Fifth Guards Tank Army. Everybody across the Eastern Front followed developments over the radio net: Operation Citadel, designed to cut off the Kursk salient, saw the biggest armoured battle of the war. Yet it seemed the Russians had known in advance that the German attack would fall near Kursk, and by the middle of July, the Germans had lost the initiative. The vast Red Army was poised to advance west. In their eventual path stood Lublin, Poland, the General Government, and the camps of Operation Reinhard. Globočnik and his men had to terminate operations, and do it as fast as they could.

The SS now began to dispose of the bodies of Jewish and other inmates gassed at Majdanek by burning them on large funeral pyres, as well as in crematoria. They transported 42,000 extra Jews to the camp, the majority of those arrested by Jürgen Stroop's men during the Warsaw Ghetto uprising. Only 7,000 were taken to the camp called 'T II' in Stroop's signals. A Jewish prisoner had secreted a hand-grenade in his clothes, and detonated it when he got to the Treblinka unloading ramp. Afraid of a similar incident, and a larger revolt by prisoners, Hermann Höfle's men took the majority of those from the ghetto to Majdanek.

By the end of June operations had ceased at Belzec, with a total of 480,000 prisoners killed there by the SS. Chelmno had suspended operations in the middle of April, while both Sobibor and Treblinka II continued to kill trainloads of mainly Polish Jews. Then, in July and August 1943, five completely different but interlinked events took place in Poland, Ukraine, the Atlantic and Italy which would decide how Hermann Höfle, Odilo Globočnik and their fellow SS officers were to spend the remainder of the war. The first was the Battle of Kursk, and the fact the Red Army seemed to have been forewarned about its location and the German tactical aims. The second took place in the Mediterranean: on 9 July the Allies landed in Sicily, as the Italian Fascist Council deposed Benito Mussolini; the King then issued orders for his arrest, as Germany's former allies arranged an armistice with the British and Americans. Italy's military leaders either chose to sign this armistice, and side with the Allies as partisans against the Germans; to remain loyal to the Third Reich, or to relinquish their arms, disappear into civilian clothes and vanish back into the countryside. Hitler ordered the SS and the

Wehrmacht to occupy the country from mid-May onwards, and ten divisions thundered through the Brenner Pass, from Slovenia and from France. The Germans took over Rome in August, as the Allies were fighting their way across the scorching fields and hills, and through the lemon and peach groves of Sicily in a hundred degrees of heat. The third incident was Himmler's decision to tell Odilo Globočnik to provide a thorough written accounting of the economic 'proceeds' of Operation Reinhard.

The fourth took place far away in the Atlantic, where Admiral Karl Dönitz ordered the remaining U-boats from the Kriegsmarine to withdraw from patrol, following a month where his losses, of 41 submarines compared to 34 Allied merchant ships sunk, proved that Nazi Germany had lost the Battle of the Atlantic. The fifth incident was on 2 August at Treblinka. As Mondays in the camp had been designated as 'no-gassing days', German and Ukrainian guards had gone swimming in the nearby River Bug. Seven hundred Jews broke into the Treblinka arsenal, removed rifles, pistols, and hand-grenades, and stormed the wire. Eighty-five guards remaining in the camp shot or dispersed most of them, but two hundred prisoners escaped, most of whom were quickly recaptured. Seventy escaped and survived. Globočnik, Wirth and Stangl decided afterwards to close the camp, and not repair the damage caused. The complex at Auschwitz-Birkenau was large enough to handle all of the Third Reich's extermination operations from now on. Operation Reinhard would draw to a close. The SS officers embarked on the absolute destruction of the camps.

The SS Harvest Festival in Lublin

One day in summer 1943, before the prisoners' uprising and escape attempt, SS-Untersturmführer Kurt Franz was waiting on Treblinka station for a convoy of cattle cars to arrive. They were carrying both Polish Jews, and some remaining ones from Vienna, Slovakia and Germany. Franz Stangl was still in command of the camp, and SS-Untersturmführer Franz was one of his deputies. The thirty-year-old officer had previously worked as a concentration camp guard, and then, promoted to sergeant, or Oberscharführer, as a cook in the headquarters of the T4 euthanasia programme in Austria. Chosen to work on Operation Reinhard, the first posting for the him had been at Belzec, and then at Treblinka II. Franz wanted to make the physical movement of Jews from the unloading ramp at the station to the inside of the camp as fast as possible; he had decided that one way not to panic the Jews being disembarked from the railway freight cars was to pretend that Treblinka was a routine, fully functioning railway station, simply a junction stop for the Jews on their way to re-settlement elsewhere. So he ordered Jewish labourers from one of the camp's work details to paint signs for a ticket-office, a waiting-room, a restaurant, even a fake destination board announcing departures to Vienna or Berlin.

One day, a Jewish inmate working on the station watched as an elderly woman approached SS-Untersturmführer Franz, took out a document, and announced she was the sister of Sigmund Freud. She had just disembarked from a train from Vienna, and she begged Franz to give her light work in an office: Franz read through the document she showed him and said that there had clearly been a mistake.[xvi]

Franz led her to the board announcing the fake train schedules,

---

xvi   Anna Freud was the eldest of the five sisters of the pioneer of psychoanalysis, Sigmund Freud, their parents Ashkenazi Jews from Galicia, on the border of western Ukraine and Poland. The others were called Rosa, Marie, Adolphine and Paula. Anna, born in 1858, was arrested by the Gestapo in Vienna in 1938 and interrogated. Her brother was at the time trying to evacuate the family and close friends to Great Britain. The American consul-general in Vienna, John Cooper Wiley, had telephoned SS headquarters during Anna's questioning. All four of her sisters died in concentration and extermination camps – it is unclear from the witness statement at Nuremberg as to which sister it might have been that Franz saw on Treblinka station that day.

and told her that there would be a departure for Vienna in two hours' time. In the meantime, she should leave all her documents and valuables with him, and go to a bathhouse, to take a bath. She never returned.[155]

After the prisoners' revolt, Kurt Franz became the new commandant of Treblinka II. He was regarded as a sadist, even by the comparative standards of sadism of the other SS and Ukrainian personnel serving on Operation Reinhard. He had inherited ownership of a dog from another SS man who had worked in Sobibor, and who had wanted to leave his pet in good hands in Poland. Franz decided to take care of him. The dog was a large Saint Bernard, whose head came up to a man's waist. His name was Barry. Franz trained him to attack and maul Jewish prisoners on his command. Barry would bite and maul parts of prisoners at the same height as his mouth, hence the abdomen, genitals and stomach were common target areas.[156] The prisoners in Treblinka were terrified of Kurt Franz: apart from their fear of Barry, they would see the SS officer walking or riding around the camp on a horse, shooting people at will with a shotgun, rifle or pistol. Franz had a baby-face, and was nicknamed '*Lalke*', or 'doll,' by the Polish prisoners. Despite orders from Hermann Höfle about maintaining secrecy in the Operation Reinhard camps, and firm orders never to take photographs, Franz disobeyed. He kept a photo album in his quarters, filled with pictures of Treblinka, called *Schöne Zeiten*, or 'Happy Days'.

On 18 and 19 August 1943, observers from the Polish Home Army counted two railway locomotives passing through the village of Treblinka. One pulled thirty-seven cattle-cars, the second thirty-nine. They were the last Jewish inmates of the Bialystok ghetto, and the last Jews on their way to be gassed at Treblinka II.

At the same time, von Herff's Personnel department was stepping up investigations into allegations of corruption and breaches of discipline among the SS officers who oversaw the operations of the camps across Poland. Kurt Franz was not the only SS man who was guilty of disciplinary offences. In August 1943, SS police working for Judge Konrad Morgen were still investigating Karl-Otto Koch, and his wife Ilse. The former was in Lublin, the latter still at Buchenwald. An officer from the Sicherheitsdienst, the SD, in Lublin then tipped off Morgen's office that SS officers operating under Odilo Globočnik had, allegedly, held a large wedding ceremony, involving the SS and Jews, at the camp at Sobibor. Morgen investigated and reportedly interviewed Christian Wirth, who showed him some of the valuables taken from Jewish prisoners. Morgen realised that a small number of SS personnel were using extermination operations as a form of personal enrichment. This suspicion was partially confirmed when German postal officials opened two parcels of dental gold sent home by a dentist serving in an SS concentration camp.

In the meantime, the SS judge was beginning investigations into two officers who served at Majdanek, Hauptsturmführer Hermann Hackmann and Standartenführer Hermann Florstedt. This would lead onwards into a widening operation involving eight other SS officers, up to the rank of Obersturmbannführer (lieutenant-colonel), in Auschwitz, Buchenwald, Flossenburg, Płaszów, Sachsenhausen and Dachau. Himmler, considerably displeased by what he saw as a betrayal of SS standards, ordered that once Operation Reinhard and its institutions – i.e. extermination and labour camps – had been terminated, Odilo Globočnik and several of his subordinate officers would be transferred to the front line in Italy, where they would continue operations against Jews and partisans. The posting was to Trieste, a strategically vital port on the upper Adriatic, on the boundaries of Italian, Yugoslav and Austrian territory. It was also Globočnik's home city, now the centre of a vicious insurgency campaign by Italian and Yugoslav partisans against the Germans and their Italian Fascist allies, soldiers, policemen and civilians. Stangl, Wirth and Franz, along with ten SS men from Treblinka and a selection of Ukrainian Trawniki guards, were among Globočnik's group who travelled to Trieste between July and September. Among these officers and NCOs who had served in Poland, there was a persistent fear that Himmler and the RSHA had sent them to such a hostile area in the hope they would be killed in action, and thus the first-hand incriminating knowledge of Operation Reinhard would perish with them. 'We were an embarrassment to the higher ranks,' said Stangl. 'They wanted to find ways of getting rid of us.'[157]

On the 22 September 1943, Himmler wrote to Oswald Pohl and Globočnik about the outstanding Reinhard accounts:

The transfer of Gruppenführer Globočnik necessitates an adjustment for the settlement of the account Reinhard 1 . . . I order herewith that Gruppenführer Globočnik is to take over the settlement of the account 'Reinhard 1' up to 31 December 1943, after which he is to hand it over to SS-Obergruppenführer Pohl . . . on the whole, an effort should be made to balance the account 'Reinhard 1' until then . . .[158]

Hermann Höfle, meanwhile, would not be travelling to Italy. His performance on Operation Reinhard, and in the Warsaw Ghetto, had pleased Himmler and Maximilian von Herff, and he appeared disconnected from the illegal expropriation of Jewish property. His future was now pinned to another SS general, neither as sadistic as Globočnik nor as criminal, but still incessantly brutal. He would now operate under Jürgen Stroop's command, and between them they would complete the destruction of the extermination camps, ghettos and labour camps around Lublin and in the General Government, and execute all the remaining Jews in them. The operation to do so was codenamed Aktion Erntefest, or Harvest Festival, and took place outside Lublin between 3 and 4 November. Höfle was second-in-command to Stroop. One of several reasons they decided to complete the final destruction of the camps and executions of the remaining prisoners was because of a mass prisoner breakout from Sobibor on 15 October. Seven hundred prisoners escaped, and the SS police leader in Lublin sent a message to his counterpart in the town of Lutzk:

> About 700 Jews have broken out from the SOBIBOR camp.
> It is anticipated that these will flee over the train border.
> It is requested that appropriate action is taken against this.
> SOBIBOR is located in the Lublin District, 5 km from the train between Chelm and Włodawa.[159]

The signal was intercepted by one of the Y stations, and decrypted at Bletchley Park. It was of significant interest for two reasons, the first being that the message was enciphered in the same coding system used for administration messages from the concentration camps outside of the Lublin system, and was what de Grey's colleagues had dubbed a 'HOR-HUG report'. The second point of interest was that it was one of the few messages picked up which directly mentioned Jews being in a camp at Sobibor – one of few instances where the draconian secrecy regulations around Operation Reinhard slipped.

The mass killing of 43,000 Jews was not just the largest individual execution of Jews in the entire war, it was meant to be secret. However, Hermann Höfle may have escaped being incriminated in Globočnik's criminal enterprise, but not in Harvest Festival. By a stroke of irony, he was seen by officials from his own side. Judge Konrad Morgen, investigating SS corruption, was in Lublin on

5 November, and spoke to eyewitnesses who described what had happened in the killings led by Höfle and Stroop.

> The men went first, filing into one trench, and later the nude women had their own separate trenches . . . all passed silently and methodically through the trenches, so the executions went very quickly.[160]

CHAPTER XI

THE KEY TO RUSSIA

Bletchley Park and London, July 1943–September 1944

On 23 June 1943, Generalfeldmarschall Maximilian von Weichs wrote a signal at his headquarters on the Eastern Front. The message concerned the Wehrmacht and SS predictions for how the Red Army might react to a forthcoming offensive, codenamed *Zitadelle* (Citadel). Weichs was the commander of Army Group South, and he sent Wehrmacht High Command in Berlin his appreciation of the Russian defensive positions two weeks before the attack. The Russian salient at Kursk bulged westwards of the Russian front line, and the Germans estimated that if they cut off the top and bottom of the pocket in an armoured pincer movement they could surround, and destroy, the Russian forces stationed within it. Von Weichs's signals staff took his written plain text, and transmitted it on one of the new Lorenz-enciphered teleprinters which the headquarters of the army group now used to send and receive messages to and from Berlin. If the sender was in a mobile, as opposed to a fixed location, the transmission required two lorries. One contained the radio transmission equipment, the second lorry the teleprinter, and the two Lorenz cipher attachments, one for sending and one for receiving.

Weich's transmission passed down the radio link between Königsberg, in East Prussia, and the OKW, or Oberkommando der Wehrmacht. Königsberg was the radio transmission hub for all Lorenz traffic coming from Poland, Ukraine and Russia. SS-Brigadeführer Jürgen Stroop's messages from Warsaw to SS headquarters in Krakow, with his daily updates about the clearing of Jews from the ghetto, would almost certainly have been routed from Warsaw-Königsberg-Krakow-Berlin. From his daily reports, it is not certain whether he was transmitting his teleprinter messages via radio or telephone landline link: on 21 April 1943 he mentions communications on a telephone line. Neither Generalfeldmarschall von Weichs nor Jürgen Stroop were aware that British cryptanalysts and engineers at Bletchley Park had created their own computer systems, codenamed Colossus, which enabled them to read into the Lorenz traffic. They could intercept and read messages sent over a radio link, but not over a telephone link, so if Stroop's messages were not sent via radio, there would have been no possibility of intercepting and reading them. Nigel de Grey and his colleagues at the GC&CS had given codenames of a variety of fish to the different Lorenz radio links across the Third Reich's European network. Bletchley called the Lorenz traffic 'Tunny'. There were five main links from the Eastern Front into Königsberg, respectively from Riga, Central Byelorussia, North, South and Central Ukraine. Hut 3 called them Whiting, Perch, Squid, Octopus and Stickleback. The line from Königsberg to Berlin was Dace. Bletchley Park intercepted von Weich's message on the Squid link.

To OKH/OP. ABT. and to OKH/Foreign Armies East, from Army Group South IA/01, No. 411/43, signed von Weichs, General Feldmarschall, dated 25/4:[161]

Comprehensive appreciation of the enemy for 'Zitadelle'

In the main the appreciation of the enemy remains the same as reported in Army Group South (Roman) IIA, No. 0477/43 of 29/3 and in the supplementary appreciation of 15/4. [In Tunny transmissions the word 'Roman' was used to indicate a Roman numeral; '29/3' and '15/4' are dates.]

The main concentration, which was already then apparent on the north flank of the Army Group in the general area Kursk--Ssudsha--Volchansk--Ostrogoshsk, can now be clearly recognised: a further intensification of this concentration is to be expected as a result of the continuous heavy transport movements on the lines Yelets--Kastornoye--Kursk, and Povorino--Svoboda and Gryazi--Svoboda, with a probable (B% increase) ['B%' indicated an uncertain word] in the area Valuiki--Novy Oskol--Kupyansk. At present however it is not apparent whether the object of this concentration is offensive or defensive.

At present, (B% still) in anticipation of a German offensive on both the Kursk and Mius Donetz fronts, the armoured and mobile formations are still evenly distributed in various groups behind the front as strategic reserves. There are no signs as yet of a merging of these formations or a transfer to the forward area (except for (Roman) II GDS [Guards] Armoured Corps) but this could take place rapidly at any time.

According to information from a sure source the existence of the following groups of the strategic reserve can be presumed:- [there follows a lengthy breakdown of every Red Army unit involved].

In the event of 'Zitadelle', there are at present approximately 90 enemy formations west of the line Belgorod--Kursk--Maloarkhangelsk. The attack of the Army Group will encounter stubborn enemy resistance in a deeply echeloned and well developed main defence zone, (with numerous dug in tanks, strong artillery and local reserves) the main effort of the defence being in the key sector Belgorod-Tamarovka.

In addition strong counter attacks by strategic reserves from east and southeast are to be expected. It is impossible to forecast whether the enemy will attempt to withdraw from a threatened encirclement by retiring eastwards, as soon as the key sectors [literally, 'corner-pillars'] of the bulge in the frontline at Kursk, Belgorod and Maloarkhangelsk, have been broken through. If the enemy throws in all strategic reserves on the Army Group front into the Kursk battle, the following may appear on the battle field:- On day 1 and day 2, 2 armoured divisions and 1 cavalry corps. On day 3, 2 mech and 4 armoured corps. On day 4, 1 armoured and 1 cavalry corps. On day 5, 3 mech corps. On day 6, 3 cavalry corps. On day 6 and/or day 7, 2 cavalry corps.

Summarising, it can be stated that the balance of evidence still points to a defensive attitude on the part of the enemy: and this is in fact unmistakable in the frontal sectors of the 6 Army and 1 Panzer Army. If the bringing up of further forces in the area before the north wing of the Army Group persists and if a transfer forward and merging of the mobile and armoured formations then takes place, offensive intentions become more probable. In that case it is improbable that the enemy can even then forestall our execution of Zitadelle in the required conditions. Probably on the other hand we must assume complete enemy preparations for defence, including the counter attacks of his strong mot [motorised] and armoured forces, which must be expected.

The intelligence was passed to Stewart Menzies and SIS, and thence to Churchill.[162] On 30 April, an intelligence memo was sent to Stalin, via the British Military Mission in Moscow. Since 1941 Menzies had always been reluctant to share with Moscow any information obtained exclusively from Ultra. He was afraid that German decryption of the Red Army, the GRU and KGB's ciphers could betray the source of Soviet intelligence received from the British. Churchill had insisted he make an exception in November 1942, during the battle for Stalingrad. Nigel de Grey and Brigadier John Tiltman had assisted in establishing Number 4 Intelligence Section at Bletchley Park as early as 1940, and one of its tasks by the time of the Kursk offensive was to decide what information could be shared both with allies such as the Russians and the French, and with neutral countries. Nigel de Grey, in his summary of the operations to intercept and break into Domino, said in spring 1942 that this was 'the beginning of a year's abortive liaison with Russia'.[163] By the time of the Battle of Kursk, the British hoped this situation had changed.

In January 1941, the personal envoy of President Roosevelt had visited London, and the Prime Minister had agreed with Harry Hopkins that the American intelligence apparatus could exchange and share information about Enigma, and American cryptanalytical successes, as soon as possible. When the American signals intelligence experts Abraham Sinkov and Leo Rosen had visited Bletchley Park in January 1941, Churchill agreed that the United States could now share information concerning Enigma. As mentioned earlier, the American team brought with them a Japanese Foreign Office Purple cipher machine and other codebreaking items to Bletchley, and liaised with John Tiltman in connection with his work on Japanese ciphers. The Brigadier had then paid a reciprocal visit to OP-20-G, the US Navy's cryptanalytical headquarters in Washington. In April 1942, as written, five months after the attack on Pearl Harbor, de Grey's colleagues were 'blind to Shark', after the Kriegsmarine added a fourth rotor to the naval

Enigma machines they were using. For Churchill, the secrecy of Ultra was of overriding, constant importance, and he checked with Stewart Menzies to ascertain what the Americans knew about the British decryption system.

'Do the Americans know anything about our machine? Let me know by tomorrow afternoon,' he wrote on 8 February 1942.[164]

The Director-General of SIS answered on the 9th: 'The American Naval Authorities have been given several of our Cypher Machines.'

OP-20-G had then helped to build and reconstruct possible Shark keys, using their version of the four-rotor bombe machine. They solved 2,940 German Naval Enigma, and 1,600 Germany Army and Air Force Enigma keys. Compared to the four Domino keys which had produced the most intelligence from the German Police decrypts, this represented a phenomenal amount of decryption. Reich, Russian and Raster alone had yielded most of the German Police intelligence, none of it having necessitated the use of bombes or Colossus machines, being derived from hand-held encryption systems. Churchill briefed General Dwight D. Eisenhower about the operations at Bletchley Park when he arrived in Britain in June 1942, to assume command of the Allied forces that were eventually to invade mainland Europe. Eventually, long after active operational collaboration had begun, on 17 May 1943 the British-United States Agreement, or BRUSA, was signed between Bletchley Park and the United States War Department. This was a form of written constitution of Anglo-American cryptanalysis. Its aim was 'to exchange completely all information concerning the detection, identification and interception of signals from, and the solution of codes and ciphers used by, the Military and Air forces of the Axis powers, including secret services (Abwehr).'

The United States assumed the main responsibility for the reading of Japanese military and air codes and ciphers, codenamed

Magic, the British for reading the German and Italian signals traffic, called Ultra. There would be total reciprocity, and total secrecy. Following this agreement, Colonel Alfred McCormack and Lieutenant-Colonel Telford Taylor, from the United States Army's Special Branch, were sent to Bletchley to see how the system there operated. They liaised with Commander Edward Travis, the operational director of Bletchley Park, and with de Grey, as the Intelligence Coordinator. It was not until September 1943, however, that Churchill finally persuaded Menzies that the BRUSA agreement should be operated without any form of restrictions on the material both sides could exchange. The United States Army and Navy in Washington should be sent all British Signals Intelligence material, including the Enigma and Lorenz decrypts. The key intelligence product which the Americans could offer was their decryption of the Japanese Purple cipher, which enabled the Allies to access the coded signals of the network of Japanese ambassadors and diplomats worldwide, such as those in Rome and Berlin, and some of the coded messages of the foreign ministry in Tokyo. Yet the British were determined to make an intelligence-sharing agreement function with the Soviet Union, as well. Any information that could be shared with Stalin should be, and there seemed no greater sign of confidence than by proposing to share information gathered through Bletchley Park's decryption of the German Police ciphers. If Moscow had been decrypting any of the other keys used in Domino, and were prepared to trade this with Nigel de Grey and his team, available information on SS and Order Police activities could be theoretically doubled.

Bletchley Park and their cooperation with Moscow

When in June 1941 the Germans invaded Russia and the Prime Minister made the declaration that any state that fights

Nazism will have our aid, the British Signals Intelligence authorities considered it their duty to try and establish some sort of liaison with the Russians. First suggestion was to send RAF and Army 'Y' units, but then this was changed to simply sending them Luftwaffe tactical codes with nothing in return – a test of sincerity.[165]

Nigel de Grey summarised his thoughts and analysis of Bletchley Park's cooperation with Moscow, writing memos and documents both during and after the war. When in August 1941 an RAF officer was sent to Moscow he was given nothing. Bletchley persisted. What they most wanted was a Y station on Russian territory, if possible on the North Cape, near Murmansk or Arkangel, to monitor German naval surface and submarine signals, and incoming German air attacks on Arctic convoys.

Apart [de Grey continued] from the supposition that Russian signals intelligence would be less efficient than British, that they would need British help and 'such help would serve to kill Germans', the British began the liaison without any very clear idea of what they were trying to achieve.

They eventually received permission to launch a Y station at Polyarnoe naval base, in Murmansk Sound. A staff member from Bletchley who had perhaps lived in or visited mid-Wales or Herefordshire codenamed this chill, bleak outpost Wye Cottage. In February 1942, a War Office representative gave the Russians the technical means to solve the German Police ciphers in use in the rear areas of the Eastern Front: at no point did the British think of letting them know about their successes with Enigma. Then in February 1943, without warning, the Russians shut down the transmitters at the British station at Polyarnoe.

Next, in August 1943, the Russians offered un-decoded German intercepts in return for help on Japanese decryption, and cooperation on army and air force ciphers, with regular flights from Moscow to Tehran to take the intercepts to the British. Up until December 1942, the Russians had been passing undecrypted German Police cipher material, containing information about German atrocities behind the front lines. The biggest thing Bletchley was now receiving from the Russians, however, was naval intercepts about movements of surface and submarine vessels off the north coast of Russia, Finland and Norway – the Tirpitz and Scharnhorst.

By July to August 1943, wrote de Grey, 'there was a considerable amount of revealing detail of (German) Police and Army relations and gruesome accounts of atrocities.'

To those who are familiar with post-war events, he said, the story of the Russian liaison will come as no surprise. At the time they were remarkable. Fundamentally the British interest before the strength of the Russians was known was to keep them in the field and

> . . . to help them to kill Germans. They [the Russians] were not unmindful of the fact that the Battle of Hindenberg victories of 1917 had been won on the strength of the Germans reading the Russian signals every evening, as they were sent in clear. The Russians had everything to gain and nothing to lose but they refused to play with people whom apparently they suspected of having all the aces up their sleeves.[166]

On 8 July 1943, Churchill felt encouraged by developments in the Atlantic, and so he was able to send a signal to Stalin to say that in seventy days, fifty U-boats had been sunk. On the 14th, he reported to Roosevelt that seven U-boats had been sunk in thirty-six hours, which Churchill described as the record killing of U-boats yet achieved in so short a time. Sixty British merchant ships had been sunk in March, thirty-four in April, thirty-one in May and eleven in June. In the meantime, by February 1943, the different Y Stations in the British Isles were intercepting 400 to 500 Domino signals per week, and by October 1943, more than 3,000 were decrypted in one month, the highest number of the entire war in a four-week period. Yet, by this date, and compared to the summer and autumn of 1941, almost none of the Domino decrypts contained details of German executions of Jews, nor of roundup, arrest, deportation or evacuation operations, neither on the Eastern Front nor in countries such as Greece, the Netherlands or France. By August 1943, the wide-ranging administrative messages sent from inside the concentration camp system in the Orange I code had also ceased. Occasional police signals, as noted, made mention of individual mass executions, such as the one which reported 700 Jews who were shot in July 1942.[167] The Höfle telegram of January 1943 had been the only specific communication about the killings of Jews during Operation Reinhard, and it appeared that the British intelligence analysts had failed to appreciate its significance. Yet when the Reich Security Main Office transmitted messages to the Gestapo and the SD in Rome in October 1943, after the Germans had invaded and occupied Italy, they did not do it in the Domino cipher system.

The SS signals announcing the beginning of the Final Solution in Italy

By summer 1943, the section that Oliver Strachey had created at Bletchley Park was run by a by a classicist from Oxford called Denys Page. Illicit Services (Oliver Strachey) or ISOS was still its name, and it handled the decipherment of German intelligence signals, from both the Abwehr and the SD. Nicknames, abbreviations, allusions were all used at Bletchley Park, often a combination of idiosyncratic English humour with linguistic twists. The codenames which Bletchley had given to the SS codes were based on fruit, such as Orange I and II, Quince, Grapefruit and Pear (which had been the previous name of Strachey's section). The SD was the SS's own intelligence service and as such had not just its own cryptanalytical section, but some of its own codes. Dilly Knox had formed the original team which had handled the Enigma traffic of the SD and the Abwehr, which still bore his name, 'Illicit Signals Knox' or 'ISK'. Their work was comparatively straightforward compared to the decryption of an Enigma machine with a plugboard, as used by the German navy. ISK could still be broken by hand and if they proved too complex, then the specialist 'bombes' could take over the task.

Dillwyn Knox died in February 1943 from lymphoma, and his huge contribution to the cryptanalytical successes at Bletchley Park was given a small token of governmental recognition when he was made a Companion of the Order of St Michael and St George while confined to his bed. It was he and a codebreaker called Mavis Batey who had helped break into the Italian naval Enigma, which had led to the British and Australian navies' victory at the Battle of Cape Matapan in 1941. By decrypting the Italian naval Enigma, Bletchley Park provided vital intelligence about the movements of the Italian fleet putting to sea to intercept merchant convoys headed for North Africa to supply British troops. The British and Australians intercepted the Italians south-west of Cape Matapan, in Greece, and the ensuing battle saw them sink three Italian heavy cruisers. Knox had celebrated with lines of poetry, which he called his 'Epitaph on Matapan to Mussolini':

These have knelled your fall and ruin,
    but your ears were far away,
English lassies rustling paper, through the sodden
    Bletchley day.[168]

The Allies were ashore in Sicily when the Germans occupied Rome, and Ernst Kaltenbrunner dispatched a small Einsatzkommando into the Italian capital to round up as many as possible of the city's 10,000 Jews. Adolf Eichmann was put in overall charge, and an SD officer called Theodor Dannecker coordinated the operations on the ground with the officer commanding the Rome Gestapo. Dannecker was another SS officer who had displeased his superiors: they caught him stealing property from Jewish prisoners in Paris, and then in Bulgaria his coordination operations with the interior ministry police in Sofia had meant the operation to deport Jews from Macedonia and Thrace to Lublin had proceeded slower than planned. Eichmann had given him a third chance in Italy.

Herbert Kappler, meanwhile, was a former electrician from Stuttgart who had become a police officer, and then joined the SS. Following promotion to the rank of Criminal Inspector, he worked in Vienna as one of the officers who oversaw the deportation of Austrian Jews following the Anschluss. In Rome he shared the responsibilities of commanding both the SD and the Gestapo.

The non-Enigma traffic, as written, was now handled by Page's team, and known as ISOS. Kaltenbrunner's office sent messages to the SS and Gestapo in the Italian capital in a subset of ISOS known as ISOSICLE. This was thought to be a hand-cipher system, based on keys, but it could have been sent on 'Fish,' as the Lorenz teleprinter cipher messages were called.

On 5 October, Kappler received a coded signal from Berlin from an official at Amt VI – the SD – of the RSHA. It was either encoded on Enigma in the SS Orange encryption, or in one of the non-Enigma encipherments codenamed ISOSICLE. Either way, the British codebreakers intercepted and read it:

Ref: transport of gold. Your W/T message of 5/10 without number is not clear. Are the 50kgs of gold actually being sent to CDS? HÖTTL.[169]

SS-Sturmbannführer Wilhelm Höttl worked for the SD in Berlin under Ernst Kaltenbrunner and already, in 1943, he was making his own preparations for what might happen after the war. Notes in an American intelligence file held on him described Höttl as a 'fanatic Nazi', who was 'believed to be cooperating with the Allies to save his own skin'.[170]

The gold to which he was referring had been taken by Kappler from the Jews of Rome, supposedly as a tax to prevent their deportation. Kappler was sending it to Höttl, destined for the Economic Affairs Office of the RSHA, but Kaltenbrunner himself had other designs on it. Two days later, it had still not arrived in Berlin. The SS officer mentioned below, Erich Priebke, was one of Kappler's deputies in Rome:

PRIEBKE'S trunk not arrived. Said to be still at the Embassy in Rome. As only hand dispatches[xvii] are sent to this end. HÖTTL.[171]

Then on the 6th of that month, the following recommendation was made to high German sources by a German official in Italy:

Orders have been received from Berlin by Obersturmbannführer KAPPLER to seize and to take to northern Italy the 8,000

---

xvii 'Hand dispatches' refers to enciphered signals sent using one-time pads and codebooks, as opposed to encipherment machines, like Enigma or the Lorenz enciphered teleprinter: in keeping with the piscine codings, the Lorenz line link from Rome to Berlin was codenamed 'Bream'. It suggests Höttl's office did not receive Lorenz traffic, but encoded radio dispatches with decryption keys, i.e. an Abwehr and SS key which the ISOCICLE section had decrypted prior to October.

Jews living in Rome. They are to be liquidated. General Stahel, the city commandant of Rome, will permit this action only if it is consistent with the policies of the Reich Foreign Minister. It would be better business in my opinion to use the Jews as in Tunis, for work on fortifications. Together with KAPPLER, I will present this view through Generalfeldmarschall Kesselring.[172]

One particular encrypted message, sent on 7 October 1943, back from Rome to the RSHA in Berlin, was deciphered by the ISOS section. It said that instructions had been given to the SS and SD in Rome 'to seize all Jews in lightning actions' and thus could have given forewarning to the Vatican, to Italian partisans and, if circulated, to the Jews themselves about forthcoming arrest operations:

To highest SS and Police Chief Italy Ograf WOLFF. RSHA has sent SS Hptstuf DANNECKER to this end with order to seize all Jews in lightning actions and to forward them to Germany.[173]

Ograf Wolff was SS-Obergruppenführer Karl Wolff, the Higher SS and Police Leader in Italy, based at Bolzano in the north-east of the country. A former adjutant to Himmler, he was implicated in the planning and execution of the Final Solution in Poland and Ukraine, and had visited an Einsatzkommando execution site with the Reichsführer outside Minsk. The signal from Rome and the acknowledgements sent back told Kappler and Dannecker exactly what they had to do. The arrest, deportation, then immediate and thorough eradication of the Jews in Italy. By 17 October, Swiss diplomats sent a signal encrypted in their foreign office's diplomatic cipher, which Bletchley Park read:

The SD is now pillaging Rome . . . Himmler has sent SS men who have had experience of this work in Russia to Rome.

The War Refugee Board, Hungary and Auschwitz

In January 1944, Franklin Roosevelt established the War Refugee Board, which was an American executive agency designed to help civilian victims of Germany and Italy, specifically those caught up in the Final Solution. It was founded at the behest of a trio of young, crusading lawyers from the Treasury Department, including Josiah DuBois, who had found evidence that the State Department had allegedly tried to actively suppress information about the persecution of the Jews from reaching the government and citizens of the United States. They wrote and submitted a report entitled 'Report to the Secretary on the Acquiescence of this Government to the Murder of the Jews'. The President finally acted after pressure from Henry Morgenthau Junior, and Treasury colleagues, who had grown exasperated at State Departmental and presidential vacillation in providing effective assistance to Europe's Jews. Once persuaded, however, Roosevelt embraced the idea vigorously, stressing that it was urgent that action be taken to prevent the continued persecution and extermination of Jews and other minorities in occupied Europe. Along with refugee organisations, finance groups, behind-the-lines organisations such as Britain's SOE (Special Operations Executive) and the United States' OSS (Office of Strategic Services), and the help of neutral countries such as Turkey, Sweden and Switzerland, Roosevelt was determined to act, though to many it all smacked of too little, too late.

On 4 April 1944, Flight Lieutenants Charles Barry and Ian McIntyre took off from San Severo airbase, outside Foggia in southern Italy, for a photo reconnaissance flight. The flight in their unarmed twin-engined Mosquito took five hours, as they were photographing the industrial plants of the IG Farben synthetic-rubber factory outside Oświęcim in southern Poland. They were over the target for four minutes, and made two passes, from west to east, and vice versa, as one of their cameras was malfunctioning. Left running, it caught aerial footage of what they much later were told was the concentration camp complex at Auschwitz Birkenau some two miles away.[174]

The Allies had known about the existence of the camp complex since February 1942, when the first Orange I decrypts were analysed in Hut 3. They knew by November, following reports from the Polish government-in-exile and others, that mass murder was taking place there. The Poles gave the Special Operations Executive a report in November called Aneks 58, which claimed that 468,000 Jews had already been killed there. From 1942 to late 1944, an estimated 1.1 million people would die, mostly European Jews, predominantly in the gas chambers of the Auschwitz II- Birkenau complex. Repeated intelligence from Poland, and from diplomats, intelligence agents, refugees, camp escapees, the Vatican and neutral governments, as well as hundreds of media reports, confirmed this, as Bletchley Park's analysts and other staff knew. Yet the scepticism of the British Foreign Office, epitomised by the Joint Intelligence Committee, helped to downplay the story of Auschwitz's existence, especially the existence of gas chambers. Whereas the camps in the Operation Reinhard system avoided identification by name for their entire operational duration, Auschwitz was different. Within a limited circle of intelligence officials, analysts, government ministers and defence chiefs, it was an open secret. Following on from the deportation operations in Italy in autumn 1943 and spring 1944, Auschwitz was mentioned in decrypted signals and reports from diplomats and refugees, along with the camp complex at Mauthausen in Austria, as the destination for trains of

Italian Jews. So when, in spring 1944, reports began to emerge from Budapest in Hungary that the Germans were initiating arrest and deportation operations of the country's estimated 900,000 Jews, and deporting them, Nigel de Grey and the analysts at Hut 3 strongly suspected that Auschwitz would be their intended destination. Signals decrypts confirmed this.

On 8 April 1944, Cardinal Maglione at the Vatican wrote a message and sent it to the Apostolic Delegate in Berne, which the British intercepted and decrypted: 'The Holy See has for some time been and still is concerned about the fate of Jews resident in Hungary, and is now making new efforts at the suggestion of the Nuncio in Budapest. But we are not able to hold out any – hopes.'[175]

In June, a Hungarian diplomat accredited to the Swiss government sent a signal to the Hungarian ambassador to the Vatican, Baron Vilmos Apor, a Catholic bishop, alerting him to what was happening in Budapest, and the surrounding countryside, and asking him to intervene with the papal authorities.[176] On 25 June a message was intercepted and decrypted describing the gassing of Hungarian Jews at Auschwitz. It was a so-called ISCOT decrypt, from a small section at the GC&CS which handled messages to and from Moscow, sent by the various national communist party organisations around the world, as well as by communist-aligned partisan and political groups in countries such as Italy or Yugoslavia. The name was derived from the surname – Scot – of the officer who ran the section. Only six out of an estimated 1,500 decrypts had any connection with the persecution of Jews. ISCOT 399 was one of them:

June 25 ... Service 133 ... from Poland.
To: 17 (ZAVADSKY) from 18 (VACLAV)
(A very corrupt message only readable in parts) . . . . . . in the concentration camp of OSWIECIM the Germans

are gradually killing from five to ten thousand Hungarian Jews . . .approximately . . . thousand . . . have been gassed . . . month . . . (for the removal of German prisoners of war to England) . . . Hungarian Jews about this (Last word missing presumably warn or tell or alert.)[177]

The Japanese diplomatic legation in Budapest then reported on 7 July that the operation was efficient and nearly 200,000 Jews had already been deported. The signal was intercepted twice by the British as the mission in Hungary then sent it to Tokyo via Baron Oshima in Berlin.[178]

On 14 July, with the Red Army advancing into eastern Hungary, Winston Churchill sent a message to Moscow:

FROM FOREIGN OFFICE TO MOSCOW.
No.2107 D.4.55a.m. 14th July 1944. 13th July 1944.
Repeated to Washington No.6325.
(Begins)
You will remember that on the 17th December 1942, a declaration was issued in the names of the Governments of the Soviet Union, the United States and the United Kingdom, and of the other Allies, calling attention to the bestial measures of extermination which the German authorities were applying to the Jewish population in the areas occupied by them, and solemnly affirming that those responsible for these crimes should not escape retribution.

2. In spite of an unbroken series of military reverses during the past two years and the certainty of final defeat the Germans are in no way desisting from their barbarous treatment of the Jews. Indeed the contrary would appear to be the case. All our information goes to show that since the Germans occupied Hungary measures of gassing and burning have been applied

with ever increasing ferocity by the Germans and that the present Hungarian Government are collaborating as willing accomplices in these outrages. As a result appeals are frequently made to His Majesty's Government to issue some further declaration condemning these crimes. It has occurred to me that, given the victorious advance of the Soviet Armies, a declaration by your Government couched in terms of unambiguous frankness and proclaiming that the Soviet Armies and retribution for these crimes would enter Hungary together, might have the effect of at least reducing the scale of these horrible outrages against the Jewish population.

On 4 August, a signal was intercepted from Hungary sent in one of the Domino keys, and reported by Hut 3:

Jews are still rounded up and deported to Poland. BdS Hungary informs RSHA Berlin that a second special train is leaving SARVAR (in western Hungary) 4 Aug for Auschwitz (Oświęcim) with 1296 Jews, no doubt for the concentration camp there.[179]

Meanwhile, Ralph Vrba and Alfred Wetzler were two Slovakian Jews who escaped from Auschwitz in April 1944, and managed to return safely to Slovak territory. They wrote a report which they presented to the Jewish Affairs Group in Bratislava, describing conditions in the concentration camp system. It included details of gas-chambers, the identities of SS officials who ran the extermination programme, the numbers and nationalities of the Jews, and others, who had been killed, the executions, and the preparation of half-a-million false discharge documents meant to cover up the numbers of people who had been murdered there. It was carried then to Berne, and delivered to Allen Dulles, who ran the OSS office there. He read it, and immediately cabled Washington about its contents. Another copy was wired to the Czech government-in-exile in London: the Y station system intercepted it, and the diplomatic cryptanalysts at Bletchley Park decrypted it. Arriving in the United States, the report reached Roosevelt, who threatened to continue US Air Force strikes on Budapest if the pro-German Hungarian Regent, Miklos Horthy, did not force a suspension of the SS deportations. Ralph Vrba then met with a Swiss Vatican Monsignor in Bratislava, who passed the report to Rome. On the 25th, Pope Pius XII made a personal appeal to Horthy. The Jewish Agency in Geneva telegraphed it to London, urging the Allies to hold members of the Hungarian government responsible. Hungarian cryptanalysts, who worked with a small team of SS signals intelligence staff in Budapest, intercepted it. The Prime Minister showed it to Horthy, and on 7 July the deportations temporarily halted.

Bletchley Park's intelligence offer to the Russians

At the beginning of August 1944, the Polish Home Army launched the Warsaw uprising, in the ruins of the ghetto which Hermann Höfle had tried to empty two years before. In Normandy, the Allied armies were breaking out of the hedgerow maze of bocage country, having taken Saint-Lô. Hitler had narrowly survived an assassination attempt at his Wolf's Lair headquarters at Rastenburg in East Prussia, while in Italy, British armoured car units were pushing into the outskirts of Florence, and nearing the German Gothic Line defensive position that stretched across the breadth of Italy from the Mediterranean to the Adriatic. In the Pacific US Marines had taken Tinian in the northern Marianas, giving them a further base on which to build airstrips within striking distance of Japan. In Burma, British and Indian troops took the key city of Myitkyina, while on the Eastern Front, the Red Army cut off the Baltics from east Prussia by taking Vilnius, the capital of Lithuania, and Minsk. The end of war was closing in on Berlin and Tokyo. Then, on the 24th, the Red Army liberated both Lublin, and the area of Majdanek concentration camp.

In September, Hut 3, the deputy directors and the director of the Government Code and Cypher School, in coordination with both MI6 and MI8, undertook an intelligence offer to Moscow. Gone was the hesitation of the first three years of the war: the British wanted to see if the Russians would reciprocate with any information they had obtained from decrypting German Police ciphers, or others. Churchill also wanted as close as possible a cooperation with Stalin in the execution of the final year of the war in Europe, with the British and Americans approaching from the west, the Red Army from the east. The summary of material to be offered to the Russians was comprehensive, including the codenames of German keys, radio frequencies, and extracts of Domino decrypts from across Europe. While Bletchley Park was not showing Russia their full hand, they were making it amply clear they had very strong, game-changing intelligence cards, and were prepared to show them to their sceptical, wary ally if it helped to persuade them to share some of their intelligence, to hasten the end of the war, the liberation of concentration and death camps, and the comprehensive destruction and downfall of Hitler's regime.[180] The package was prepared by de Grey and one of his colleagues, and assembled by Number 4 Intelligence Section.

> General survey – of interception, breaking, and intelligence, and a selection of prepared by the No.4 Intelligence Section from 1943, that shows how the messages used long-term can form background intelligence. The next section is a selection of German message decodes, in the original language,

from August 1943 to February 1944, showing the types of messages received.

A selection of messages in a traffic key now defunct called 'Ingot'. The total number of messages runs 'into a thousand or two'. The message then says that 'I think our friends might be interested in these as it shows them to some extent where their art treasures have gone.'

A selection from another moribund traffic, called No.11 Traffic, which 'if this is what we think it is – German D/F (Direction-Finding) on Russian agents – it might well interest them.'

The operational message showing the encirclement of Obergruppenführer Prutzmann near Rovno on February 1st, followed by the message about Tito and Anglo-Russian relations, and a note on the machine-cypher inaugurated for Police Traffic on February 1st. The message finishes with the words 'I hope these will do the trick! Wishing you the best of luck . . .'

Then followed the notes:

In one or two cases, to whet the appetite of the Russians, No.4 Section added two 'etc,etc' on the end of longer messages, to imply there was more than had been stated. The ones chosen (for the Russians) are of course the best, but by no means the only good ones. In a normal day the total number of decrypts (they could expect) would be between 80–100. The messages include ones from Himmler, Göring and Nazi Party ministers, describing Allied bomb damage, the situation in Russia and other countries, as well as in the Third Reich itself. Bletchley then slips in what it describes as 'a minor leg-pull', as it describes the decrypts of German messages describing the aftermath of a 'most unsuccessful Russian raid on Gomel' and a 'shatteringly successful' British raid on Hannover. Then there was a message about 31 escaped Russian POWs at the end – in all, the escape of 972 Russian prisoners was reported in 1943.

The first in the selection of the chosen messages for the week from 12 September to 19 September 1944 were as follows:

As a result of heavy air raids on Emden on the 6th, extra funds are available on notification to the sum of 1,500,000 Reichsmarks.

To Police President Diedenhofen: the Emden plant of the Hutten administration must be cleared as quickly as possible, namely the presses and machines. If clearing is no longer possible, the plant must be blown up. From Reichswerke Hermann Göring.

From Gauleiter Regener, Propaganda Ministry Berlin. Major damage in Osnabrück, with thousands homeless.

To Rf SS (Reichsführer Heinrich Himmler), on board the special train 'Stiermark'. Secret Matter. From the Higher SS and Police leader in the Netherlands, Rauter. First shots fired from the batteries at Walcheren. (Guarding the estuary leading to the port of Antwerp.)

To Rf SS, Personal and to SS Gruppenführer Fegelein (Commanding Officer of the SS Cavalry Regiment). From SS General von dem Bach: in a sudden and swift night attack, the Legionow Dabrowskiego fort south of Mokotow was taken. Secret![181]

Next on the list of intelligence which Bletchley Park was offering Moscow was the most technical, and the most secret. It concerned information on the decrypts of the Domino key which Bletchley had codenamed 'Raster'. The name came from the word for a matrix of tiny images making up a visual item like a digital aerial photograph, where a two-dimensional image is represented by a series of square pixels. If the Russians were to release Raster cryptography for discussion, what GC&CS wanted was any information they had on Raster, any one-time pads, and any work done on German Police traffic. Hut 3 could offer Moscow seven German army, five air force pads, and one extra, encrypted in Raster – in essence, the key to decrypting the cipher. This was the highest bid that GC&CS's intelligence section were prepared to make to the Russians, and they waited for them to match it, raise it, or show their hand. In the meantime, the advance of both the Western Allies in Normandy, Italy and the Pacific continued, while the Red Army had pushed forward across their entire 1,000 front following the success of a main summer offensive, Operation Bagration.

'It looks as if the Germans are about to collapse,' said Nigel de Grey and the Head of British Military Signals Intelligence, on 3 August, in an exchange of messages with Supreme Allied Headquarters in Europe. Thinking that the war could soon be over, de Grey started looking ahead to what might be the GC&CS requirements for interception – and by extension decryption – after an armistice with Germany? To which parts of the world would the Allies need to listen? Who would be the new enemies, and where would they be? Operation Talisman was launched to find out, and to establish a strategic listening and intelligence-gathering plan.[182] The codename was an early version of 'Eclipse', which represented the plans and operational outline to be put into action in the advent of a German surrender in north-west Europe.

De Grey wrote to Colonel J. R. Vernham at the Signals Intelligence Department, or MI8, at the War Office, agreeing that the GC&CS should have signals interception parties with British forces of occupation.

There may be a good deal of [German Police] traffic of this nature which will be unauthorised and for which careful watch should be kept ... the Russians are realists, and they will intercept our traffic and expect us to intercept theirs. They would make no bones about it though they would not be as candid as the French, who at one time gave us their TA [intercept] reports complete with 'Section Anglais!' [This being of British traffic they had decrypted.] The interception of Russian traffic is normally difficult for us, but owing to their present advance westwards, the opportunity to do so is good . . . staff must be trained in Japanese morse so as to operate in the Japanese war.[183]

On 26 September Colonel W Scott at the office of the Assistant Chief of Staff at SHAEF, the Supreme Headquarters of the Allied Expeditionary Force, wrote a memo, with 'Subject – Secret' saying that 'after a German surrender a vast quantity of documents will be captured, Bletchley should send a couple of officers to be on the SHAEF documents team looking for material that will be of information to them – we assume about decrypts.'

On the 27th Colonel Vernham listed the War Office's intercept requirements after an armistice, and passed it, classified as Top Secret Ultra, to Commander Travis, the Director of GC&CS.

First all German traffic authorised and illicit, both internal and external. Any traffic on countries outside Germany which provide a source of information on Germany, such as Spanish police, and any country such as the Argentine where the cadre of a New Wehrmacht might be formed. Next Russian traffic for information on Russian order of battle, Polish and Czech, being countries adjacent to Germany . . .

Nigel de Grey and Bletchley Park were playing a long game: simultaneously planning the interception and decryption of the messages of a current foe – Germany – who stood to be a potential ally in the near future, and an old ally – the Soviet Union – who were on the verge of becoming a new enemy. Sharing the Domino decrypts and the technical details of the Raster keys with the Russian cryptanalytical infrastructure was a gesture of supreme confidence by Bletchley Park and SIS – it backfooted the Russians, as, confronted by this new information, they would have asked themselves which of their own ciphers had the British and Americans broken? It encouraged them to share information, very particularly that which they were discovering, and about to discover, as they liberated Poland, and the existing and destroyed structures, and inmates, of the camp complexes around Lublin and Oświęcim. This information gained from any SS, Order Police, SD and Gestapo records they found could assist in forthcoming war-crimes trials – even though the Soviets would stage their own – and in helping the Allies discover technical aspects of the RSHA's infrastructure, such as signals intelligence. Additionally, if the NKVD and GRU shared any information they had intercepted and deciphered in the Domino keys, the extent to which they had or had not been successful would also tell the analysts in Hut 3 much about their cryptanalytical and interception capabilities.

The Vrba-Wetzler Report was finally published on 25 November, in tandem with two other reports, and the three together were titled *The Auschwitz Protocols*. The Executive Office of the War Refugee Board released them on 13 November, on the same day as the last thirteen prisoners, all women, were gassed or shot at Auschwitz II-Birkenau. In December, the SS Plenipotentiary for Hungary, who had overseen much of the planning and execution of the Final Solution in Budapest and surrounding countryside, sent a signal to the RSHA, the Foreign Office and the German High Command. An official in the German foreign affairs department called Fritz Kolbe was a courier who travelled with the department's diplomatic bag to Berne in Switzerland. He had been an avowed anti-Nazi since 1940, and had refused to join the party. Despite this he had become a trusted and valued staff member in the ministry: he was also a spy for the Americans. He had offered his services to MI6 in 1943 in Switzerland, who rejected him as unreliable; the American OSS in Berne took him on. Allen Dulles, who ran the operation in Switzerland, codenamed him 'George Wood'. He described Kolbe as not just their best source on Germany, but undoubtedly one of the best secret agents any intelligence service had ever had. The British, having rebuffed him, were more sceptical. Only eleven people, including Roosevelt, were allowed to see Kolbe's 'product', and his information gave the Americans crucial insights into the V1 and V2 rocket programmes, the Me 262 jet fighter, and the Wehrmacht's knowledge of potential Allied invasion sites in France. His handlers called his intelligence 'Boston', and in early January 1945 he brought with him to Berne the signal received from SS-Brigadeführer Veesenmayer on 30 December.

Veesenmayer to Berlin 30 Dec 44

From Veesenmayer, to Berlin 30th December 1944

Re: final status of Jewish questions in Hungary. Obersturmführer Eichmann was ordered back to Berlin. The remainder of the command is picking up any Jewish workers who can be found. It will then suspend activities . . .

. . . according to final figures available here we have the following picture. Clean up of the provinces in the summer of 1944: 440,000 Jews . . .

By mid-January the Red Army had entered Warsaw and begun a large offensive in East Prussia. Hitler was by now headquartered in his Führerbunker in Berlin, along with his companion Eva Braun. The Americans and Russians were closing in. In January 1945 the Jewish Agency for Palestine asked the Czech government-in-exile in London to send a message for them, to its representative in Stockholm. They wanted it to be relayed to the Soviet ambassador in Sweden, a veteran Marxist called Alexandra Kollontay, who had been part of efforts to end the war between the Soviet Union and Finland. The British, who had broken into Czech diplomatic codes, intercepted the message, decrypted it, and shared it with the Americans. It asked that the Soviets initiate some surprise military action to seize the German death camps in Poland before the Germans executed the thousands of Jews and other anti-fascists still held in them.[184]

Then, on 25 January, the Red Army's 322nd Rifle Division fought its way into the town of Oświęcim, taking 221 casualties, as it battled through the area around Monowitz, Auschwitz I and Birkenau concentration camps. The Soviet soldiers arrived in Auschwitz II at three o'clock in the afternoon of the 27th, to discover the camp mostly empty, the SS guards having fled. They had left behind 7,000 corpses, 600 living prisoners, 837,000 articles of women's clothing, and seven tonnes of human hair.

Red Army General Vasily Petrenko, of the 107th Infantry Division, said:

I, who saw people dying every day, was shocked by the Nazis' indescribable hatred towards the inmates, who had turned into living skeletons. I read about the Nazis' treatment of Jews in various leaflets, but there was nothing about the Nazis' treatment of women, children, and old men. It was in Auschwitz that I found out about the fate of the Jews.[185]

CHAPTER XII

THE END OF THE FINAL SOLUTION

Austria, Italy and Germany, 1945-62

The Third Reich was collapsing, yet German propaganda continued like a bushfire burning out of control. Hitler, Goebbels and Himmler were desperate to split the Allies against each other, and against themselves. For the preceding five months, the senior SS commander in Italy and a select team of loyal officers had been trying to negotiate a separate peace with the Americans and British that would bring an early end to the fighting in Italy. Operation Sunrise had deliberately sidelined the Russians: SS-Obergruppenführer Karl Wolff, like the American and British generals with whom he was negotiating, could see the Cold War coming, and how the Soviet Union would become the new enemy. The talks, held in secret near Berne in Switzerland, collapsed when Sergei Molotov, the Russian Foreign Minister, discovered the Soviet Union's exclusion from the ongoing negotiations and accused the Western Allies of traitorous deception. Even though the war was all but over, the Nazi Party seized on this and poured as much petrol as they could on the flames. On 6 April, Hut 3 at

Bletchley Park sent a priority decrypt from to the British Directors of Military Intelligence for each respective armed service. The signal was also sent to Major-General Terence Airey in Italy, who had been the senior British negotiator on Operation Sunrise.

Top Secret U
To: CSS Personal, / Rear-Admiral Rushbrooke, Personal / Major-General Sinclair, Personal / Air-Vice Marshal Inglis, Personal /
From: Duty Officer Hut 3
Ref: T.O.O 190854Z/5/45 passed at request of Police Section, following has now been sent as Special Un-numbered Signal specially for AIREY, bearing T.O.O 211536Z/5/45:

'Following German Police message dated 6th April:
To Reich Security Main Office (Roman) 3 Berlin from Security Police GRAZ Doktor Zehlein.

The Soviets have shot all British and Belgian prisoners in BERNDORF (XC15), Kreis Feldbach, laid them on the road and driven over them with tanks. Identity numbers determined. Scene of dead photographed.

Note from DMI. Grateful any evidence to confirm or deny above. 211616Z/5/45 [186]

Berndorf was a town ten miles south-west of Vienna, which the Red Army had reached around 6 April. British and Belgian POWs had been among groups of Allied prisoners who had been kept in camps in that area of Austria, and the information was simultaneously precise, yet extremely difficult to verify, and played to the German and Western Allies' fears about the potential and actual behaviour of the Red Army as it advanced.

On the same day, the German Propaganda Ministry were

working on a story about an escaped Allied POW, about Canadian forces' ill-treatment of German women. Hungarian state treasure, evacuated on a so-called 'Hungarian Gold Train', was to be brought into the Reich itself from Linz; Himmler ordered the commander of Mauthausen concentration camp to bring back all the prisoners (into Germany), while the Gauleiter, or regional governor, of the Carinthia area, was asking for money and weapons and ammunition to defend the area, while millions of evacuated people were moving from east Germany. Nobody, but nobody wanted to be caught by the advancing Russians. Every mayor in every town, village and city was ordered to build anti-tank barriers, every town and village and street and bridge was to be defended by Volksturm, or civilian defenders, and the Wehrmacht.[187]

'The Führer expects all Gauleiters to take strong action against cowards of both sexes, and hang them with a suitable label attached,' was a signal from Berlin sent to the headquarters of each town and city in the Reich still occupied by Germany and its allies.[188]

Himmler meanwhile ordered the last drops of fuel to be reserved for fighting troops; art treasures were stored in the castle at Langenau-an-der-Lahn, while a battle group of 300 Hungarian soldiers was disbanded after they caused trouble; enemy parachutists were expected on the Ems canal, troops moved to confront a partisan threat inside Austria, while emergency currency was issued in Nord-Rhein Westphalia. The SS, Police units and civilians were ordered to evacuate Graz in Austria and head north. Ad-hoc battle groups were being made up of any available SS and policemen as the Red Army swept into the suburbs of Vienna. The war was effectively over. Then on 30 April came news that Adolf Hitler had committed suicide in Berlin.[189]

The capture of SS-Sturmbannführer Hermann Höfle

In the aftermath of the operation codenamed 'Harvest Festival', and following Globočnik's transfer to Trieste, SS-Gruppenführer Jakob Sporrenberg had been sent to replace him in Lublin, while the SS posted Jürgen Stroop to serve as the Higher SS and Police Leader in Greece. He did not last long. On arrival in Athens a number of German and Greek police and security units were put under his direct command. Civilian administrators of both nationalities complained about Stroop's autocratic command methods, an official signal reached the German High Command in Berlin, and Himmler replaced Stroop. The SS general who took his place, Walter Schimana, was an Austrian, from Vienna, and after leaving Lublin, Hermann Höfle went to Greece join his fellow countryman. By the time both men arrived there, the majority of the country's 75,000 Jews had already been deported to Poland and Auschwitz, with most of them from the huge Jewish community in Thessaloniki. Höfle's SS record has him arriving in Greece in June 1944, although he may have started duties there prior to that. His, and the German stay would not last much longer.

Italy had collapsed in summer 1943, and the Allies were now fighting their way northwards up the country: they had liberated Rome in June 1944. The Red Army invaded Romania on 20 August, King Michael replaced the Fascist leader Ion Antonescu, and then declared war on Germany. The vital Ploesti oilfields, which had supplied the crucial majority of Hitler's fuel, were now in Russian hands. Greece was nearing open rebellion, and partisan attacks on German troops were increasing. With Romania now captured, Hungary partially occupied by the Red Army, and anti-partisan warfare in Yugoslavia approaching the north-eastern Italian border, the presence of German units in Greece was pointless. The Wehrmacht, Luftwaffe and SS pulled out of the country in mid-October, and Höfle accompanied Schimana back to Vienna. The Austrian capital was now in range of Allied aircraft based in Italy, and anti-aircraft units were stationed around the city. The beautiful Austrian capital was now touched by war, and for Hermann Höfle, back in his own country after three years in the east, of mud and wire and orders and rivers of other people's blood, the Third Reich seemed to be contracting fast.

His former colleagues from Lublin were not far away. In and around the Adriatic seaport of Trieste, Himmler had granted Odilo Globočnik, Ernst Lerch, Franz Stangl and even the psychotic Kurt Franz their own little piece of Reich empire, and told them to empty it of Jews and undesirables. Globočnik, back home with his trunks of stolen loot, a loyal cadre of his SS praetorians, and a platoon of chosen Ukrainian guards from Treblinka and Belzec, needed no second urging. Had Himmler sent the men from Lublin into an angry, complicated urban and rural combat zone, in the hope they would all be killed, taking the secrets of Operation Reinhard with them to their graves? Franz Stangl and some of the other officers and NCOs thought so, but the reality was probably more prosaic. For Himmler, his men in the SS were there to serve it in the best way they could, and if that meant that he and Maximilian von Herff from SS Personnel sent them where they were most needed, and most effective, then that was simply good leadership, and the proper use of military resources. Globočnik and Lerch and his men were past masters in conducting anti-partisan warfare in a viciously hostile urban and rural environment, while simultaneously carrying out operations of ethnic cleansing and human extermination. More simply put, they knew how to run a concentration and extermination camp located in a city where half the population would fight alongside you, the other half wanted to kill you, while pincered in between three front lines. The Yugoslav partisan armies of Marshal Tito, with the Red Army behind them, were closing in across the Slovenian and Croatian borders; the Russians, by autumn 1944, were across Hungary, and Italian and Slovenian partisans were everywhere. To the south-west were the huge Allied armies advancing up Italy, struggling to cross the defensive Gothic Line before winter arrived. To the direct south were the dark cobalt waters of the Adriatic. Globočnik and his men, operating a detention centre, extermination camp and a prison all in one, in the back suburbs of Trieste, were an operational microcosm of the Third Reich: surrounded, back against the wall, but determined to fulfil its agenda.

The converted rice-factory which they had turned into the camp was called the Risiera di San Sabba, a gloomy, five-storey red-brick building. The SS, the Ukrainians and some Italian Fascist auxiliaries rounded up Jews, communist partisans, Slovenian and Croatian anti-Fascists and either killed or imprisoned them in the camp, while deporting around 2,500-3,000 Italian and Slovenian Jews to Auschwitz and Mauthausen. The camp was the only one in Italy to have its own crematorium. The squad from Lublin took losses, as well: in May 1944 Christian Wirth was machine-gunned in a partisan ambush on a mountain road across the border in neighbouring Yugoslav territory. Back in Vienna, with possible SS postings to Holland or Sachsenhausen concentration camp on his agenda, Höfle waited until he would see his SS colleagues once more.

On the evening of 29 May 1945, troopers from the 4th (Queen's Own) Hussars were on patrol in south-eastern Austria. The war was over by more than three weeks, and the roads, villages and towns of this border region were filled by refugees returning home, displaced people from Poland and Russia, former POWs, Wehrmacht soldiers tramping west, British and American army patrols, and Austrian civilians tending to their farms in the first spring of peace for six years. One of the SS men the

Hussars questioned on that night was a sergeant called Siegfried Kummerer: he told the British soldiers that up on the slopes of a nearby mountain, above a lake, a group of high-ranking SS officers were hiding. The mountain was called the Mösslacher Alm, the lake the Weissensee. The Hussars were based in the nearby town of Paternion, and at ten o'clock at night on the same day, an arrest and ad hoc raiding party left the base. In command was Major Alex Ramsay, an officer from the Parachute Regiment, attached to the Special Air Service. He was part of a team set up by the MI6 and MI9 departments of British Intelligence in spring 1945 to track, identify and arrest Nazi war criminals inside Europe. With him were four officers from the Hussars, and twelve NCOs and troopers. The men climbed up the mountain for five hours, and arrived outside a hut set in a stand of pine trees at half-past four in the morning.[190] Ramsay pushed in through the front door with one of the Hussar NCOs, while Hedley and one of the other officers went behind the cabin: the special forces officer swept through to the inside, followed by three men. There were eight men in the building, and two women. The British soldiers took them outside, and lined them up. One of them admitted that he was Friedrich Rainer, a former Carinthian Gauleiter, or governor, who said he had arrived from Trieste. The other men said that they were in the Wehrmacht. The last man, a heavily built man with dark hair, said simply he was a merchant from Klagenfurt. The Hussars took them back down the mountain, and returned to Paternion.

The eight men were questioned by the British Hussars and the Military Police, where three of them gave their names, and their original units, as SS-Sturmbannführer Georg Michaelsen, SS-Sturmbannführer Ernst Lerch and SS-Sturmbannführer Hermann Höfle. They said they had recently arrived from Trieste. The 'merchant' from Klagenfurt kept silent. All of the men bar him were locked into a small building behind the castle in Paternion, while the man from Klagenfurt paced the small courtyard. SS-Oberscharführer Kummerer, however, told Ramsay and another officer that this man was in fact SS-Gruppenführer Globočnik. Ramsay then went to stand on a small terrace outside a first-floor entrance to the castle, and as the man walked around the courtyard, he called his name:

'Globočnik!'

The man's step did not falter, but his head moved slightly. Ramsay was watching him. He shouted in German that he had given himself away, and ordered one of the military police NCOs, Sergeant Sowler, to put him in the small locked building with the other men. This was around 11.25 in the morning. As he was being escorted out of the courtyard to the locked building, Globočnik bit down on something in his mouth: a cyanide capsule. Despite the Hussars' medical officer attempting to revive him, he was dead in under two minutes. The three SS majors then confirmed that the body was, indeed, that of Odilo Globočnik. Of Lublin, Aktion Reinhard, Trieste and Poland, they said nothing.

Höfle then spent two years in British internment camps in Austria, and by 1947 was on the Central Register of War Criminals and Security Suspects, the so-called CROWCASS Wanted List, which was published by SHAEF, the Supreme Headquarters Allied Expeditionary Force. This was a four-volume list divided into Germans, non-Germans, and two supplementary lists of people suspected of other war crimes, a total of around 60,000 people in all. The first entry on the list was Adolf Hitler: wanted for murder by Poland, Czechoslovakia and Belgium.[191] The CROWCASS list guided Allied war crimes investigators, and was their main source of information concerning wanted suspects. In 1946, the Central Jewish Historical Commission in Poland had also published information about Höfle, including testimony from Marcel

Reich-Ranicki, the former secretary of the Warsaw Judenrat. The CROWCASS Consolidated list has a 'Hoeffle' listed as a 'Gestapo functionary wanted for murder who was in Warschau 40-45, sought by Poland'.[192]

He was not, however, on the organisation's Index of War Criminals, or List of War Criminals. So in August 1947 Höfle was released by the British from the Wolfsberg internment camp in Carinthia and handed over to the Austrian justice system. At first he was imprisoned in Salzburg, by orders of the Regional Court, then he was transferred to the supervision of the People's Court in Linz. Then he was freed. It helped him substantially that his namesake SS-Obergruppenführer Hermann Höfle, who was born in 1898, came from Augsburg and served as the Higher SS and Police Commander in Slovakia from 15 September 1944 to 15 March 1945. He was sentenced to death as the person mainly responsible for the suppression of the Slovak National Uprising in Bratislava, and hanged on the 7 December 1947.

Hermann Julius Höfle, meanwhile, worked as a car mechanic until 15 December 1947, when he was interrogated by the Americans. On 9 July 1948, the Polish government applied to the Western Occupying Powers of Great Britain, France and the United States for his extradition. They wanted to try him together with Jürgen Stroop, with whom he had served in Greece after he left Lublin in early December 1943. The last entry on Höfle's SS personnel file is for July 1944, under the entry 'Griechenland' (Greece), and with his mission specified as working for the Higher SS and Police Leader, which referred to the office where Stroop was assigned. After that he served briefly at the Sachsenhausen concentration camp in Germany, and then in April 1945 travelled to join Globočnik either in, or near Trieste.

Following the Polish government's extradition request, Höfle then left Austria, and moved to Italy, where he lived under an assumed name for three years. Stroop, however, was extradited by the Americans, and the Poles sentenced him to death. He was hanged in 1951. Höfle returned to Austria from Italy at the beginning of 1951. In March he tried to get into West Germany secretly and was arrested for illegal border crossing. He gave his real name and told a Munich court that the Poles were searching for him and that he feared being kidnapped. He then received new identity papers and a West German residence permit.

It was at this point that the US Army's Counterintelligence Corps contacted and recruited him in 1954. Höfle had met up with some former SS members, who themselves were under surveillance by the Americans. The CIC then approached Höfle as an agent who could potentially provide information about organisations of former SS men. The Americans gave him the codename 'Hans Hartmann'. He was paid 100 Reichsmarks per month.

> Subject is punctual, militant in action, truthful and trusting in a person only after his trustworthiness has been proven. Subject has been found to be most appreciative and courteous . . . Based on information received from subject, he can be evaluated as fairly reliable at this time. Subject is considered 'usually reliable' insofar as past activity of the SS and Gestapo is concerned. It is pointed out, however, in the majority of cases that subject must be asked specific questions during meetings because he is prone to minimize an occurrence or event rather than to magnify it.[193]

Höfle's name was then mentioned during Eichmann's trial, as were those of several of his fellow SS colleagues. Eichmann was kidnapped in Brazil by Mossad agents, and taken back to Israel for trial, after which he was executed on 1 June 1962. Partly due to the publicity generated by the trial of Adolf Eichmann, the Salzburg

Public Prosecutor's Office initiated proceedings against the perpetrators of Aktion Reinhard in 1961. The principal defendant was Hermann Höfle. Eichmann had claimed in court that when he first visited Lublin in late summer of 1941, it had been Höfle who had shown him the gassing facilities on behalf of Globočnik. The Israeli Ministry of Justice and the Austrian legal officer observing the trial in Jerusalem then contacted the Central Office of the German State Justice Administrations in Ludwigsburg. After studying the available information on Höfle, the senior German public prosecutor sent a telegram to the Austrian Minister of Justice, Christian Broda. He sent an arrest warrant to Salzburg by courier, and on 31 January 1961 Hoefle was arrested by Austrian police in his home town.

The prosecutor indicted him on charges of the deportation of over 300,000 Jews from the Warsaw Ghetto to Treblinka. A lack of staff in Salzburg saw the case transferred to Vienna, where Höfle hanged himself in his cell on the evening of 21 August 1962, the night before his trial was to begin. The proceedings continued, however, with sixty-four other defendants in the trial. It was only in 1971 that Ernst Lerch and Helmut Pohl were charged by the Klagenfurt Prosecutor's Office. However, in May 1976, the prosecution withdrew the charges, and Klagenfurt Regional Court dismissed the cases against Pohl and Lerch on 11 May 1976.

WHAT HAPPENED TO THE MAIN CHARACTERS?

Nigel de Grey. Following on from the war, he stayed at Bletchley Park, working on Russian intercepts and decrypts. In 1946, GC&CS became the Government Communication Headquarters (GCHQ), and de Grey its first director. His memo on post-war interception became the basis for the formation and establishment of the new headquarters. His and his colleagues' successful overseeing, technical mastery and management of the decryption of the Domino cipher group meant that large amounts of information were available to the British and United States governments and intelligence communities about the persecution of Europe's Jews.

Nigel de Grey retired in 1951, and died suddenly that same year, dropping dead from a heart attack in London's Oxford Street.

Stewart Menzies (Major-General Sir Stewart Graham Menzies, KCB, KCMG, DSO, MC) stayed with SIS until 1953 when he retired, transforming the service for the Cold War, and dealing with the scandals and problems caused by Soviet spies infiltrating the service, such as Guy Burgess and Donald Maclean. He died in 1968.

John Cairncross was a British graduate of Cambridge, and a Russian spy at Bletchley Park, who worked in the section dealing with Luftwaffe decrypts. He had been recruited by the Russians while working for the Foreign Office in 1936. Codenamed Liszt by the Russians, Cairncross's principal success with his Soviet handlers was smuggling decrypts of Lorenz cipher material out of Bletchley Park, and passing them on to his handler in London. The most important ones were documents relating to German preparations for the Battle of Kursk. The Russians claim in their archive that between 1941 and 1945, both at Bletchley and with MI6, Cairncross handed some 5,832 documents to the Soviet Union.

Victor Cavendish-Bentinck became Britain's post-war ambassador to Poland, and then was offered the ambassadorship in Brazil. He was obliged to relinquish it, however, following publicity surrounding his divorce. He had to resign from the Foreign Office, and lost his pension. In 1980 he succeeded his brother as ninth Duke of Portland, and died in 1990.

Ernst Kaltenbrunner was arrested on the run in the Austrian Alps in 1945, with a considerable amount of a personal haul of gold buried in a farmer's field nearby. He was tried for war crimes at Nuremberg, sentenced to death, and hanged in October 1946. His ashes were scattered in a tributary of the River Isar, which flows through Salzburg.

WHAT HAPPENED TO THE MAIN CHARACTERS?

Ernst Lerch escaped justice, after a court case against him collapsed in 1972. After the war he had returned to his father's café in Klagenfurt, called Café Lerch, and ran it as a music bar until his death in 1997.

Kurt Daluege After a major heart attack in May 1943, he retired and spent the rest of the war living on an estate in Pomerania. He was arrested by the British in May 1945, charged with war crimes at Nuremberg, and handed over to the Czech government, who put him on trial for the atrocities committed at Lidice. Protesting that he was only following orders, and that three million German policemen loved him, he met his death in October 1946, hanged in Prague.

Christian Wirth was transferred to Trieste in September 1943 with Odilo Globočnik, and together with other SS officers who had served on Operation Reinhard, established a small concentration and extermination camp at a disused rice-processing plant in the Adriatic port. Some 2,500–3,500 Jews and partisans were killed there, while Wirth and colleagues deported another 3,000 to concentration and extermination camps. He was shot dead in a partisan ambush in neighbouring Slovenian territory in May 1944.

Franz Stangl went to Trieste as well, and in 1945 began a chain of escape that led to Italy, then Syria and finally Brazil. Authorities there arrested him in 1967, and a Düsseldorf prosecutor sentenced him to life imprisonment in 1970. He died in gaol from a heart attack in June 1971.

Karl-Otto Koch and his wife Ilse were indicted by an SS court in August 1944, and in April 1945 Koch was executed by firing squad within the camp at Buchenwald.

Kurt Franz was arrested in 1959 in Düsseldorf, and appeared at the 1965 Treblinka Trials, on 35 separate individual counts of murder of 109 people, as well as the collective responsibility for the killing of 300,000 Jews. He was sentenced to life imprisonment, then released in 1993, dying in 1998.

CONCLUSION

Excellence in one area can sometimes lead to assumptions of excellence in others. Bletchley Park decrypted so many messages from the Einsatzkommandos, SS and police units operating with Army Group Centre in 1941, that it seems pertinent to ask why they did not show such numerical success with decrypts from the special units operating with the other two army groups – both in the period before and after General der Polizei Daluege ordered a change of codes, and a clampdown on the reporting of executions by radio.

The answer lay in the number of radio intercept sets available to the British, the percentage of decrypts per key they were able to achieve per day, and the decision by the SS and Police commanders behind Army Groups North and South to dispatch updates of executions by courier or telephone. It appears, from available archive material, that vastly more signals were intercepted from behind the lines of the German central army group than the ones to the north and south. That the German Police and SS did not change their cipher security in the Domino cipher group post-September 1941, and for the rest of the war, meant that Bletchley Park were able to continue to break into the Domino system uninterrupted until 1945, as written.

Meanwhile if Jürgen Stroop had not been so keen to ingratiate himself with Himmler, and had not sent such long update signals, and had used radio, rather than enciphered teleprinter, then it is likely that de Grey and his colleagues would have decrypted his signals from the Warsaw Ghetto in April and May 1943, and gained a slightly more comprehensive picture of the deportations from there to Treblinka.

The British decryption of the Lorenz system, which yielded such high-grade intelligence about German High Command decisions later in the war, was possibly not sufficiently advanced to handle Stroop's messages. The SS capacity for reducing interceptable radio traffic from the Reinhard camps to a bare minimum, and from the Auschwitz-Birkenau camps to the Code Orange signals, meant that GC&CS's knowledge of the operations of both camp systems was extremely limited. The delivery of the regular, courageous and urgent information from the Poles themselves was not always matched by a similar sense of determination or conviction on the part of the Foreign Office, Home Office, or Joint Intelligence Committee.

The Ultra secret was kept safe: the British, working and living in a wartime democracy, largely knew how to keep secrets. The Germans, fighting and existing under a hideously brutal dictatorship, largely couldn't, and didn't. The operations to decrypt signals from the Final Solution also stand as proof of an old intelligence adage, that it is one thing to gather it effectively, another thing to be able to deploy it in an operationally, strategically and tactically effective manner. The secret of Ultra and Enigma had to be protected, whatever the cost. Even the horrifying intelligence about the Final Solution gathered by decrypting the SS ciphers codenamed Domino could not be allowed to compromise this secrecy, and had to be deployed in other ways. For the Allies, finding out about the Holocaust was one thing, being able to alert the world was sometimes very much another.

At the end of and after the war, the Allies published an internal report that contained many of the details about the German camp system. This information was collected from multiple sources before and after the liberation of the camps, such as prisoner escapes, reports from the Polish government-in-exile, Jewish and refugee groups, as well as military, diplomatic and intelligence messages. Very little of it appears to cross over with any information gathered from Ultra decrypts.

Titled, 'Basic Handbook: KLs: Axis Concentration Camps and Detention Centres Reported as such in Europe', the report is 120 pages long, and while extensive mention is made of some concentration camp systems – Sachsenhausen, for instance – the references to Treblinka and Sobibor are much briefer. The former is described as having been reported in September 1941, as consisting of three camps, comprising a punitive camp for forced labour, a KL (the German abbreviation of *Konzentrationslager*, or concentration camp), and an extermination camp for Jews. The entry for Sobibor says it was reported in September 1942 as a KL and extermination camp for Jews. The report was only declassified in January 1974.[194]

To understand what kind of strategic information would be at risk if Ultra were compromised can be of help in understanding the vital necessity of keeping it secret. Just a dozen or so of the principal pieces of intelligence the Allies gathered from Ultra would include the following. In April 1940, Ultra gave the British a detailed picture of parts of the disposition of Wehrmacht units in preparation for their attack on the Low Countries. During the Battle of Britain in summer 1940, Air Chief Marshal Sir Hugh Dowding received Ultra intelligence from Bletchley Park over a teleprinter link to the headquarters of RAF Fighter Command at Bentley Priory, in Middlesex. This gave him information about the strength and locations of German fighter and bomber units in France, and their readiness for bombing missions over southern England. Decrypts from the Luftwaffe Enigma revealed indirect information about the German preparations for Operation Sealion, the proposed invasion of Britain, and its cancellation.

Ultra helped the British army defeat the Italians in North Africa during Operation Compass in Libya, and the Royal Navy's destruction of parts of the Italian navy at Cape Matapan and Taranto in March 1941. Decrypts of the German army and air force Enigma gave the Allies detailed information about the preparations for Operation Barbarossa. Stalin, unfortunately, did not believe them, when he saw the information loosely disguised as emanating from another source. The huge and conflict-swaying contribution of Ultra to the Battle of the Atlantic has been documented in previous pages, but in the Mediterranean, decryptions of army, navy and air force Enigma meant the Allies sunk half the ships supplying troops, fuel, food and other supplies to the Germans and Italians in North Africa. Abwehr decrypts in the ISOS and ISK series showed that MI5 had captured, imprisoned or 'turned' all of the German agents in Britain and that the Double Cross system was operating.

Ultra contributed to Montgomery's successes at the battle of Alam Halfa and the second battle of El Alamein, while the decryption of the German naval Enigma enabled HMS *Duke of York* to sink the German battleship *Scharnhorst* at the Battle of the North Cape in December 1943. It showed German defensive preparations in Sicily in 1943, and that Allied deception efforts had proved effective, and similarly, that vital efforts prior to Operation Overlord had misled the Germans as to where the invasion landings would actually take place. The list is long, and impressive.

The German compromise of Britain's naval codes and its effect on Ultra security

Nigel de Grey and his colleagues involved in the decryption and analysis of the German naval Enigma would have been aware that the Germans, in turn, would be making efforts to break into the codes of Britain's Royal Navy and Merchant Navy. The Naval Intelligence Division were also aware of this, as was by extension Winston Churchill. It is unclear how much the NID knew, and exactly when, yet a safe answer is too little, too late. The Royal Navy themselves would ultimately provide the answer, in an authoritative analysis, assessment and report which appeared in November 1945.[195] The Germans were reliant on machine cipher systems like Enigma, which they were sure the British could not or had not decrypted, and on hand-held codebook systems, which they changed when they feared they were compromised, as in the case of Domino.

As the war progressed, repeated security assessments of the Enigma led the Kriegsmarine to add a fourth rotor to the system in February 1942. The Germans also assumed that if they could not break into the British Typex – their rotor-based encryption device, equipped with five rotors – which was more complex than Enigma, then the British could not penetrate Enigma. Yet while the Germans almost certainly never knew Enigma was compromised, and the British never let them find out, when they realised their own ciphers were being broken, they changed them. Part of this imbalance of knowledge and action came from the fact, described earlier, that the British, living, working and fighting in a democracy, could largely keep a secret, while the Germans, in a dictatorship, largely couldn't.

The Beobachtungsdienst, or B-Dienst, was the German Kriegsmarine's signals intelligence agency, its 'observation service'. They broke into the Royal Navy's long subtractor system early in the summer of 1938, and they did this through the secret reciphering tables which were used with another cipher, called the Administrative Code. This had been in use, unchanged, since 1934. In 1938 and 1939, the Germans broke into the Naval Cypher, used by all Royal Navy warships; the British then changed it, but the Kriegsmarine compromised it again, and by spring 1940 the German work on the Naval Cypher had progressed to the extent 'they could read almost everything of importance to the (1940 British invasion of) Norway operation'.[196]

This state of affairs continued till 20 August 1940, when the old Naval Cypher in use since 1934 was replaced by Naval Cypher No. 2, and the British introduced the Naval Code, which was identical. This achieved its purpose, which was to confuse the enemy codebreakers, trying to separate different signals sent in one of two almost identical codes. The B-Dienst suffered from a repetitive shortage of staff, which slowed their decryption times of British codes. In October 1941, the Royal Navy introduced Naval Cypher No.3, which used a combination of British and American call-signs: as this was used almost exclusively for merchant shipping and their escorts crossing the Atlantic, the Kriegsmarine called it 'the Convoy Code'. Cracking it meant that U-boat wolfpacks would know the location of the crucial convoys trying to reach Britain: it had the potential to sway the outcome of the Battle of the Atlantic.

By the middle of February 1942 very substantial progress had been made by the enemy in reading messages made in Naval

Cypher Number 3, the Convoy Cypher . . . and the cypher had been reconstructed by him with astonishing rapidity, and in February and March 1942 [when Bletchley Park were 'blind' to Shark] the enemy had achieved such a degree of success that he was reading after the briefest of time-lags a great proportion of all signals connected with convoys not only in the north Atlantic but in other areas where the cypher was used.

This state of affairs continued till 15th December 1942. The recyphering tables used with Naval Cypher No 3 were, between early 1942 and 15th December 1942, broken into by the enemy so successfully that there were times during this period when he appeared to have succeeded in reading as much as 80% of volume of intercepted traffic. On 15th December, disguised 'starting point indicators' [a more complex encipherment of each word] were reintroduced for all traffic in Naval Cypher No 3. This was a setback, but not much as he [the B-Dienst] increased staff and by February 1943, having more, he was well on his way to his former degree of success. *[This meant being] Often able to read all convoy traffic in the North Atlantic that interested him, so quickly that sometimes he had movement information [of convoys] some ten to twenty hours in advance, assisted by Signals from Western Approaches and Halifax* [Author's italics].

The signals in the Merchant Ships Code [were] all sent to U-boats, and the most disturbing feature in this connection is that from February 1942 till 10th June 43 the enemy was nearly every day able to read the Admiralty U-boat Disposition Signal often as early as midnight on the day it was made. By this he could forecast the probable routes of convoys which would be followed in order to avoid U-boat concentrations referred to in disposition signals. Then on

10th June Naval Cypher No 5 replaced the British - U.S Cypher No 3 and Naval Cypher 4. After this the enemy had no further success with the Naval Cypher.[197]

In summary, the German U-boats could be directed by their naval headquarters in western France and Kiel to the exact locations of almost every Allied convoy for seventeen months at the height of the Battle of the Atlantic, at a point when the British cryptanalysts did not have the advantage of being able to read German naval signals. It said much for the Allied deployment of aircraft, sonar and other anti-submarine warfare assets by autumn 1942 that they managed to survive this period with their merchant and escort fleet even half or a third intact: had this sequence of events occurred, say, for the whole of 1941, it is likely that Britain would have had, at the least, to relinquish any form of workable operational freedom of movement in the Atlantic, as the convoy and escort system collapsed. Had the crews of both Royal Navy and Merchant Navy ships been informed that their ciphers had been broken, and that U-boats were almost certainly waiting for them on each voyage, the operational ramifications of this on the naval crews – being told they were sailing straight into the eyes of a wolfpack – would have been highly damaging.

It was not just the Royal Navy's codes which the Germans could decrypt; the Luftwaffe's signals intelligence agency, for instance, could read into the Bomber Code used by the American 8th Bomber Command and US Air Force IX Bomber Command operating over Europe and North Africa in 1941 and 1942. The daily change to the codes was made at six o'clock in the evening, so it often happened that captured codes from shot-down aircraft were recovered so promptly they were available for use the following morning against 8th Air Force operations.[198]

Yet the British did not let the Germans or Italians know that they were aware, or suspected that the B-Dienst had compromised their convoy codes: in the ironic and inverted logic that cryptanalysis sometimes displays, because the Germans could read nothing in their decryptions of the British naval codes that gave them an idea that their own Enigma might be compromised, this made them feel more secure about their own cipher systems, thus strengthening the British hand. Yet in terms of the overall security of Ultra, the partial compromise of the Royal and Merchant navy's cipher systems made it all the more of an imperative for de Grey and his colleagues to hang on 'by their coattails' if necessary,[199] to the German ciphers whose keys they were decrypting. It made Enigma all the more valuable, all the more of a strategic advantage, all the more an asset that Britain could not, under any circumstance, lose. If that meant that intelligence gathered from the decryption of systems like Domino could not be overtly deployed, then that was the price of protecting Ultra.

It also obliged British intelligence to find ways in which they could use the information from the Domino decrypts, and the behind-the-scenes work of the UN Nations War Crimes Commission, and the December 1942 UN Declaration, and the November 1943 Moscow Declaration, were backed up by this intelligence. The Jews of Europe were a priority, but not the priority: winning the war was, and that was how Churchill and Roosevelt had decided the Jews could best be helped. The point when the differential between knowledge and possible action had been the closest had been at Evian in 1938 – the failure of the conference was when the ghostly, macabre shakes of the death rattle were heard most loudly, before the Wannsee Conference, before Kristallnacht, before Poland, and before Barbarossa.

Evidence at the Nuremberg Trials

On 21 November 1945, the trial of twenty-two senior Nazi leaders opened at the Nuremberg Palace of Justice. It was the first, and major war crimes trial, and another 183 of the Third Reich's leaders would face trial on charges such as crimes against humanity, war crimes and crimes against peace. The evidence against the German accused often came from their regime, their own people, and was of their own making. Films, photographs, diaries, orders, documents. This was part of the prosecution's plan to demonstrate and prove that Nazi Germany had intended to destroy Europe's Jews. One of the items, for instance, submitted as evidence in the opening statement of American Justice Robert H. Jackson was Jürgen Stroop's lengthy report about the destruction of the Warsaw Ghetto. Bound in embossed black leather, with carefully captioned photographs inside it, three copies of the 125-page report had originally been commissioned by Friedrich-Wilhelm Krüger, the Higher SS and Police Leader in Krakow. One was given to Himmler, one to Stroop, while Krüger kept the third. An unbound copy was held by Stroop's SS chief of staff, Max Jesuiter. After the war, the Allies captured Himmler's and Jesuiter's copies, the latter of which was given to British military intelligence in London; while Himmler's went to the headquarters of the US 7th Army. Both copies were shown to the judges as evidence by the prosecution in their opening address.

The Allies captured millions of pages of documents as they advanced into Germany in spring 1945. The Americans found tens of thousands of individual records in the Kaiseroda salt mine in Merkers. Gestapo and SS headquarters across Germany, Austria and Czechoslovakia yielded more, as did the headquarters of German industrial consortiums like Krupp, and the government ministries of the Third Reich. At the RSHA headquarters in

Prague, the SS tried to burn the documents in the basement; Eichmann himself had overseen the partial destruction in Berlin of the documents of the department IV B4, the Jewish Affairs office. The Allies also captured reports and daily records from the different Einsatzkommandos which operated across Eastern Europe after the beginning of Operation Barbarossa. Also admitted as evidence was a single copy of the minutes of the Wannsee Conference from 1942, known as the Wannsee Protocol. The SS commander of Einsatzgruppe D, Otto Ohlendorf, testified too to his unit killing 90,000 Jews in the southern Ukraine in summer and autumn 1941. When British prosecutor Sir Hartley Shawcross asked a witness to describe a mass execution in Ukraine, the incident chosen from available evidence was a witness statement to a killing which took place at Dubno, in Ukraine, in October 1943.[200]

It was not on the list of mass executions detailed in any of the Domino intercepts from 7 July 1941 onwards. While the British Joint Intelligence Committee, under Victor Cavendish-Bentinck, had submitted a selection of Domino, and other decrypts to the United Nations War Crimes Commission, the need to protect Ultra sourcing over-rode Domino's use at Nuremberg. However, evidence from the UN Commission was subsumed into some of the evidence used at the war crimes trials, so the material finally stood tall as a weapon of international justice, albeit one that had to remain secret. By the time Nazi leaders went on trial at Nuremberg, the Allies had sufficient material from hundreds of other sources to prosecute the Third Reich's leaders, without having the added concern of revealing the covert origins of material whose initial sources and methods of decryption could easily compromise future intelligence operations, particularly against the Soviet Union.

The material evidence captured in the possession of some senior SS officers revealed details of their orders, and means of secret communication. Hans-Bernd Gisevius was a German Abwehr agent, diplomat and Allied intelligence asset who gave evidence for the defence in two trials at Nuremberg:

> We asked ourselves whether it was possible that an even worse man could possibly be found after such a monster as Heydrich . . . Kaltenbrunner came . . . and things got worse every day . . .We had the experience that perhaps the impulsive actions of a murderer like Heydrich were not as bad as the cold legal logic of a lawyer who was handling such a dangerous instrument as the Gestapo.

On 12 May 1945, when the Americans arrested Kaltenbrunner and his adjutant, Arthur Scheidler, they were hiding in a mountain cabin above the village of Altaussee in southern Austria. Acting on a tip-off from the mayor of the village and a mountain ranger, US infantrymen surrounded the house and led the former head of the RSHA and his assistant back down to Altaussee. Kaltenbrunner's mistress, Gisela von Westarp, and Scheidler's wife Iris saw the two men being brought back by the American soldiers, and called out to welcome them. This provided a formal identification of both. When the military police searched Kaltenbrunner and his luggage, they found a copy of a message he had sent on a teleprinter.

> Please inform the Reichsführer SS and report to the Führer that all arrangements as to Jews, political and concentration camp internees in the Protectorate have been taken care of by me personally today.[201]

This was understood to be a reply to a preceding order issued by Himmler to the office of the Higher SS and Police Leaders in the General Government:

Should the situation at the front necessitate it, early preparations are to be made for the total clearance of the prisons. Should the situation develop suddenly, in such a way that it is impossible to evacuate the prisoners the present inmates are to be liquidated and their bodies disposed of as far as possible (burning, blowing up the building, et cetera). If necessary, Jews still employed in the armament industry or on other work are to be dealt with in the same way. The liberation of prisoners or Jews by the enemy, be it the Western enemies or the Red Army, must be avoided under all circumstances. Nor may they fall into their hands alive.[202]

The decryption of the Holocaust codes

The decipherment of the Domino and Orange code systems, of the various Lorenz encipherment attachments, the Illicit Signals Knox, the Illicit Signals Oliver Strachey, the Abwehr and SD one-time keys, of the Japanese Purple code, of all the Holocaust Codes and the cipher systems in and via which information about the Final Solution was transmitted, was not a straight, linear and chronologically sequential process, defined by approximate volumes of finite information that could be automatically intercepted or decrypted. It was not like the Battle of the Atlantic, which was a much more mathematically delineated decryption operation, of permutations of numbers, of submarines, square miles of ocean, permissible rotor cipher permutations of Enigma, of convoy whereabouts. The naval Enigma was a cryptanalytical challenge bar none: but the rules of the game were laid out. W number of submarines operating in X square miles of ocean had to send Y numbers of signals in Z number of cipher permutations, and there were A or B or C or D ways of successfully decrypting them and benefiting from, inverting or neutralising their electronic advantage. To intercept the merchant ships, U-boats *had* to send signals reporting convoy whereabouts, the convoys in turn *had* to cross the Atlantic, and there were only a finite number of mechanical ways – i.e. the rotor permutations on an Enigma – in which the signals could be sent. In the Atlantic, the rogue cryptanalytic variable was not whether the signals existed, or the information was being transmitted, it was whether de Grey and his colleagues could intercept and decrypt them. With the Holocaust, the rogue variable was whether there were even any signals to start with.

The Double Transposition and Double Playfair systems codenamed Domino were considerably less complex to decipher than the Enigma encoded signals, and it is one of Bletchley Park and British intelligence's pieces of supreme fortune that the Germans did not change the Domino keys after September 1941. This allowed the British to decipher information for four years not just about the persecution of the Jews, but about such things as partisan warfare in Ukraine, morale in SS guard units at concentration camps, the operational number of tanks in a given Panzer division, or the daily movements of the thirty most senior members of the SS. But the numbers of signals were finite – there was only such a large volume of them in summer and autumn of 1941 and spring and summer of 1942 because there were dozens of Einsatzkommando, SS and Police units operating, and they regularly had to report their execution tallies. Himmler and Heinrich Müller at the Gestapo, and Heydrich and Daluege and, ultimately, Hitler, had to know that sufficient numbers of Jews were being killed. Ergo, information had to be sent by one form of radio or machine transmission, by telephone or by courier.

The information available for interception and decryption by the British depended on the volume of transmissions, and in the months of July 1941 to June 1942 across Army Group Centre, and parts of the areas to the north and south of it, huge numbers of signals were sent, and then decrypted. The same was not the case for the Baltics, Army Groups North and South: a considerably smaller number of signals were intercepted, and after September 1941, much of it was not sent in any of the keys decrypted by Hut 5. It is also unknown how much was sent and simply not intercepted at Beaumanor or any other Y station, because there were not enough receiving sets and not enough operators. So from the Domino decrypts in 1941 and the first half of 1942, the British cryptanalytical and intelligence apparatus knew that the Germans were executing vast number of Jews. When the means and places of execution shifted from rifle and machine-pistol, and mass-graves dug in a Ukrainian forest, to a wire-enclosed camp and Zyklon B or carbon monoxide gas, the information about it was not being sent in radio or teleprinter signals that the British could decrypt, if at all. Encrypted radio communications to and from Operation Reinhard in Lublin about the operations of the four camps, plus Chelmno, were, as we have seen, practically non-existent.

Is there a separate body of SS, SD or Gestapo signals to and from the Auschwitz II-Birkenau complex that were neither intercepted nor decrypted by the British, Americans or Russians but which give information about the operations of the two camps between mid-1942 and November 1944? No, says the Head of Archive at the State Museum Auschwitz-Birkenau in Oświęcim, what they have are copies of what is in the British National Archives. Yet 95 per cent of the camp files and records were burned by the SS as they left the camp, and the remaining five per cent is in their archives, but with no decrypted signals distinct from those the British have.[203] While large and varied reports about Auschwitz from Polish prisoners, escapees, resistance fighters and others reached the Polish government-in-exile up to and including the Vrba-Wetzler report, there appears, at the time of writing, to be no available intercepted, decrypted German signals to or from Auschwitz, to or from the Reich Security Main Office, Heinrich Himmler or other SS officials concerning execution operations of Jews at the Auschwitz II- Birkenau complex.

Compared to the abundance of intelligence available from Domino about executions on the Eastern Front, this absence of hard, cryptanalytical intelligence about Auschwitz left an information vacuum which was only partially filled by reports from Poles and Jews inside Poland. It left space for the draconian scepticism of the likes of Victor Cavendish-Bentinck and the British Joint Intelligence Committee. The knowledge-to-action differential narrowed considerably in 1943 and 1944: the decrypted signals about the Holocaust in Italy and Hungary became more numerous, the SS operations more visible in plain sight, the Allied military options more available from the air and on the ground as British, American and Red Army troops closed in on the camp apparatuses. The decryption of such sensitive material as that in the Domino, naval Enigma and other ciphers was often a very fragile advantage at any given time, like a king or ace or queen on the green baize of the card table that could blow away in the wind or evaporate unexpectedly. One approach is to ask why the entire cryptanalytical infrastructure of the British, Americans, French and other countries did not or could not reveal more about the ongoing persecution of Europe's Jews. A more sanguine, pragmatic and perhaps positive approach is to be thankful that it revealed even what it did, such were the material and technical odds and obstacles sometimes stacked against it, combined with the vicissitudes of science, human nature and a world at war.

THE WHISTLE-BLOWER OF TREBLINKA

SS-Untersturmführer Kurt Gerstein and the night train to Warsaw

On the night of 22–3 August 1942, a Swedish diplomat named Baron Friedrik Goran von Otter was travelling on a train from Warsaw to Berlin. He was thirty-six years old, and worked at the Swedish legation in Berlin. After the train pulled out of the station in the Polish capital, von Otter noticed an SS officer with black hair standing in the corridor, looking extremely nervous. The soldier explained that he had not been able to find a sleeping compartment or berth, or even a seat, so the two men ended up sitting next to each other on the crowded train. The SS officer started to tell the Swedish diplomat what he had been doing during the past week.

His name was SS-Untersturmführer Kurt Gerstein, he said, he was thirty-seven, and he had studied mining engineering and medicine at university. He had achieved excellent grades, so following two successive postings, he was promoted to work as the head of the technical disinfection services in the Waffen-SS Institute for Hygiene. As the men talked, Gerstein was still in a state of agitation and some shock, and he explained to von Otter why. One part of his job was to obtain supplies of hydrogen cyanide bought from the German chemical corporation Degesch, and deliver them to SS camp facilities at places in Poland called Treblinka and Belzec. In fact, said Gerstein, he had just come from Treblinka the day before, and had been in Belzec that same week. Degesch, he said, was short for *Deutsche Gesellschaft für Schädlingsbekämpfung*, or German Corporation for Pest Control. One of its products was a hydrogen cyanide-based pesticide called Zyklon, and Degesch now produced a variant of this called Zyklon B, which humans could not smell. One of their biggest customers were the Schutzstaffel, who were buying large quantities under the auspices of the RSHA, or Reich Security Main Office. Gerstein was the liaison between the two parties.

The previous week, on the 17 August, he had travelled to a camp at Belzec, north of Lvov on the Ukrainian border. Two senior SS officers there, Odilo Globočnik and Christian Wirth, were refining ways of killing large numbers of Jews in camps, either using the carbon monoxide exhaust gases from specially adapted lorries and coaches, or Zyklon B. It was there, at Belzec camp, said Gerstein, that he had witnessed a shipment of 6,700 Polish Jews from Lvov and Lublin arriving at seven o'clock in the morning. Around 1,450 of them were dead on arrival, he said, and the remainder were whipped out of the cattle cars of the train transport by two hundred Ukrainian guards. The Jews undressed, handed over their clothes, shoes, suitcases and valuables, and then had their heads shaved, after which their hair was put in potato sacks.[204]

Then the Jews – who Gerstein told von Otter were mostly old men and women, and children – queued up on a ramp to enter a gas chamber. When some 750 had been forced in by the Ukrainian guards with riding whips, the doors were closed, and gas from the exhaust of a diesel engine was pumped in. On the day of Gerstein's visit, however, the diesel motor broke down, and despite SS-Hauptmann Wirth whipping one of the Ukrainian SS guards in the face, it took two hours and fifty minutes to start it. It took another thirty-two minutes to gas 3,000 people in four chambers, with 750 in each. After he had witnessed this, and provided advice to Wirth and Globočnik about how the use of Zyklon B could speed up the killings, Gerstein drove with Wirth to a camp at Treblinka, north-east of Warsaw. He arrived on the 19th. There he saw piles of suitcases, shoes and clothes, and eight gas chambers. After this visit, Wirth's SS driver took Gerstein to Warsaw, where he remained before catching the night train to Berlin.

Did the SS lieutenant have any person he could provide as a form of reference? asked Von Otter, as they sat on the floor of the train. After talking for several hours, the SS officer had asked the Swede to inform his country's embassy and foreign ministry about what he had told him, and also to try to bring the information to the attention of the Vatican and the Red Cross. Gerstein explained his motives to von Otter. He was a committed and devout Christian, who had joined the German Confessing Church, which tried to resist efforts by the Nazi Party to control German Protestant and Evangelical congregations. Yet Gerstein and his family were also deeply attracted by the nationalist authoritarianism of the Nazi Party, and so Kurt had joined the SA in 1933. A conflicted man, his Christianity rebelled against his attraction to National Socialism, and on two occasions he was thrown out of the Party, once for distributing anti-Nazi pamphlets. He spent time in SS prisons, but each time he came back. He himself had joined the SS in 1941, partly, he said, out of a desire to see things from the inside and to expose them, and partly to avenge the death of a close female relative. She was disabled, and had been murdered by the SS under its Aktion T4 Euthanasia programme. The person whom he recommended as a reference to von Otter was Karl Otto

Dibelius, a German Evangelical bishop and committed opponent of Nazism.

On arriving in Berlin, von Otter went straight to the Swedish Legation, where he described his meeting with Gerstein. His ambassador advised him to save his report until he had returned to Stockholm, and could then brief the foreign ministry. Von Otter wanted to send an encrypted account of his meeting with Gerstein, both to his home capital, and if necessary the Vatican nuncio in Berlin and, also, in Sweden. The Swedish foreign ministry, however, was concerned that the German foreign ministry's codebreakers might be targeting Swedish diplomatic signals, so restrained von Otter. Ursula Hagen at Pers Z had targeted Swedish signals but had reported making no progress with them: the Swedes, however, under the expertise of Arne Beurling, had managed to decrypt the German T52 teletypewriter.

Von Otter then met Gerstein twice more in the following week, but he sent no information to his own capital. The Swedes in Berlin were concerned that the Germans were intercepting and reading their diplomatic signals traffic, so did not want to transmit von Otter's information by radio. The verbal report from Gerstein stayed in Berlin. The renegade SS officer himself, meanwhile, had approached the office of the papal nuncio to Berlin, and tried to make an appointment. He arrived in the lobby at the Vatican delegation in uniform, and Cardinal Orsenigo asked his staff to inform him whether Gerstein was a soldier. The nuncio had already been told the purpose of Gerstein's visit by one of his deputies, and sent a message to his reception staff that he refused to meet with the SS officer. He also announced that he refused to read Gerstein's report or forward it to Rome. The SS officer was the first to give direct eyewitness testimony about the gassing of Jews in a concentration camp, providing an example of definitive proof of everything that the Allied leadership, world

Jewish organisations and the Vatican had been told was happening. Thus the most telling, first-hand piece of information about the annihilation of the Jews was lost between Orsenigo's compliant, subservient approach to the Nazi regime, and the hesitancy and lack of determination by the Swedes, fearful of protecting their tenuous, often compromised neutrality.

Two weeks before the end of the war, he gave himself up to the French commander of the now-occupied town of Reutlingen. The officer was welcoming, and gave Gerstein a place in a hotel in which to write his report. On 25 July, he was transferred to the Cherche-Midi military prison in Paris, where he was treated as an SS war criminal. He was found dead in his cell from an apparent suicide.

NOTES AND SOURCES

Abbreviations/keys frequently used:

TNA – The National Archives (formerly the Public Record Office (PRO) and Historical Manuscripts Commission (HMC))

HW (as cited here) – General records of the Government Code and Cypher School (later inherited by Government Communications Headquarters (GCHQ))

BP – Bletchley Park; BPGP – Bletchley Park German Police

1   TNA/HW16/1 BPGP Early Reports /German Language / Information from German Police Codes V/1 7pp, p.2. 18.11.39, circulated to MI8 25.12.1939.

2   TNA/HW16/1 BPGP Early Reports /German Language / Information from German Police Codes IV/3pp, p.1 18.11.39, circulated to MI8 25.11.1939.

3   TNA/HW3/155 GCCS German Police Decrypts: The History of the German Police Section 1939–1945 pp.1–5.

4   TNA/ HW16/1 BPGP Early Reports /German Language / Information from German Police Decodes VI/2, 3pp, p.1, 24.11.39, circulated to MI8 19.12.39.

5   TNA/ HW16/1 BPGP Early Reports /German Language / Information from German Police Decodes V, 3pp, p.1, 24.11.39, circulated to MI8 19.12.39.

6   TNA/HW16/1 BPGP Early Reports /German Language / Information from German Police Wireless Traffic GB221/ 18.10.39. Compiled by 4 Int Sec GCCS 25.11.39/ 7pp, p.7, circulated to MI8 28.11.1939.

7   TNA/ HW16/1 BPGP Early Reports /German Language / Information from German Police Decodes V, 3pp, p.1, 24.11.39, circulated to MI8 19.12.39.

8   *The Military Service and Intelligence Career of Lieutenant-Commander Nigel de Grey,* by David King and Mark Lubienski, document courtesy of Bletchley Park archives, BPR2022/168, 20pp, p.8.

9   Ibid.

10   Michael de Grey, quoted in 'Bletchley Park celebrates codebreakers who changed the course of First World War', *The Guardian*, London, 29 July 2015.

11   The words of the historian, chemist and biographer Stephen Budiansky in his *Battle of Wits: The Complete Story of Codebreaking in World War II*, the Free Press, Simon & Schuster, 2002, p. 135.

12   *The Lost World of Bletchley Park: An illustrated history of the wartime codebreaking centre* by Sinclair McKay, Aurum Press London, 2013, p.28.

13   'A Black Day for Germany', *The Times*, London, 11 November 1938.

14   *The Nazi Holocaust,* by Ronnie S. Landau, I.B Tauris, New York, 2006, pp.137-40.

15   'Evian and Geneva' by Walter F. Mondale, *New York Times*, 28 July 1979.

16   *Churchill: A Life* by Martin Gilbert, Heinemann, London, 1991, p.598.

17   Quoted by Gilbert, a historian and leading Churchill biographer, in a speech to the International Churchill Society at the United States Holocaust Memorial Museum, Washington, 8 November 1993.

18   Winston Churchill MP to the House of Commons, April 1937.

19   Ibid. Gilbert referred to an interview with an anonymous British official carried out around 1968.

20   Ibid.

21   TNA/HW16/1 German Police Decrypts 1939 V, GB 342, p.6, Occurrences in Poland.

22   *Hitler 1936-1945: Nemesis*, by Ian Kershaw, Penguin Books, London, 2001, pp. 242–43.

23   TNA/HW16/1 BP GPD V Occurrences in Poland GB 221, p.1. Sent 19/10/39, seen by MI8 28.11.39.

24   Hermann Höfle's SS Personnel File is in the United States National Archives, in RG (Record Group) 242, HOEFLE, HERMANN J – AE544848WJ, and in the Berlin Document Centre, Microfilm A-3343, SSO-102A.

25   The words were spoken by Eichmann in Israel during his trial in 1963, and appear, inter alia, in Hannah Arendt's narration of the legal proceedings: 'Eichmann in Jerusalem' Part 1, the *New Yorker*, 16 February 1963.

26   From the Final Interrogation Report of SS-Obersturmbannführer Arthur Scheidler, one of Kaltenbrunner's later assistants in the RSHA; carried out by the US Counter-Intelligence Corps on 11 July 1945 in Munich, TNA/WO 208/4478. It is stamped and countersigned as annotated by the British Director of Military Intelligence for Germany (MI14) on 25 July 1945.

27   'Eichmann in Jerusalem' Part 1.

28   Written testimony given at the trial of Adolf Eichmann by former SS-Sturmbannführer Wilhelm Höttl, 4 July 1961, Jerusalem. US Holocaust Memorial Museum Archive, Record Group 60 / 2100, Film Footage ID number 2112.

29   *Heydrich: The Face of Evil*, by Mario R. Dederichs, Casemate Publishing, Havertown PA, 2009, p.92.

30   *Hitler's Hangman: The Life of Heydrich* by Robert Gerwarth, Yale University Press, 2011, p. 61.

31   Ibid.

32   *The Third Reich Sourcebook*, by Anson Rabinbach and Sander Gilman, University of California Press, 2013, p.335.

33   *The Path to Genocide: Essays on Launching the Final Solution*, Christopher Browning, Cambridge University Press, 1995, p.194.

34   TNA/ HW16/1 BPGP Early Reports /German Language / Information from German Police Decodes VI GB406, 14.1.40, 5pp, p.1, circulated to MI8 16.1.40.

35   TNA/ HW16/1 BPGP Early Reports /German Language / Information from German Police Decodes VI GB406, 14.1.40, 5pp, p.3, circulated to MI8 16.1.40.

36   TNA/ HW16/1 BPGP Early Reports /German Language / Information from German Police Decodes VII, GB 457, 28.1.40, 6pp, p.1.

37   TNA/ HW16/1 BPGP Early Reports /German Language / Information from German Police Decodes VII GB457, 28.1.40, 6pp, p.1, circulated to MI8 16.1.40.

38   TNA/HW 3/155 German Police Section, GCCS: History of the German Police Section, 1939–1945, 9pp inc. personal notes, pp.1–4.

39   Ibid.

40   Ibid. p.4.

41   *Eminence Grise of Bletchley Park: Nigel de Grey and the Intelligence Exchange*, by Kenneth Macksey, 2003, not published, MS courtesy of Bletchley Park archives. Ch 6, p.1, January 1940, also 'The History of Hut 3', TNA/HW3/120, p.75.

42   War Office papers, TNA WO 199/911A, 4 and 9 October 1940.

43   'Secret and Confidential' and 'Prime Minister Only'. 21 October 1941, F. H. Hinsley and others, *British Intelligence in the Second World War*, Volume 2 (HMSO: London 1981), p.655.

44   *Ian Fleming: The Complete Man*, by Nicholas Shakespeare, Harvill Secker 2023, p. 212, with the 'access' quotes from TNA/HW 14-4; ADM 223/851 8 April 1940.

45   The Papers of Sir John Colville, Churchill Archives Centre, University of Cambridge, diary entry, 4 May 1941.

46   UK National Archives Document File HW16/6 Bletchley Park German Police Summaries 3 July–14 August 1941, Message Group 27, 28.8.41, 3 pp., p.1, hereafter written throughout as TNA/HW16/6 BP GP MSGP 27 Summaries 3 July-14 Aug p.1.

47   Ibid. p.3.

48   UK The National Archives Document File HW16/6 Bletchley Park German Police Summaries 15–31 Aug 1941 Message Group 28 12.9.41, page 1, hereafter written throughout as TNA/HW16/6 BP GP Summaries 15–31 Aug 41 / p.1.

49   Ibid. p. 2.

50   Ibid. p. 5

51   Ibid. pp. 6–7.

52   Ibid. p.7.

53   TNA HW16/32 1/40, German Police Decrypts (GPD) decrypted 28 August 1941.

54   The German message decrypt and the additional GC&CS comment are in TNA/ HW3/ 155/ GCCS: History of the German Police Section, 1939–1945, 9pp. inc. personal notes, p.5.

55   *Odilo Globocnik: Hitler's Man in the East,* by Peter Poprzeczny, McFarland & Co, New York, 2015, p.99.

56   *Marching into Darkness: The Wehrmacht and the Holocaust in Belarus*, by Waitman Wade Beorn, Harvard University Press, pp 95–6.

57   *Fegelein's Horsemen and Genocidal Warfare: The SS Cavalry Brigade in the Soviet Union.* Henning Pieper, Palgrave Macmillan, London, 2015, p. 62.

58   Ibid. pp. 86–90.

59   Ibid. p.190.

60   Yitzhak Arad, *The Einsatzgruppen Reports: Selections from the Dispatches of the Nazi Death Squads' Campaign Against the Jews July 1941–January 1943*, Holocaust Library, 1989, doc. 133, pp. 234–5. Cited here from Yitzhak Arad, *The Holocaust in the Soviet Union*, (University of Nebraska Press, Lincoln and Yad Vashem, Jerusalem, 2009), p.188. The passages are cited from the Einsatzkommando's war diary, see 'An ort und Stelle Erschossen' ('Shot on the spot'), *Der Spiegel*, 26 October 1986, p. 44: http://www.spiegel.de/spiegel/print/d-13521618.html.

61   TNA/HW16/6 GPD 1 – 30 September 41 / MGP 29, from 22/10/41.

62   T NA/HW16/GPD MSGPs 30, 1 Oct–14 Nov 1941, no distribution date mentioned.

63   Ibid.

64   Ibid.

65   Ibid.

66   Memo from Nigel de Grey, 11 September 1941, TNA/HW1/62.

67   PRO HW 1/135/ GPD.

68   21 October 1941: Sir Harry Hinsley and others, *British Intelligence in the Second World War*, volume 2, (HMSO: London 1981), p.655.

69   Ibid. p.657.

70   PRO HW16/32 German Police Messages July–December 1941 / ZIP/ GPD 515 of 25/12/1941, with traffic from 17 November 1941, messages 35 and 36.

71   PRO / ZIP/GPD 467/30.11.41: German Police Decodes, No. 1, Traffic 20.11.41.

72   Letter of 22 September 1941: Secret Intelligence Service papers, HW1/86, Winston Churchill to Stewart Menzies.

73   Documents of Hut 6 of GC&CS, held at Bletchley Park and in the National Archives in Record Group HW43/72, 1-3pp, numbered Sec.1.8132 / 1942 'The Orange Age', paras 1&4. Author's documents courtesy of Bletchley Park.

74   The quote was from Sir Victor Cavendish-Bentinck, the head of the Joint Intelligence Committee, commenting on the massacre at Babi Yar outside Kiev of some 33,000 Jews in September 1941.

75   TNA/HW12/272/32 Decrypts of intercepted diplomatic communications: January 1942.

76   *Eichmann: His Life and Crimes*, by David Cesarani, Vintage, London, 2005, p.114.

77   The operation was named after Reinhard Heydrich, so the formal spelling of it was without a 't' on the end; the 't' is, however, frequently used in messages. Heydrich was known to spell his name both ways.

78   *Eichmann: His Life and Crimes*, by David Cesarani

79   www.belzec.eu. The original document is in the Yad Vashem archive, and a copy is on: https://www.holocausthistoricalsociety.org.uk/contents/ aktionreinhardt/aktionreinhardtdocuments.html.

80   *Odilo Globocnik: Hitler's Man in the East*, by Joseph Poprzeczny, McFarland & Co. Jefferson, North Carolina, 2004, pp. 95,99.

81   *Die Tagebücher von Joseph Goebbels: Sämtliche Fragmente*, by Joseph Goebbels, Munich, 1996, Partie II, Volume 3 (Jan–Mar 1942), p. 104.

82 *Into That Darkness: from Mercy Killing to Mass Murder, a study of Franz Stangl, the Commandant of Treblinka* by Gitta Sereny, (2nd edition.) Pimlico Books, London, 1995, p.54.

83 TNA/HW16/ GPD MGP 36, 1 May to 30 June 1942, circulated 17.7.1942.

84 Ibid.

85 *Country of Ash: A Jewish Doctor in Poland, 1939–1945,* by Edward Reicher, Bellevue Literary Press, New York, 2013. pp.100, 105–6.

86 Ibid.p.67.

87 Zygmunt Warman, a Polish Jew from Łódź, was a member of the Jewish Council who attended the meeting and was in the office that morning. He gave testimony on 24 January 1947, recorded on Chronicles of Terror, at https://www.zapisyterroru.pl/dlibra

88 *The Healing Wound -- Reflections on Germany 1938–2001,* by Gitta Sereny, Norton, New York, 2001. p.117.

89 *The Good Old Days: The Holocaust Through the Eyes of the Perpetrators and Bystanders,* eds. Ernst Klee, Willi Dressen and Volke Riess, Hamish Hamilton, London, 1991 p. 245.

90 FCO Telegram Geneva-Berne-London 10 August 1942, No.174 / C7853, the telegram sent to America to Stephen Wise, and some details quoted here of its path from Riegner in Geneva to New York, are in the United States Holocaust Memorial Museum.

91 Foreign Office transcript of decrypted message FO371/30917, 11 August 1942.

92 *Jewish Refugees from Germany and Austria in Britain, 1933–1970,* by Anthony Grenville, Mitchell, London, 2010, p.58.

93 'The Holocaust, America and American Jewry' by Yehuda Bauer, *Israel Journal of Foreign Affairs* VI (1) 2012, p.66. The author is Emeritus Professor of History and Holocaust Studies at the Hebrew University of Jerusalem. He interviewed Riegner in the 1970s.

94 Letter from Myron C. Taylor to Cardinal Maglione, 27 August 1942, reproduced on https://www.jewishvirtuallibrary.org/taylor-letter-to-cardinal-maglione-describing-holocaust-september-1942.

95   Montini would later become Pope Paul VI.

96   *Actes et Documents du Saint Siège relatifs à la Seconde Guerre Mondiale*, Volume 8, pp. 665, 669-670, notes 493, 496 and 497. *Actes et Documents*, or ADSS, is an 11-volume series of archived messages, signals and letters from the period of the wartime papacy of Pope Pius XII, between him, his Cardinal Secretariat of State, and hundreds of external correspondents, ranging from ambassadors, papal nuncios, heads of state, foreign ministry staff, intelligence officials to civilians from countries ranging from the United States, Britain, France and Germany, to Russia, Sweden, Yugoslavia, and Brazil. At 2,014 pages, they are in four languages – Italian, French, German and English – were authorised by Pope Paul VI, and were published between 1965 and 1981 by LEV, the Libreria Editrice Vaticano.

97   Ibid. Notes 496 and 7.

98   These codebooks are now in the archives of the German Ministry of Foreign Affairs. They were stolen by the Gestapo in 1941 from the Vatican, then captured by the Americans at the end of the war, and handed to the British, who returned the files to Germany in the year 2000 as part of the declassified resources of the US Target Intelligence Committee.

99   European Axis Signal Intelligence in World War II as revealed by TICOM Investigations – Volume 6, The Foreign Office Cryptanalytic Section / US Army Security Agency / National Security Agency Library file S47-61. (TICOM stands for Target Intelligence Committee, a secret Allied group formed to capture German intelligence resources.)

100   *The Finnish SS volunteers and atrocities against Jews, civilians and prisoners of war in Ukraine and the Caucasus region 1941–1943*, An Archival Survey by the Finnish National Archives, Helsinki 2019, 249 pp.

101   Ibid. p.104.

102   *Actes et Documents*, Vol.8, pp. 669–70, note 497.

103   Ibid. Notes 496 and 497.

104   *Actes et Documents*, Vol.8, p.687, note 20.

105   *The Catholic Church and the Holocaust: 1930–1965*, by Michael Phayer, Indiana University Press, 2000, p.45.

106   See Appendix: 'The whistle-blower of Treblinka'.

NOTES AND SOURCES

107   *Blind Eye to Murder, Britain, America and the Purging of Nazi Germany: A Pledge Betrayed*, by Tom Bower, Picador, London, 1983, p.43.

108   Victor Cavendish-Bentinck to Sir Alexander Cadogan, Permanent Undersecretary at the Foreign Office, October 1942 TNA/HW14/54.

109   TNA/FO371/30923.

110   'The Mass Extermination of Jews in German Occupied Poland'. Document by the Polish government-in-exile based on Jan Karski's reports, addressed to the wartime allies of the then-United Nations, 10 December 1942.

111   TNA/HW16/10, GPCC ZIP OS6, 28.1.1943, Section III, Paragraph (i).

112   Ibid. GPCC ZIP OS5, 28.12.1942, Section II, Msg (a).

113   PRO HW 16/23, Signal GPDD 355a, SS Lublin Telegrams 12, 13, 14 and 15 intercepted 11 January 1943, distributed 15 January 1943.

114   *Belzec, Sobibor, Treblinka: The Operation Reinhard Death Camps*, by Yitzhak Arad, Bloomington, Indiana University Press, 1987, pp. 187–8.

115   *Odilo Globocnik: Hitler's Man in the East*, p.120.

116   TNA/HW16/10 GPCC OS1 21.8.1942, p.21, Section d), 'Salvage'.

117   Testimony at Nuremberg given by former Treblinka II inmate Samuel Rajzman, on Wednesday, 27 February 1946, Nuremberg Trial Proceedings Volume VIII, recorded on Yale Law School's The Avalon Project: https://avalon.law.yale.edu/imt/02-27-46.asp.

118   Listing from Globočnik SS Gruppenführer and Lieutenant-General of Police, to Personal Staff Reichsführer SS Ref. No Secret / 115; used as evidence at Nuremberg; in Document 4024PS-Economic Evidence of Action Reinhardt, Part 01–09, Evidence presented by British and American Prosecutors, in 'Nazi Conspiracy and Aggression' – District of Columbia GPO 1947, pp. 744–70.

119   TNA/HW ZIPOS3 29/10/42

120   TNA HW-16 /10 Bletchley Park/German Police Concentration Camp / GPCC/ ZIP OS3. 29/10/42.

121   Ibid.

122   Ibid.

123   Ibid – ZIP OS5 28/12/1942.

124   Ibid – ZIP OS4 27/11/1942.

125   Ibid – OS5 28/12/1942.

126   GPCC ZIP OS6 28/01/1943.

127   Ibid – OS6 28/01/1943.

128   Ibid – OS6 28/01/1943.

129   HW12/272/32: Archbishop Spellman's visit to the Vatican: Report from Japanese Minister, Vatican, Signal no: 115425, dated 9/3/1943, decrypted 14 March 1943.

130   HW12/272/32: Archbishop Spellman's visit to the Vatican: Report from Turkish Ambassador, Rome, Signal no. 115258, dated 10/3/1943, decrypted 14 March 1943.

131   'Roncalli in the Second World War' by Peter Hoffmann, *Journal of Ecclesiastical History*, 1989, no.1, pp. 74–99.

132   Alec Dakin, 'The Z Watch in Hut 4', in Sir F.H Hinsley and Alan Stripp (eds.) *The Codebreakers*, Oxford University Press 2001, p. 52.

133   TNA/HW12/286/25 Jewish Agency seeks Vatican intervention on behalf of Slovak Jews March 1943, 13 March, signal no. 99, decrypt and translation typed 17 March 1943, no. 115364; the plaintext of the message that the GC&CS decrypted is in The Historical Archives of the Vatican and was published in *Actes et Documents* Vol.IX, messages 185-6.

134   *Actes et Documents VIII, messages 597–8,* 13 July 1942, Cardinal Domenico Tardini, Head of the Congregation for Extraordinary Ecclesiastical Affairs.

135   TNA/HW12/286/25: Jewish Agency seeks Vatican intervention on behalf of Slovak Jews March 1943, 13 March 1943, msg no.71. Translated and decrypted and read by 16 March 1943 record no. 115328.

136   He put this in writing on 5 May, and the message is in *Actes et Documents IX*, messages 275–7.

137   Speech supporting immediate aid to Jewish refugees, by William Temple, Archbishop of Canterbury: Hansard, House of Lords Debates, 23 March 1943, vol.126 cols. 811–60.

138   Ibid - Temple quoted these, and other reports in his speech.

139   *Battle of Wits,* by Stephen Budiansky, p.282.

140   *Station X,* by Michael Smith, p.117.

141   TNA/HW16/10 internal memo from Nigel de Grey, 28 March 1943.

142   *Facing a Holocaust: the Polish Government in exile and the Jews, 1939–1945*, by David Engel, University of North Carolina Press, 1993, p.71.

143   The Jürgen Stroop Report – Nuremberg Trials document P-1061 / Exhibit U.S.A 275.

144   'A New Ordering of Space and Race: Nazi Colonial Dreams in Zhytomyr, Ukraine, 1941–1944', by Wendy Lower, in *German Studies Review* Vol. 25, No. 2 (the Johns Hopkins University Press, May 2002), pp. 227–254.

145   TNA/HW16/GPDD summary from 1–31 October 1942, MSGP 40, 9.11.42.

146   Ibid.

147   *The Good Old Days: The Holocaust as Seen by its Perpetrators and Bystanders*, by Ernst Klee, Willi Dressen, Volker Riess, the Free Press, New York, 1988, pp.180–1.

148   Report No.51 of Reichsführer-SS Heinrich Himmler to Hitler about mass executions in the east, 1942. *Trials of War Criminals before the Nuernberg Military Tribunals* – Washington, US Government Printing Office, 1949–1953, Vol. XIII, p.269–72.

149   *The Final Solution: The Attempt to Exterminate the Jews of Europe*, 1939–1945, G. Reitlinger, Elstree, 1968, p.233.

150   Ibid. p.133.

151   *The Good Old Days*, p.67.

152   *A Report on the Duty Journey through POLAND from 4–16 May 1943 by* SS-Sturmbannführer ALBERT FRANKE-GRICKSCH, TNA/WO 309 / 2241.

153   Ibid.

154   Ibid.

155   Witness testimony of former Treblinka inmate Samuel Rajzman at Nuremberg, 27 February 1946.

156   At the 1965 Treblinka Trials, three of the 309 charges against Franz included the biting, mauling and killing of prisoners by Barry.

157   *The Destruction of the European Jews*, Vol. II, by Raoul Hilberg, Quadrangle Books, Chicago, 1961, p.134.

158   Prosecution Exhibit Code 485 / Evidence Code NO-3034, letter from SS-Reichsführer Heinrich Himmler to Oswald Pohl, 22/9/43, submitted as evidence at the Nuremberg trial of Pohl.

159   TNA/HW16 ZIP GPD 1956 CC-HH Transmitted 15 October 1943 from Police Führer Lublin to PF Lutzk

160   International Nuremberg Military Tribunal's *Nazi Conspiracy and Aggression*, the Red Series (three volumes) Supplement Vol. B, pp. 1309–11.

161   *General Report on Tunny*, written at Bletchley Park in 1945 by Jack Michie, Geoffrey Tims, Donald Good, and declassified from the National Archives in 2000. TNA/HW 25/4, 25/5 for Vols.1 and 2.

162   TNA/HW1/1606 and 1648 13 and 30 April 1943.

163   TNA/HW16/ History of German Police Section, p.5.

164   The Churchill Papers, Set 20 / Group 52 / Jan – May 1942.

165   TNA / HW43/78 Nigel de Grey's *History & Memos of Wartime Signals Intelligence*, Ch X – Part II, pp. 17-30, 'Russian Liaison'.

166   Ibid.

167   TNA/ HW16/6 GPD MSGP 37 1–31 July 1942.

168   From Mavis Batey, quoted in *The Bletchley Park Codebreakers*, Ralph Erskine and Michael Smith (eds.), Biteback Publishing, 2011, pp. 79–92.

169   Signal from Wilhelm Höttl, RSHA, Berlin, Amt VI, to Herbert Kappler in Rome, Signal XIII/52 Berlin to Rome, RSS 107, 7 October 1943, held in NARA RG 226 of the messages of the OSS, contained in the declassification in 2000 by the Nazi War Criminal Records Interagency Working Group.

170   'Background of Dr Wilhelm Höttl, 5 August 1949', p.2: https://www. cia. gov/readingroom/docs/HOETTL%2C%20WILHELM%20%20%20 VOL.%20 3_0061.pdf.

171   Signal from Wilhelm Höttl – Signal RSS 118, 187 – 7 October 1943.

172   OSS message held in National Archives, RG 226, Entry 212, Box 40, Folder J: 6 October 1943. Declassified 28 June 2000, Office of Strategic Services, Washington DC, Boston Series No. 9, Copy No. 8.

173   US NARA RG Group XIII/52/ROME TO BERLIN/RSS32/7/10/1943.

174   It was only in 1978 that the CIA identified the footage as being of Auschwitz-Birkenau.

175   TNA/HW12/299/18 Vatican Interest in Fate of Jews resident in Hungary, Msg 130638, summary dated 20 April 1944.

176   NARA Multinational Decrypts Geneva to Vatican City, 15 July 1944, H131282. NARA, RG457, HCC, Box 425. 111.

177   TNA/HW17 39-118 / COMINTERN-ISCOT decrypts.

178   NARA MND Translation, Budapest to Tokyo, via Berlin (Oshima), 7 July 1944, H-127152, NARA, RG 457, HCC, Box 420.

179   TNA/HW16/6 GPD MSGP 1 – 31 Aug 1944 CIRO/PEARL No number, 7 Sept 4.

180   TNA/HW 16/16 GPD extracts for Russia: German language decrypts selected by 4 Intelligence Section for passing to Russians from 12 September 1944 onwards, plus internal notes.

181   'A selection of texts from GPD sources' from TNA/HW16/16 – Intelligence Sharing with Moscow by No.4 Intelligence Section of GC&CS.

182   Operations Talisman and Eclipse, and Post-War Interception', Bletchley Park Document BOP27, 10pp, p.2.

183   Ibid.

184   Multinational Diplomatic Translation of the Boston series, from London (Czech Government) to Stockholm (Czech Representative), 27 January 1945, H-169498, NARA RG 457, HCC, Box 470.

185   *The Liberation of the Camps: The End of the Holocaust and its Aftermath,* by Dan Stone, Yale University Press 2015, p.46.

186   TNA/HW16/77 Two high interest GP reports sent by Duty Officer Hut 3 to C and the 3 Service Directors of Intelligence. 6 April 1945.

187   TNA/HW16/6 GPD Summary 4045 for 6 and 10.4.1945.

188   TNA/HW16/6 GPD Summaries No.4065 for 6 and 10.4.45.

189   Ibid.

190   War Diary of the 4th (Queen's Own) Hussars 29.05.1945–31.05.1945.

191   The lists were declassified in 2005, although originally the date was set at seventy-five years after 1943, or 2018.

192 CROWCASS Consolidated List, Reel 44, 1948 Final Consolidated Wanted List, United Nations War Crimes Commission, www.unwcc.org.

193 Report on the IRR File of Hermann Julius Höfle for the Nazi War Crimes Interagency Working Group, written by Professor Richard Breitmann, Consultant Historian to the IWG. The US CIC quote is from Höfle's Personnel file at the US National Archives & Records Administration, at Hermann Julius Hoefle, Record Group 242, Berlin Document Center, Microfilm A-3343, SSO-102A.

194 Supreme Headquarters Allied Expeditionary Force Selected Records, Box 27, SHAEF – Evaluation and Dissemination Sections (G-2) German Concentration Camps; NAID #17368747.

195 Admiralty 1/27186 / Admiralty 195/45 'Review of Security of Naval Codes and Cyphers September 1939-May 1945', issued by the Signals Division of the Admiralty in November 1945, 130 pages, Part II: Enemy Cryptanalytical Successes, pp. 62–68.

196 Ibid.

197 Ibid.

198 US Target Intelligence Committee (TICOM) File I-109.

199 As one of Bletchley's cryptanalysts said in 1941, quoted in Ch. V.

200 Nuremberg Trial Proceedings Vol. 19 Day 188, closing statement of Sir Hartley Shawcross, British Chief Prosecutor at Nuremberg, Document No.2992-PS.

201 International Military Tribunal proceedings at Nuremberg, prosecution document 2519-PS, trial of Ernst Kaltenbrunner.

202 Ibid. prosecution document L-53.

203 Email between the author and Wojciech Plosa PhD, Head of Archive, State Museum Auschwitz-Birkenau at Oświęcim, 8 September 2023.

204 The Gerstein Report, written on 4 May 1945, while Gerstein was under house arrest in Allied custody in the German town of Reutlingen. On the website of the Jewish Virtual Library: https://www.jewishvirtuallibrary.org/the-gerstein-report.

SELECT BIBLIOGRAPHY

Arad, Yitzhak *Belzec, Sobibor, Treblinka: The Operation Reinhard Death Camps*, Bloomington, 1999

Arad, who died in 2021, was originally from modern-day Lithuania, and fought as a teenage partisan with a Soviet unit against the Germans during the war. He emigrated to Israel after the war, served in the Israel Defence Forces, becoming a brigadier-general, and was also an author and Holocaust historian. He was director of the Yad Vashem Remembrance Centre 1972–93.

Arad, Yitzhak, Shmuel Krakowski and Shmuel Spector (eds) *The Einsatzgruppen Reports: Selections from the Dispatches of the Nazi Death Squads*, Holocaust Memorial Museum, Washington, 1989

Bankier, David (ed.) *Secret Intelligence and the Holocaust*, New York, 2005

Published in conjunction with the Yad Vashem Remembrance Centre in Jerusalem, a collection of essays from a conference on

'The Holocaust and Intelligence' held at the City University of New York in 2003.

Breitman, Richard and Lichtman, Allan J. *FDR and the Jews*, Harvard, 2013

An investigative account of the complex and internecine relationship between Roosevelt and the different factions of American Jews during the war.

Browning, Christopher *Ordinary Men: Reserve Police Battalion 101 and the Final Solution in Poland*, London, 1998, reprint 2017

An in-depth study of how a group of German reserve policemen became one of the units responsible for carrying out mass executions on the Eastern Front.

Calvocoressi, Peter *Top Secret Ultra*, London, 1980

The author was an RAF signals intelligence officer based at Bletchley Park, and in this first available account, tells a complicated and mostly accurate story of some of the Government Code and Cypher School's operations to decrypt both German police and SS signals from the Eastern Front and concentration camps.

Cesarani, David *Final Solution: The Fate of the Jews 1933–49*, London, 2016

One of the most authoritative and wide-ranging histories of the Holocaust, the author also focuses on two of the fundamental preconceptions of it: its inevitability, and its organisation.

Eger, Dr Edith Eva *The Choice: Embrace the Possible, A Memoir*, London, 2018

A Czech Jew deported from Hungary to Auschwitz in 1944, Edith Eger was a teenage gymnast and ballerina. After selecting her mother for the gas chamber, Josef Mengele made Edith dance for him. She barely survived the Holocaust. She later emigrated to the United States, eventually to become a famous psychologist.

Erbelding, Rebecca *Rescue Board: The Untold Story of America's Efforts to Save the Jews of Europe*, New York, 2018

The inside story of the War Refugee Board, and how it tried to save Europe's Jews.

Favez, Jean-Claude *The Red Cross and the Holocaust*, Cambridge, 1999.

An investigation into what the International Committee of the Red Cross knew about the workings of the Holocaust, and what it did – and didn't – do about it.

Frank, Anne *The Diary of a Young Girl*. First published in Dutch in 1947 (expurgated and edited by her father, Otto Frank); French and German versions were published in 1950, and English translations in the UK and the US in 1952. Later editions included material originally cut by Otto Frank, and more recent ones include additional material found later, some of it text edited out by Anne herself.

It has been translated into over seventy languages and more than 35 million copies have been sold worldwide. The story of the Dutch teenager hiding for some two years from the Germans, with her family and others in a top-floor annex of a house, is one of the finest books on the Holocaust there is.

Hilberg, Raul, *Perpetrators, Victims, Bystanders: The Jewish Catastrophe*, London, 1995

— *The Destruction of the European Jews*, Yale, 2003
An Austrian-born Jewish American scholar and professor, Hilberg narrowly escaped the Holocaust in 1939. He is now reckoned to be one of the pre-eminent scholars on the subject, and his book *The Destruction of the European Jews* is one of the seminal works on it, at 1,300 pages and in three volumes.

Hinsley Sir Harry and others (eds) *British Intelligence in the Second World War: Its influence on Strategy and Operations* Volume II, London, 1981

From the five-volume official history of wartime intelligence, it contained the first information to be made available about how Bletchley Park decrypted German police ciphers from the Eastern Front in 1941 and 1942. Hinsley was a history undergraduate at Cambridge recruited by the GC&CS in 1939, and worked on the plan to seize Enigma materials from German weather ships. He also liaised with the US Navy in Washington about the sharing of intelligence from decrypted Japanese naval signals.

Lower, Wendy *The Ravine: A family, a photograph, a Holocaust massacre revealed*, New York, 2021

An investigation into the family and the background of a mother and two children pictured in a photograph taken at a massacre site in Ukraine.

Medoff, Rafael *Blowing the Whistle on Genocide: Josiah E. DuBois, Jr. and the Struggle for an American Response to the Holocaust*, West Lafayette, 2008

The author is a leading American professor of Jewish history, and the book examines the governmental resistance to granting visas to Jews, and the work of one Treasury lawyer in helping set up the War Refugee Board.

Plesch, Dan *Human Rights After Hitler: The Lost History of Prosecuting Axis War Crimes*, Georgetown, 2017

The story of the United Nations War Crimes Commission, from its archives, only fully declassified and released in 2017.

Rees, Laurence *The Holocaust: A New History*, London and New York, 2017

One of the standing classic histories of the Final Solution.

Rubinstein, William D. *The Myth of Rescue: Why the Democracies Could Not Have Saved More Jews from the Nazis*, London and New York, 1997

The author takes the stance that there was almost nothing more that the Allies could have done to save Europe's Jews than that which they actually did.

Smith, Michael *The Emperor's Codes: The Breaking of Japan's Secret Ciphers*, New York, 2001

The author has written a number of books about wartime codebreaking, including *Station X: the Codebreakers of Bletchley Park* (London, 1988). *The Emperor's Codes* stands as the definitive work to date on the deciphering of Japanese codes, and the impact this had not just on the war in the Pacific, but globally.

Snyder, Timothy D. *Black Earth: The Holocaust as History and Warning*, New York, 2016

Named after the soil of Ukraine, Snyder's book argues that the Holocaust contains multiple, vital warnings and lessons for modern international geopolitics.

Wachsmann, Nikolaus *KL: a History of the Nazi Concentration Camps*, London and New York, 2016

The definitive, par excellence story of the entire economic, detention, extermination and penal business run by Himmler and the SS.

Wyman, David S. *The Abandonment of the Jews: America and the Holocaust*, New York, 1984

A dry, rigorous and well-investigated account of American policy towards the Jews during the Second World War, and probably the best documentation of what the US and Britain didn't do.

ACKNOWLEDGEMENTS

'History with its flickering lamp,' said Winston Churchill, 'stumbles along the trail of the past, trying to reconstruct its scenes, to revive its echoes, and kindle with pale gleams the passion of former days.'

Any author of modern history trying to follow this trail, to reconstruct these scenes, could ask for no better literary agent than Andrew Lownie, and no finer editor than Toby Buchan. To both, many thanks. At the convergence of the trail that is the Second World War, the Holocaust and the world of cryptography, history is simultaneously complicated, technical and very human, and often it seems that under the tip of the iceberg written about here there lie even more and bigger stories.

Thanks and acknowledgements are due to several people for help and encouragement in keeping the lamp shining. In Italy, Giulia Avataneo, Alessandro Avataneo and Clara Gastaldi. My niece Lily McMeeking helped with clear-minded and efficient archive research, my brothers Anthony and James were stalwart, fox-like and very sharp with editing advice, while David Kenyon at Bletchley Park and Ela Kaczmarska at The National Archives were extremely helpful. Writing investigative books like this always reminds me of the examples I followed from my colleagues while on the road in such countries as Rwanda, Burundi, Democratic Congo, Kosovo and Bosnia. These include Beth Kampschror, Corinne Dufka and Nerma Jelacic. For example and inspiration, however, few can exceed that of the *stella cadente,* Sylvia Scheul.

CHRISTIAN JENNINGS

PIETRA LIGURE, TURIN, AND LONDON

INDEX

INDEX

INDEX